Essays and Studies 2003

Series Editor: Peter Kitson
Associate Editor: Helen Lucas

The English Association

The objects of the English Association are to promote the knowledge and appreciation of the English language and its literature, and to foster good practice in its teaching and learning at all levels.

The association pursues these aims by creating opportunities of co-operation among all those interested in English; by furthering the recognition of English as essential in education; by discussing methods of English teaching; by holding lectures, conferences, and other meetings; by publishing journals, books, and leaflets; and by forming local branches.

Publications

The Year's Work in English Studies. An annual bibliography. Published by Oxford University Press.

The Year's Work in Critical and Cultural Theory. An annual bibliography. Published by Oxord University Press.

Essays and Studies. An annual volume of essays by various scholars assembled by the collector covering usually a wide range of subjects and authors from the medieval to the modern. Published by D. S. Brewer.

English. A journal of the Association, *English* is published three times a year by the Association.

The Use of English. A journal of the Association, *The Use of English* is published three times a year by the Association.

Newsletter. A *Newsletter* is published three times a year giving information about forthcoming publications, conferences, and other matters of interest.

Benefits of Membership

Institutional Membership

Full members receive copies of *The Year's Work in English Studies*, *Essays and Studies*, *English* (3 issues) and three *Newsletters*.

Ordinary Membership covers *English* (3 issues) and three *Newsletters*.

Schools Membership includes copies of each issue of *English* and *The Use of English*, one copy of *Essays and Studies*, three *Newsletters*, and preferential booking and rates for various conferences held by the Association.

Individual Membership

Individuals take out Basic Membership, which entitles them to buy all regular publications of the English Association at a discounted price, and attend Association gatherings.

For further details write to The Secretary, The English Association, The University of Leicester, University Road, Leicester, LE1 7RH.

Essays and Studies 2003

Victorian Women Poets

**Edited by
Alison Chapman**

for the English Association

D. S. BREWER

© The English Association 2003

ESSAYS AND STUDIES 2003
IS VOLUME FIFTY-SIX IN THE NEW SERIES
OF ESSAYS AND STUDIES COLLECTED ON BEHALF OF
THE ENGLISH ASSOCIATION
ISSN 0071–1357

First published 2003
by D. S. Brewer, Cambridge
Reprinted 2005

Transferred to digital printing

ISBN 978-0-85991-787-2

D. S. Brewer is an imprint of Boydell & Brewer Ltd
PO Box 9, Woodbridge, Suffolk IP12 3DF, UK
and of Boydell & Brewer Inc.
668 Mt Hope Avenue, Rochester, NY 14620, USA
website: www.boydellandbrewer.com

A CiP catalogue record for this book is available
from the British Library

This publication is printed on acid-free paper

Contents

Illustrations

Acknowledgements

Peter Kitson, the Essays and Studies series editor, not only commissioned this volume, but also advised with the editing, no doubt far beyond the call of duty. I owe my greatest thanks to his editorial skills and robust good humour, which made the work on the collection a pleasure. For her gracious assistance throughout, I am indebted to Helen Lucas at the English Association. Thanks are also owed to the contributors for their co-operation and patience with the editing process. My colleagues and graduate students in the Department of English Literature, the University of Glasgow, provide a collegial and lively research environment for which I am deeply grateful. The final work on the collection could not have been completed without the kindness and support of my parents and Robert Miles.

Introduction

ALISON CHAPMAN

As RECENTLY AS 1992, Angela Leighton lamented that, despite the successful feminist recovery of women's writing, nineteenth-century women's poetry continues to be neglected.[1] Within the space of a decade, the publication of anthologies and scholarly editions has brought to light the diversity, complexity and richness of Victorian women's poetry. Two major anthologies in particular, Leighton and Margaret Reynolds' 1995 Blackwell edition of *Victorian Women Poets* and Isobel Armstrong and Joseph Bristow's Oxford University Press 1996 edition of *Nineteenth-Century Women Poets*, have radically changed the shape of Victorian poetry. More recently these antho-logies have been complemented by Virginia Blain's annotated antho-logy for Longman.[2] Alongside the canonical Elizabeth Barrett Browning and Christina Rossetti, a host of new women poets have been recovered, such as Felicia Hemans, Caroline Norton, Dora Greenwell, Adelaide Anne Proctor, Augusta Webster, Margaret Veley and Mathilde Blind. The specially commissioned essays in this volume take their point of departure from this important moment in Victorian studies, all in various ways responding to recent develop-ments and either offering new readings of canonical poets, or bringing into critical focus recently re-discovered writers.

The critical effects of the recovery of forgotten voices are still making their mark and the work of uncovering women's poetry is by no means completed. While a variety of Victorian women poets are newly accessible in anthologies, only Christina Rossetti has a complete modern edition of her poems; in particular, scholars and students urgently need a variorum edition of the works of Elizabeth Barrett

---

[1] See Angela Leighton, *Victorian Women's Poetry: Writing Against the Heart* (Hemel Hempstead, 1992), p. 1.

[2] Angela Leighton and Margaret Reynolds (eds), *Victorian Women Poets: An Anthology* (Oxford, 1995); Isobel Armstrong and Joseph Bristow with Cath Sharrock (eds), *Nineteenth-Century Women Poets: An Oxford Anthology* (Oxford, 1996); Virginia Blain, *Victorian Women Poets: A New Annotated Anthology* (Harlow, 2001). See also Margaret Randolph Higonnet, *British Poets of the Nineteenth Century* (New York, 1996).

Browning.[3] Additionally, although Letitia Landon and Augusta
Webster have recently enjoyed selected critical editions of their
poetry, this is only just the very beginning of the on-going process of
making accessible women poets who are emerging as the important
writers of the period.[4] Furthermore, despite their wonderful range of
coverage, the anthologies of the 1990s had some unfortunate blind-
spots. As Joseph Bristow points out in his essay for this collection,
working-class women poets such as Ellen Johnston and Janet Hamilton
have not been well served.[5] Women poets from other nations in the
United Kingdom – Scotland, Wales and Ireland – are also poorly
represented in existing anthologies.[6] Another type of women writer has
also been by-passed: those who wrote extensively or exclusively for the
periodicals, magazines and newspapers. The exception is partly the gift
annual or album, whose significance for the woman poet has been
noted since Andrew Boyle compiled his *Index to the Annuals*, but there
still remains to be completed a large-scale uncovering of women poets
whose principal outlet was this form.[7] Women poets involved in
periodical culture present a challenge to the conceptual basis of the
poetry anthology, structured as it is upon the category of the author, for
many of these women published anonymously and very few authored

[3] R. W. Crump (ed.), *The Complete Poems of Christina Rossetti: A Variorum
Edition*, 3 vols (Baton Rouge and London, 1979–1990); Penguin published this
edition as a single volume in paperback, introduced by Betty Flowers. There are
excellent separately published scholarly editions of Barrett Browning's *Sonnets
from the Portuguese*, *Aurora Leigh* and *Casa Guidi Windows* and a complete
critical edition of her *oeuvre* is in its early stages, edited by Sandra Donaldson.
[4] See Jerome McGann and Daniel Riess (eds), *Letitia Elizabeth Landon: Selected
Writings* (Ontario, 1997); Christina Sutphin (ed.), *Augusta Webster: Portraits
and Other Poems* (Ontario, 1997). Both these volumes are published by
Broadview Press, who deserve enormous credit for their commitment to
women's poetry.
[5] See also Blain's comments on the exclusion of working-class women in the
introduction to her anthology, in which she suggests that, rather than being
included as a token gesture in general poetry anthologies of the period,
working-class women poets require a separate anthology of their own (p. 4).
For an excellent series of essays on Victorian working-class poetry, see the
special issue of *Victorian Poetry* for 2001 (39: 2), edited by Florence Boos.
Another excellent introduction to the field is her essay on 'Working-Class
Poetry' in Richard Cronin, Alison Chapman and Antony H. Harrison (eds), *A
Companion to Victorian Poetry* (Oxford, 2002).
[6] See Matthew Campbell 'Poetry in the Four Nations' in Cronin, Chapman
and Harrison.
[7] See Andrew Boyle, *An Index to the Annuals, 1820–1850* (Worcester, 1967),
vol. 1.

poetry collections.[8] The recent volumes on British Victorian women's poetry in the *Dictionary of Literary Biography*, for example, underline the problem. Although both offer a generous selection of women's poetry from a variety of classes, and with some attention to the 'Celtic fringe', its organisation structure is based on the authorial individual who publishes poetry volumes, ignoring the important alternative outlets of periodical print that challenge this conception of writing.[9]

This transitional period in Victorian studies is an exciting one for scholars who are continuing to develop the critical paradigms for understanding the dazzling wealth of women's poetry, as well as for those who are continuing to discover and edit new voices. It is also, however, a fruitful period for reflecting on the renaissance of Victorian women's poetry and our methodologies for recovery. The essays in this volume consider a diverse range of issues inherent to Victorian women's poetry and the mechanics of its recovery, and offer new dialogues, networks and literary histories.

Patricia Pulham's essay, '"Such jewels – delights – perfect loves": Victorian Women Poets and the Annuals', explores the relationship between the professional identity of the woman poet and the rise of the annual in the 1830s and 1840s. The connection, she argues, is not entirely happy or unproblematic, for women are both the consumers and, symbolically, the commodities in annual publications. Thus, while offering their women contributors a lucrative publishing outlet, the feminisation of the annuals commodified both poet and poem. Pulham reads a latent eroticism at work in such a gendered medium, which made annual publication both tempting and also dangerous. Women poets, she argues, negotiated this problematic sensuality through the figure of Sappho as the primordial woman poet who is also subjected to the objectification process. Through an inter-artistic reading of two poems by Lady Emmeline Stuart Wortley and Lady Blessington on engravings of society beauties, Pulham teases out these contradictions and suggests how women poets fragment the feminised body on display,

---

[8] An important recent anthology of women's contribution to magazines, including poetry, is Margaret Beetham and Kay Boardman (eds), *Victorian Women's Magazines: An Anthology* (Manchester, 2001).
[9] *Dictionary of Literary Biography*, Volume 199, *Victorian Women Poets*, ed. William B. Thesing (Detroit, 1999), and Volume 240, *Late Nineteenth- and Early Twentieth-Century British Women Poets*, ed. William B. Thesing (Detroit, 2001). It is important to add, however, that the essays do provide bibliographies of selected periodical publications that are uncollected, after a list of the published poetry volumes.

against the 'whole' of the engraving, suggesting the anxiety about the annual's feminisation and eroticism. Women poets writing for annuals, Pulham argues, adopt a '"sapphic gaze" which erotices the exchange between themselves and the women in the illustrations', but this also involves a 'fragmentary poetics that fetishise[s]' (p. 30) the object of gaze, a masculinist and Petrarchan poetic strategy. Such a problematic double manoeuvre is even at work in the poem that, for many critics, transformed and reconfigured women's poetry, Elizabeth Barrett Browning's *Aurora Leigh*.

Barrett Browning's 'The Runaway Slave at Pilgrim's Point' is the focus of the following essay in the collection. Marjorie Stone offers an extended analysis of the intimate and complex relationship between the dramatic monologue and the circumstances of its initial publication in the 1848 issue of the Boston *Liberty Bell*. Stone demonstrates how an understanding of Barrett Browning's literary and political relationship to this anti-slavery movement radically alters the reading of the poem. She contests the tendency to prioritise biographical over the historical and inter-textual contexts in the critical reception of 'The Runaway Slave'. Even when critics have reviewed Barrett Browning's relationship to slavery, she argues, they have largely ignored the specific abolitionist transatlantic networks with which the poem engages. Stone traces these networks in detail, reading 'The Runaway Slave' alongside other abolitionist poems in the *Liberty Bell* and mapping Barrett Browning's various transatlantic connections, in particular with reference to Harriet Martineau and the Garrisonians. The second part of the essay turns to link these issues with the poem's textual history. Stone analyses the phases of poetic composition as suggested by the Wellesley manuscript of 'The Runaway Slave', arguing that the evolution of the poem evinces the poet's developing relationship to the abolitionist politics of the Garrisonians and anti-slavery *topoi*.

Barrett Browning's investment in another political movement for liberty is the starting point for Alison Chapman's essay on 'The Expatriate Poetess'. This essay uncovers the work of expatriate poetesses in Barrett Browning's Florentine circle who vigorously support the Risorgimento: Isa Blagden, Eliza Ogilvy and, in particular, Theodosia Garrow Trollope. The first section of the essay unravels the hidden hybrid nationalism embedded in the monolithic figure of the English poetess defined by reviews and essays in the 1840s. Although explicitly positioning English national identity and women's poetry as equivalent, and defining the woman poet herself as the epitome of

English domestic character, mid-century commentators nevertheless invest their discourse in the foreign bodies of Sappho and her modern counterpart, Corinne. The newly Anglo-centric poetess is thus both a signifier for English nationalism and domesticity and yet, also, foreignness. While this means that Felicia Hemans (who died in 1835) was posthumously denied a political and public agency by the reviewers of the 1840s, women poets writing in this decade and the 1850s, however, self-consciously claim the agency and foreignness for themselves. The figure of the poetess, Chapman argues, is mobile and subversive, always in transit, signifying her fractured patriotism ambivalently through devotion to nations not her own. The second section of the essay suggests that expatriate woman poets of the Risorgimento motivate the hybrid nationality within the figure of the poetess, often against British interests abroad. Focusing on Theodosia Garrow Trollope, the discussion uncovers a very different configuration between feminine poetics and revolutionary politics than the one adopted by Barrett Browning. Trollope, the analysis suggests, works within the discourse of feminine sensibility to forge a radical political poetics through the rhapsodic form.

Glennis Byron's essay concerns a more canonical poetic form, the dramatic monologue. Her analysis urges us to reconsider the impact made by women poets to the genre. The essay notes that the contribution of women poets to the development of the dramatic monologue in the Victorian period has been repeatedly overlooked in the major critical studies of the genre. The rediscovery of women's poetry, however, forces us to reconsider the form's traditional definition. Byron asks whether the re-emergence of women's poetry re-writes the story of the dramatic monologue's origins and whether men and women poets conceptualise the form in different ways. In the 'transitional period' of the 1820s (p. 81), Letitia Landon and Felicia Hemans found the genre productive, especially in its intrinsic assertion of a speaker's (and thus not necessarily the woman poet's) subjectivity. Byron, however, sees this strategy as problematic, for it re-affirms and not challenges the erasure of female subjecthood and, furthermore, situates the voice of the female poet within universal definitions of womanhood. For Hemans, in particular, the use of context in her dramatic monologues reinforces rather than undermines these essentialist gender values. In contrast, however, later women poets of the century use the form in different ways. The discussion turns to consider a wide range of other women poets – such as Augusta Webster, Barrett Browning, Dinah Craik, Amy Levy, Adah Menken, Constance Naden and Charlotte Mew – who established and refined a line of generic development that endured: social critique. This is where the subtle differences can be located, Byron argues, between men and women's dramatic monologues.

Michele Martinez's essay uncovers the extensive and detailed Italian scholarship of Christina Rossetti. The discussion begins with Rossetti's comments in her preface to the sonnet sequence *Monna Innominata* (1881) that give preference to Dante over Petrarch, whom she terms 'a great tho' inferior bard'. Martinez traces Rossetti's reservations about Petrarch to the 1850s, in particular to her biographical entry on Petrarch for John F. Waller's *Imperial Dictionary of Universal Biography* (1857–63). Through a negotiation of the long and complex history of Petrarch criticism, and a search for portraits and monuments of his beloved Laura, her essay implicitly challenges the allegorical scholarship of her father and re-fashions Laura as an ideal Anglo-Catholic Christian. The conclusion of Rossetti's essay leaves the question of Laura's real historical existence open-ended. Instead, she offers an 'iconicist moment' (p. 103) in the form of a quatrain by Petrarch that parabolically suggests Laura's spiritual significance as a guide to the Italian poet. Martinez links such iconicism to one of Rossetti's most enigmatic lyric poems, 'Memory'. Part one of the poem, composed in 1857, she argues, explores Petrarch's obsession with memory and idolatry, while part two, written in 1865, reflects the conclusion of her essay for Waller and represents redemption through the Anglo-Catholic doctrine of reserve. The extended reading of 'Memory' offered by Martinez suggests new ways of understanding the link between Rossetti's intellectual investment in her Italian heritage, the poetics of the lyric form, and religion.

Susan Brown's essay also presents a new approach to poetics, but in this case through the political poetry of an unjustly neglected atheist poet. In '"A still and mute-born vision": Locating Mathilde Blind's Reproductive Poetics', Brown uncovers the relationship between political poetics and the gendered body. The essay begins by charting Blind's political commitment to the cause of Italian national liberty, in particular the poems to her mentor Mazzini that echo Barrett Browning in their fluid imagery. Blind associates the nationalist leader with images of reproductive processes associated with fruitfulness and also destruction; furthermore, such images are closely linked to the difficulties of poetic inspiration and vocation. The discussion then considers Blind's *The Heather on Fire: A Tale of the Highland Clearances* (1886), which evolved out of the political poetics forged through her investment in the Risorgimento. In this narrative poem, Blind represents the suffering of the Scottish crofters through tropes of reproduction and miscarriage that again echo and revise the poetry of Barrett Browning. Brown argues that the tradition of women's political poetry, which articulates a poetic voice through the generative female body, is intensified by Blind's poem, for her 'emphasis on reproductive process is more tightly interwoven with the contemporary political debate' (p. 132). Furthermore, Blind's new reproductive political poetics incorporates the discourses of materialism and Darwinism, and the poem contributes to the contemporary debate about Scottish land reform through an evolutionary framework that raises questions about the relationship between the natural and the social, causality and agency. What Blind finally achieves in *The Heather on Fire*, Brown concludes, is a new poetic mode and a new form of historical epic.

The following essay by Natalie M. Houston concerns another poetic form, the Victorian sonnet. 'Towards a New History: *Fin-de-siècle* Women Poets and the Sonnet' begins with a challenge to the process of historical recovery of poetry by women. Drawing on John Guillory's *Cultural Capital* (1993), Houston suggests that a new material history of literature, one which presents a challenge the traditional male-centred canon, is at odds with the feminist project of recovering women writers. Masculinist notions of canonicity, according to Guillory, attach value to the individual writer. He argues instead for a new kind of literary history that would begin by questioning 'what genres of writing count as "literature"'. Houston points out, however, that the recovery of women's poetry and associated issues of literary history are still closely linked to methodological tools that 'tend invariably to rely upon lists of writers' (p. 146). The essay forges an alternative approach through analysis of the *fin-de-siècle* sonnets by Mathilde Blind, Michael Field and Rosamund Marriott Watson. Houston's analysis of the sonnet form challenges bio-historical critical categories such as the woman poet and, instead, offers a new materialist literary history of the genre, linking issues of cultural value to the politics of gender.

Value is also the starting-point of Joseph Bristow's essay, which begins with a reflection upon the recent anthologies of women's poetry, including his own 1996 collection, edited with Isobel Armstrong. Bristow considers the vexed questions raised by the work of reclamation, in particular the editorial principles of inclusion and exclusion. Rather than estimating value and worth through a poet's diversity of forms, Bristow suggests instead a concentration on a diversity of outlets.

In particular, he charts the importance of the periodical press in forging Anglo-American readerships for Victorian women's poetry. The essay's focus is *Harper's New Monthly Magazine*, an illustrated periodical which achieved a massive circulation and gave prominence to a select group of English women writers whose poetry enjoyed renewed attention in the anthologies of the 1990s, such as A. Mary F. Robinson and Margaret Veley. Bristow explores how poetry was valued in *Harper's* and why its worth was so very transitory. The second part of the essay concentrates on Margaret Veley, whose success with *Harper's* was impressive but brief. A reading of her poems published in the magazine suggests Veley's progressively liberal and democratic ideals and her awareness of a transatlantic public, just as the accompanying illustrations by American artist Edwin Austin Abbey underline the high transatlantic value *Harper's* placed on her poems. After her premature death in 1887, however, her poetry quickly faded into obscurity. Bristow concludes with a discussion of how her swift decline into invisibility ironically gave her renewed value as a subject for psychical research in the 1920s.

These essays collectively celebrate the phenomenal diversity, inventiveness and richness of Victorian women's poetry. While the poetry of Barrett Browning and Rossetti is re-assessed and given surprising new readings and inter-texts, poetry by writers of emerging importance are given prominence and contexts. The themes interwoven throughout the essays – literary history and canonicity, political poetics, print culture, and genre – chart new and innovative journeys through the recently expanded map of Victorian women's poetry and also suggest further paths for exploration and discovery. This is an exhilarating literary renaissance, and the process of poetic recuperation, reflection and adventure has only just begun.

'Jewels – delights – perfect loves': Victorian Women Poets and the Annuals

PATRICIA PULHAM

IN 1823, THE FIRST ANNUAL, Rudolph Ackermann's *Forget Me Not, a Christmas and New Year's Present*, appeared in the literary marketplace. Its popularity fostered a variety of imitations sporting names such as *The Keepsake*, *Friendship's Offering*, *The Literary Souvenir*, the *English Bijou Almanack*, *The Diadem*, *The Book of Beauty*, and by 1832 'sixty-three gift books were in production'.[1] Aimed 'at the Christmas and New Year market in Britain and its colonies', the annuals were modelled on the continental literary almanacs popular in Germany and France and based in part on the English 'ladies' pocket-books' – elegant diaries containing 'small engravings of landscapes, country houses, picturesque villages, or sentimental scenes', which had appeared from time to time in previous years.[2] They became a phenomenal publishing success which lasted over thirty years and continued to find readers both in England and in America long after initial interest had waned.

Between 1823 and the late 1830s, these collections became 'the period's main vehicle for publishing verse'.[3] The reasons for this were manifold but include demographic and economic alterations, geographic migration, and changes in printing techniques which 'all worked to form new audiences and new relations between author, supporters, and text'.[4] Whereas, in the past, publication of one's poetry had often depended on the goodwill of a patron or patroness, it now relied on that of publishers or editors.[5] Moreover, changes in education

---

[1] Susan Brown, 'The Victorian Poetess', *The Cambridge Companion to Victorian Poetry*, ed. Joseph Bristow (Cambridge, 2000), p. 190.
[2] Alison Adburgham, *Silver Fork Society: Fashionable Life and Literature from 1814 to 1840* (London, 1983), p. 250.
[3] Brian Goldberg, '"A Sea Reflecting Love": Tennyson, Shelley, and the Aesthetics of the Image in the Marketplace', *Modern Language Quarterly: A Journal of Literary History*, 59: 1 (1998), pp. 71–97 (p. 75).
[4] Linda M. Shires, 'The Author as Spectacle and Commodity', in Carol T. Christ and John O. Jordan (eds), *Victorian Literature and the Victorian Visual Imagination* (California, 1995), p. 199.
[5] Shires, p. 199.

9

and the growing affluence of certain sectors of the community resulted
in an audience which was no longer 'composed of members of the same
class or profession. Rather the public splintered into audiences: a large
and diverse public, rural and urban, marked by divisions of status, class,
and gender and specific readerships'.[6] And, as several commentators
have noted, the annuals appealed to a particularly significant reader-
ship – the increasingly prosperous and aspirational middle classes, and
especially its female members. This study of the annuals will examine
the marketing strategies employed to solicit this audience, before
exploring the effects of such strategies on their presentation, and on
the women poets whose works formed a vital part of their attraction.

Consumers and Contributors

Showily bound, 'with covers of embossed or gilt leather, or of watered
silk, or of floral designs inlaid with mother-of-pearl', the annuals
created an illusion of exclusivity belied by their ubiquity and were
aimed primarily at a female market: either purchased *by* women, or
given *to* women as gifts.[7] Alison Adburgham describes them as the
nineteenth-century equivalent of the 'coffee-table book' and notes
that it was 'social snobbery [which] secured the success of the
annuals'.[8] In her introduction to *Victorian Women Poets: An Anthology*,
Margaret Reynolds adds that a main factor of their social cachet lay in
the publishers' custom of seeking out 'well-known society hostesses to
edit their volumes as if the contents of the annual itself mimicked a
select fashionable gathering'.[9] Among these were the Countess of

---

[6] Shires, p. 199.
[7] Donald Hawes, 'Thackeray and the Annuals', *Ariel: a Review of International
English Literature*, 7: 1 (1976), pp. 3–31 (p. 4). In *Friendship's Offering: An Essay
on the Annuals and Gift Books of the 19th Century* (London, 1964), Anne Renier
notes that young women found the annuals much more to their liking than the
conduct manuals which had previously been regarded as the ideal literature for
the young lady, and in 1828 Southey was to write that 'The Annuals are now
the only books bought for presents to young ladies' (p. 16). One of the annuals,
The Keepsake, is famously given as a gift to Rosamund Vincy by her suitor, Ned
Plymdale, in George Eliot's *Middlemarch* (1871–72).
[8] Adburgham, *Silver Fork Society*, p. 248; Alison Adburgham, *Women in Print:
Writing Women and Women's Magazines from the Restoration to the Accession of
Victoria* (London, 1972), p. 236.
[9] Margaret Reynolds, introduction to *Victorian Women Poets: An Anthology*, eds
Angela Leighton and Margaret Reynolds (Oxford, 1995), p. xxvi.

Blessington and Caroline Norton both of whom attracted as much attention for the scandals in which they became involved as praise or otherwise for their literary contributions.[10] Yet, despite the gossip, both wrote for and edited annuals considered morally acceptable reading for young ladies.

The contents of these annuals were varied, featuring short stories, essays, and poems, but they were valued more perhaps for the steel engravings of sentimental or pastoral subjects the writing was often commissioned to accompany. Nevertheless, at the height of their popularity, they contained works by an impressive range of authors. Frederic Mansel Reynolds, the editor of *The Keepsake* (1829–35) solicited for work by many famous names. The 1829 edition published a prestigious array of writers and poets including Wordsworth, Sir Walter Scott (listed as 'Author of *Waverley*'), Percy Bysshe Shelley, Samuel Taylor Coleridge, Robert Southey, and Mary Shelley (listed as 'Author of *Frankenstein*'). The appearance of male poets such as Wordsworth in what was considered a somewhat 'trivial' publication, owes much to the financial changes affecting the literary market. In contrast to the novel, poetry was fast losing its hold on the popular imagination. Faced with the public's growing indifference and haunted by insecurities fostered by the financial crisis of 1826, publishers were reluctant to publish first editions of poetry. By the 1830s and 1840s Edward Moxon was one of the few publishers in England of new collections of poetry by individual poets and his firm survived mainly due to his precaution that poets should agree to underwrite part of the publishing costs incurred.[11] In this literary climate, fledgling poets had to find new outlets for their talents and established poets had to make certain concessions. Wordsworth was no exception. Despite his later disdainful dismissal of the annuals as 'those greedy receptacles of trash, those Bladders upon which the Boys of Poetry try to swim', Wordsworth found himself unable to reject the considerable sum of a hundred guineas for twelve pages of verse, the amount paid for his contribution

---

[10] Blessington was criticised for living in a ménage-à-trois with her daughter and her husband, Count d'Orsay, a situation exacerbated by her daughter's subsequent departure from the home. Norton, like Blessington, was often the subject of scurrilous rumour, most notoriously as a result of the divorce action brought against her by her husband in 1837 which cited Queen Victoria's Prime Minister, Lord Melbourne, as her lover. For further details see Adburgham, *Women in Print*, pp. 236–49.

[11] Dino Franco Felluga, 'Tennyson's *Idylls*, Pure Poetry and the Market', *Studies in English Literature 1500–1900*, 37: 4 (1997), pp. 783–803 (p. 785).

to *The Keepsake* of 1829.[12] For Alfred, Lord Tennyson, young and 'on
the verge of a literary career in which writing poetry would be his
primary source of income', the gift books provided a useful and
fashionable introduction to the literary milieu.[13] As Anne Renier
observes, Tennyson, like many others, saw in them an excellent
means of gaining publicity and eagerly complied with requests for
poems from annual editors. During the 1830s, three short poems of his
appeared in *The Gem*; sonnets in *Friendship's Offering* and *The Yorkshire
Literary Annual*; 'The Eve of St Agnes' in *The Keepsake*; [and] a poem in
The Tribute that was later to be transmogrified into 'Maud'.[14] Yet, like
Wordsworth, he was soon to forswear 'all annuals provincial or
metropolitan', feeling 'beGemmed and beAmuletted and be-forget-
me-not-ted' to the point of profound professional dissatisfaction.[15]
Male poets, it appears, were quick to condemn the annuals even as
they reaped the financial benefits of their contributions.

For women poets, however, the annuals provided a safe space in
which to publish. Seemingly protected by the apparent propriety of the
annual form, important female poets such as Felicia Hemans and
Letitia Landon (L.E.L.) contributed regularly to a number of titles,
and poems by Elizabeth Barrett Browning are to be found among the
pages of *Finden's Tableaux* for 1838, 1839, and 1840, as well as *The
Keepsake* for 1855 and 1857. A cursory glance at some of the current
anthologies of nineteenth-century women's poetry will provide a long
list of names, such as Mary Howitt, Maria Jane Jewsbury, Joanna
Baillie, Amelia Opie, Helen Dufferin, Sarah Stickney Ellis, and
Louisa H. Sheridan, whose primary outlet was the annual, or who
contributed to the annuals at some point in their professional careers.
Indeed women editors requesting contributions often highlighted the
annual's role as a springboard to literary success. Writing to a 'Miss
Harrison' in 1837, Mary Russell Mitford, editor of *Finden's Tableaux of
the Affections*, informs her potential contributor: 'The real advantage is
being included in the most splendid of these works with a very few . . .
of the choicest poets of the day, and [it is] sure to be seen upon the table
of almost every rich person of taste in England; so that it is the very best

[12] Peter J. Manning, 'Wordsworth in the *Keepsake*, 1829', in John O. Jordan
and Robert L. Patten (eds), *Literature in the Marketplace: Nineteenth-Century
British Publishing and Reading Practices* (Cambridge, 1995), pp. 68, 49–50.
[13] Goldberg, p. 72.
[14] Anne Renier, *Friendship's Offering*, p. 15.
[15] Alfred, Lord Tennyson, letter to William Henry Brookfield, 3 August 1831,
quoted in Goldberg, p. 78.

possible introduction to authorship.'[16] In many ways, the annuals were, as Reynolds points out, instrumental in creating 'a professional sisterhood', and Lady Blessington, Caroline Norton, Letitia Landon, and Catherine Gore, were among the exclusively female circle labelled the 'Regency Blues' in honour of their blue-stocking status.[17] As Susan Brown observes:

> the fact that women edited as well as published in [the annuals] fostered a network of women's writing that rippled down through the entire Victorian period. The sense of association with sister writers whose work appeared alongside their own, the opportunity to publish in a large-circulation market . . . and the correspondence between authors and editors all laid the foundation for a community of women writers. (p. 191)

Brown adds that the annuals also 'posed a challenge to anthologists and critics attempting to institute separate spheres in the literary domain, since female and male authors appeared in them side by side, and women most often took the role of editor' (p. 191). While this is in some sense true, it is clear that the predominance of female poetry, female editorship and female readership associated with the annuals was inevitably responsible for what was deemed the 'feminisation' of the product. The fact that the annuals appeared to promote 'a small and trivialized style of poetry in which women were presumed to specialize' also explains perhaps the contempt which underlay comments made by male contributors such as Sir Walter Scott who 'regretted having meddled in any way with the toyshop of literature'.[18] Fearing feminisation by association, Scott, like Wordsworth and Tennyson, distanced himself from the annuals. In making the gift books their own, women, it seems, had stamped them with their femininity. Women poets and women's poetry were both marketed together in the feminised culture of the annual.

Feminine Sensuality and the Annual Form

This slippage between product and producer is insistently present in the literary annual, as 'woman' becomes a commodified artifact. This

[16] Quoted in Adburgham, *Silver Fork Society*, p. 258.
[17] Reynolds, p. xxx; Adburgham, *Women in Print*, p. 253.
[18] Reynolds, p. xxx; quoted in Goldberg, p. 78.

resonates interestingly with contemporary descriptions of the gift
books, which are based on an analogy between text and woman: in
an 1826 review, Christopher North was to compare 'four virgin
volumes' to four beautiful girls entering his room, all of whom are
'jewels – delights – perfect loves'.[19] Like those female poets whose work
graced its pages, and whose public personae were already predeter-
mined by conventional conceptions of decorum, The Keepsake 'was a
bound product before distribution to the bookseller', its presentation
'[a]ppropriately simple and understated, yet beautiful', and sold in
fabric that displayed a 'soft shiny grain . . . [that was] clearly
feminine'.[20] Renier speaks of the annuals' 'elegant garb': 'The Amulet
appeared in green silk in 1828, and The Keepsake began and continued
its career in red watered silk': normally a dress fabric, this material was
used to give the annuals, 'a strikingly feminine look that also appeared
expensive'.[21] In 1838, The Keepsake's 'femininity' was enhanced still
further, for the rubber utilised in the new backing techniques in which
binders had invested 'was also being used in women's corsets to tighten
the stays'.[22]

The 'femininity' and sensuality of the annual form played a central
part in the marketing strategies of its publishers and did so from its
inception. In his introduction to the first Keepsake (1827), Leigh Hunt
creates a fantasy vision of the 'ultimate gift book'.[23] Ascribing 'to a lock
of hair a value above all other keepsakes' he astutely suggests that the
most fitting container for that lock would be a bejewelled edition
whose

> cover should be thick with emeralds and crystal: Keepsakes of all
> kinds should glitter without and within; hearts in ruby, and fervid
> letters in opal . . . a border of the exquisitest flowers on ivory should
> run round it; and . . . there should be a crystal with a key to it in the
> midst, that when the heart was full, the locks of hair might be
> kissed.[24]

[19] Quoted in Manning, p. 62.
[20] 'Introduction to The Keepsake', Electronic Editions, Romantic Circles http://
www.rc.umd.edu/editions/lel/intro.htm (August 2000), p. 2.
[21] Renier, p. 12; 'Introduction to The Keepsake', Electronic Editions, p. 2.
[22] 'Introduction to The Keepsake', Electronic Editions, p. 3.
[23] Cynthia Lawford, 'Bijou Beyond Possession: The Prima Donnas of L.E.L.'s
Album Poems', in Isobel Armstrong and Virginia Blain (eds), Women's Poetry,
Late Romantic to Late Victorian: Gender and Genre, 1830–1900 (London, 1999),
p. 104.
[24] Quoted in Lawford, p. 104.

In spite of the annuals' apparent propriety, and their publishers' efforts to present themselves as moral guardians, it would seem that at the heart of the annual form there lies a latent eroticism that compromises their probity. The medium's implicit sensuality problematises the woman poet's association with the annual form. If the annual is a woman, what kind of woman is she? Is she the kind of woman with whom the female poet may associate without damaging her reputation? On the surface it would seem so – respectability, taste, and femininity being her avowed concerns. Yet, she is a commodity, sold in the marketplace, and, like the eponymous prostitute in Dante Gabriel Rossetti's 'Jenny' (1870), she is 'Apparelled beyond parallel' and knows not 'what a book' she seems as her 'lifted silken skirt/ Advertis[es] dainties through the dirt' of the market economy, as her, 'silk ungirdled and unlac'd' reveals 'warm sweets' of literary and artistic delight.[25] Straddling the boundary between innocence and sin, the annual is not only like Rossetti's Jenny but also like her customer's cousin Nell: 'fond of dress, and change, and praise': it is 'So pure' yet, simultaneously, 'so fall'n!' (pp. 63–4).

A Dangerous Vocation

Such moral ambiguity was evidently a latent concern and discussed in the fiction of the day. In Catherine Gore's *Women As They Are* (1830), Lady Theodosia Mitford states: 'Authorship is a dangerous temptation to a woman; – I would have none in whom I am interested incur such a dangerous publicity, till she has attained her fullest years of discretion.'[26] Some were to feel the truth of these words. While the gossip and interest which surrounded some high-class contributors and editors were often instrumental in their appointment or solicitation, such attention could be permanently damaging to those in less secure social positions such as Letitia Landon. Having no family background to speak of, Landon was in an equivocal position, and her professional associations with men were sometimes interpreted unfavourably. In the case of her association with William Maginn, who helped her with the editorship of the *Drawing-Room Scrapbook*, the scandal led to personal misfortune and the breakdown of her engagement to John Foster with

---

[25] Dante Gabriel Rossetti, *Selected Poems and Translations*, ed. Clive Wilmer (Manchester, 1991), pp. 68, 59, 62, 59.
[26] Quoted in Adburgham, *Silver Fork Society*, p. 249.

whom she was deeply in love.[27] Regardless of class or status, however, the woman poet engaging in public display and visibility was in a precarious position. Despite the fact that the annuals often concentrated on domestic, sentimental subjects, woman poets nevertheless risked unsavoury associations in being paid for their art. According to Angela Leighton, the concept of fallenness was capacious: 'for the Victorians, the fallen woman is a type which ranges from the successful courtesan to the passionate adulteress, from the destitute streetwalker to the seduced innocent, from the unscrupulous procuress to the raped child. To fall, for woman, is simply to fall short.'[28] In Victorian society, one might argue, the woman poet, too, is seen as 'falling short'. Her entry into the public sphere for monetary gain was incompatible with contemporary constructions of femininity. Middle-class conventions required that men should support women and any woman supporting herself was perceived to be a victim. This image of the working woman appears in *Aurora Leigh* (1856), Elizabeth Barrett Browning's bildungsroman of the Victorian woman poet. Describing her attempts to support herself through her poetry Aurora writes:

> The midnight oil
> Would stink sometimes; there came some vulgar needs:
> I had to live that therefore I might work,
> And, being but poor, I was constrained, for life,
> To work with one hand for the booksellers
> While working with the other for myself
> And art: you swim with feet as well as hands,
> Or make small way.[29]

It is significant that Aurora makes a distinction between writing 'for the booksellers' and working for herself 'and art'. She seeks the elevation of poetry beyond the contaminating touch of the literary marketplace, and, perhaps, the lucrative but ostentatious gift books. It is clear that, in writing a book-length poem which addressed contemporary subjects, Barrett Browning also wished to distance herself from what Margaret Reynolds calls 'the sentimental, picturesque mode'

---

[27] Adburgham, *Women in Print*, p. 247.
[28] Angela Leighton, '"Because men made the laws": The Fallen Woman and the Woman Poet', in Angela Leighton (ed.), *Victorian Women Poets: A Critical Reader* (Oxford, 1996), p. 217.
[29] Elizabeth Barrett Browning, *Aurora Leigh*, ed. Margaret Reynolds (New York, 1996), 3: 299–306.

of women such as Felicia Hemans and Letitia Landon who wrote for the annuals.[30] Yet their spectres are raised in *Aurora Leigh*, for it is difficult to avoid reading Barrett Browning's account of a maverick woman poet without being aware of the text as a paradigmatic exposition of the difficulties encountered by women poets in general. Moreover, despite her success, Aurora remains subject to the common perception that there is an implicit relationship between the woman poet who enters the financial world selling her wares and the prostitute who is driven to the streets and exhibits herself to make her living. In Barrett Browning's text this relationship is located not only in economics, but also in the realms of desire.

In *Aurora Leigh*, Barrett Browning acknowledges the sublimation of a woman's sexual desire in poetry. As Aurora muses on her fame she concedes that her poems contain the 'very heart of passionate womanhood',

> Which could not beat so in the verse without
> Being present also in the unkissed lips
> And eyes undried because there's none to ask
> The reason they grew moist.   (5: 443–7)

This, however, creates an unsettling paradox. If women's poetry acts as a container for the woman poet's sexual desire, then both poetry and the woman poet are necessarily eroticised in the process. Dorothy Mermin argues that this heady coalescence of poetry and desire in women's poems stems from traditional images of women as love objects in poetry by men. She writes: 'Since women had appeared in poetry almost exclusively as amatory objects, it was generally assumed that when they wrote poems themselves love should be their theme.'[31] As Mermin points out, Felicia Hemans and Letitia Landon evidently agreed, always insisting that 'love, not fame, is woman's only source of happiness and that the two are incompatible' (p. 75). Despite striking a blow for the emancipation of the woman poet, Barrett Browning's Aurora Leigh capitulates similarly when she acknowledges that 'Art is much, but love is more' (9: 656).

Yet there is perhaps another reason behind the woman poet's association with desire. In the figure of the Greek poetess Sappho, the female poet becomes not only the object of desire, but the desiring

---

[30] Reynolds, *Victorian Women Poets*, p. 64.
[31] Dorothy Mermin, 'The Damsel, the Knight, and the Victorian Woman Poet', *Critical Inquiry* 13 (1986), pp. 64–80, p. 75.

woman, and it is perhaps no accident that 'Sappho emerges as the proper name for the Poetess' in Victorian Britain for women poets and for literary critics who 'constantly evoked Sappho as the precedent for the poetess'.[32] Until the lesbian eroticism of her poetry was highlighted by the publication of Swinburne's 'Anactoria' in 1866, Sappho, according to Brown, was generally read 'in the biographical tradition promulgated largely by Ovid's *Heroides*, which emphasised her suicidal leap from the Leucadian cliff after her male lover Phaon abandoned her' (p. 182). This story of desire and fatal love struck a chord with the Victorian woman poet: 'Sappho's suicide became an allegory for women poets' dilemmas and an alibi for their voices: it focused their sense of the conflicts between art and love, vocation and gender, and the desire for literary fame and the demands of social convention' (p. 182). But more importantly perhaps Sappho represents the active love of a desiring subject, not merely the passivity of a desired object. Even the invocation of Sappho as a talismanic force for female poetry is complicated, however, by the Greek's femininity. While, as Brown suggests, Sappho provides the woman poet with 'a prime vehicle for poetic utterance', exemplified not only indirectly, but directly in poems such as Felicia Hemans's 'The Last Song of Sappho' (1834) and Caroline Norton's 'The Picture of Sappho' (1840), she does not fully evade the objectification which hampers the woman poet's subjectivity and this is made clear by the poems themselves. In each poem Sappho is associated with a work of art (p. 183). The inspiration for Hemans's poem is a sketch by Richard Westmacott Jr. which 'represents Sappho sitting on a rock above the sea, with her lyre cast at her feet', and Norton's poem opens with the words:

> Thou! whose impassion'd face
> The Painter loves to trace,
> Theme of the Sculptor's art and Poet's story –
> How many a wand'ring thought
> Thy loveliness hath brought,
> Warming the heart with its imagined glory.[33]

Sappho is represented here as both desiring subject and erotic object, a

---

[32] Yopie Prins, *Victorian Sappho* (Princeton, 1999), p. 14; Brown, p. 183.
[33] Felicia Hemans, 'The Last Song of Sappho', in *Victorian Women Poets*, p. 4; Caroline Norton, 'The Picture of Sappho', in *Victorian Women Poets*, pp. 136–7.

sexualised female on display. If the Victorian woman poet identifies herself, and is identified by others with Sappho, such an association has significant implications. In a society that aimed to confine women exclusively to the private sphere, where they were expected to be 'modestly unself-conscious and shun the gaze of men' the female poet, modelling herself on Sappho – the desired and desiring woman – found her life and work construed as a form of 'highly sexualised self-exposure'.[34]

Women on Display

In the annuals this over-determined self-exposure and visibility is often complicated by the subject matter of the engravings and the poetry which accompanies them, as well as by the nature of the contract between them. The engravings were of paramount importance to the success of any annual: they were usually chosen in advance and the poems then written to complement them. Adburgham informs us that:

> All the illustrations in the first *Keepsake* were by Thomas Stothard and F. P. Stephanoff, both of whom could claim large fees; and it was made clear in the introduction that the pictures were chosen first, then the poems and stories commissioned to go with them. This prostitution of the pen to the picture was the usual practice with all the annuals. (p. 253)

During her time as editor of the *Drawing-Room Scrapbook*, Letitia Landon was the sole contributor contracted to provide poems for each of the thirty pictures collected for each volume. In her introduction to the first volume published in 1832, she voices the difficulties experienced in such a process: 'It is no easy thing to write to prints selected rather for their pictorial elegance than their poetic capabilities, and mere description is certainly not the most popular species of composition.'[35] It is clear that Landon is not fully comfortable with the demands of the process despite her success in providing what the public wanted, and it has been suggested that her contributions were 'often penned . . . with the loathing of a slave – a literary slave – to the

---

[34] Mermin, p. 65.
[35] Quoted in Adburgham, *Silver Fork Society*, p. 254.

enforced subject'.[36] In his essay 'A Word on the Annuals', William
Makepeace Thackeray condemns this waste of Landon's talents: 'It is
the gift of God to her – to watch, to cherish, and to improve: it was not
given her to be made over to the highest bidder, or to be pawned for so
many pounds per sheet.'[37] Interestingly these comments are informed
by the language of the market, of prostitution and enslavement, which
both contaminates and reflects the woman poet's professional engage-
ment with the literary economy. Moreover, the content of these
engravings was also often subtly erotic, consisting primarily of images
of women in either exotic or sumptuous domestic settings. This
eroticism seeped from cover to content, for bound in the annuals'
silken binding are images constructed by artists from what was referred
to as 'a little boudoir school' of painters: engravings of women
displaying 'varieties of ringlets, eyelashes, naked shoulders, and slim
waists ... ladies in voluptuous attitudes and various stages of déshabillé,
to awaken the dormant sensibilities of misses in their teens, or tickle
the worn-out palates of elderly rakes and roués.'[38]

In The Diadem: A Book for the Boudoir, published in 1838, the title
page displays an engraving in which three women are grouped
together in an aesthetic pose. The central figure holds her left
hand to her breast, and looks pensive. To the right another, in
conventional Victorian garb, her white shoulders exposed, looks
directly at the first and exhibits her beautiful back and neck to the
viewer. To the left of the central figure is a third woman with long
hair, who wears an oriental headdress and looks into the distance.[39]
The poem which accompanies this engraving is called, 'Love's
Inquest', and is written by 'The Hon. Mrs J. C. Westenra'. Westenra's
poem transforms the women into allegories of prudence, caprice and
joy who vie for the figure of 'Love', a young boy who arrives in their
midst. The erotic undercurrent is evident in the subject matter of the
poem, in the representation of the women's figures in the engraving,
and particularly in the description of Joya's treatment of the boy. The
speaker tells us:

[36] Quoted in Adburgham, Silver Fork Society, p. 254.
[37] William Makepeace Thackeray, 'A Word on the Annuals', Fraser's Maga-
zine, XVI (1837), pp. 757–63 (p. 763).
[38] 'Introduction to The Keepsake', Electronic Editions, Romantic Circles, p. 6;
Thackeray, p. 758.
[39] The Diadem: A Book for the Boudoir, ed. Louisa H. Sheridan (London, 1838).

This Maiden only sought to *please*
Her charge, by soft luxurious ease,
Honey, rich fruits, and luscious wine,
With silken couch, and raiment fine.[40]

While the end of the poem subverts this luxury by stating that '*too much kindness killed this Love!*' (p. 28), it is the sensuality of this stanza and the female figures in the illustration which remain in the reader's imagination. A similar effect occurs in 'The Sultan's Daughter and the Slave' by Agnes Strickland. The engraving the poem accompanies features the sultan's 'child', a beautiful and luxuriously dressed young woman wearing a necklace of pearls, who holds a butterfly in her hand. She shows the butterfly to her servant, 'Leila', an older woman, still lovely, who gazes down at her. The poem sets the scene in the 'guarded bound/ Of royal Acbar's harem bowers' in which the speaker tells of 'The listless languor, and despair/ Of young warm hearts, that pine in vain'.[41] Despite the exotic (and erotic) context of the poem, the scene is domesticated and Leila's longing looks are associated with thoughts of home 'The blessed home of infancy' that she may never see again (p. 17). Yet such sorrows quickly disappear as her gaze is captured by the sultan's 'beauteous child' who with 'glowing cheeks' and 'loosened tresses floating wild' directs her attention at the fragile butterfly she cradles in her hand.

While both of these poems ostensibly work within the parameters of morality and domesticity, they are problematised both by the volup-tuous quality of the female figures in the illustrations and by the sensuality of the poetry. In addition both poems draw attention to the beautiful women in the engravings and are set in intimate female locations: each poem appears in *The Diadem*, which advertises itself as a 'book for the boudoir', and 'The Sultan's Daughter and the Slave' is set in that most exclusive of female spaces – the harem. Both the 'boudoir' and the 'harem' sexualise the poetry and the women depicted in the pictures it accompanies and I suggest that an anxiety regarding content is evident in the anonymous poem which appears on the title page of the annual:

A Diadem, by Fancy lightly placed
Upon the brow of Genius, Beauty, Taste:

---

[40] J. C. Westenra, 'Love's Inquest', in *The Diadem*, pp. 26–8 (p. 27).
[41] Agnes Strickland, 'The Sultan's Daughter', in *The Diadem*, pp. 17–18 (p. 17).

No symbol glaring with factitious light, –
But a pure Golden Circlet, chaste and bright!

The Diadem must be seen to be 'chaste' and concede to matters of
'taste'. Yet its inclusion of oriental subjects in its engravings and its
poetry offers its readers an exciting and semi-sexual encounter for, as
Edward Said has argued, in the fantasies of the West, the East is
'feminine' providing sexual delight and revelling in moral laxity.[42]
Furthermore, in each of the poems and engravings we, as readers and
viewers, are placed in the position of voyeurs, favoured with a peek into
a feminine world of sensuality and eroticism. What complicates the
representations still further is the relationship between the women
presented in the illustrations. In each, the female gaze is directed at
another woman, and this gaze becomes even more problematic in *The
Book of Beauty*, an annual which blurs the line between female beauty
and female poetry.

In 1833, Charles Heath designed a new annual 'whose illustrations
were to consist of beautiful and fashionable ladies'.[43] It was originally
edited by Letitia Landon, and subsequently by Lady Blessington. The
book appeared in a variety of elegant bindings including 'figured silk,
[and] velvet' echoing the luxurious fabrics worn by the mainly
aristocratic females in its illustrations.[44] Although, under Blessington's
editorship, *The Book of Beauty* also contained essays and articles which
were independent of the plates and written by famous names such as
Thackeray, Edward Bulwer Lytton and Sir Walter Scott, these were
interleaved with poems which extolled the beauties and virtues of the
society women who appeared in its engravings.[45] Among these are 'The
Lady Ashley' (1836) by Lady Emmeline Stuart Wortley, 'The Countess
of Coventry' (1836) by Letitia Landon, and 'Lines on the portrait of the
Lady Fanny Cowper' (1839) by Lady Blessington.[46] The engraving of
Lady Ashley faces Wortley's poem so that the text 'looks' at the portrait

[42] Edward W. Said, *Orientalism* (London, 1995), p. 207.
[43] Andrew Boyle, *An Index to the Annuals*, 2 vols (Worcester, 1967), preface to
vol. 2 (unnumbered).
[44] Ibid. Although most of the images in *The Book of Beauty* are of society
women, some, such as Blessington's 'Felicité', which depicts a maid, do show
other classes. What is interesting, however, is that in Blessington's poem the
sense of luxury is maintained as the maid is trying on her mistress's clothing and
jewels (see *The Book of Beauty* [1837], pp. 223–4).
[45] Adburgham, *Women in Print*, p. 250.
[46] The limited availability of editions of *The Book of Beauty* has restricted my
choice of poems. Those chosen, however, are representative of the genre.

mirroring the gaze of the speaker in the poem (figure 1). The picture is 'framed' in portrait style, and the beautiful woman within it wears a deep décolletage and gazes directly at the viewer. Her shoulders are bare and her brunette hair falls loosely about them. The poem begins with a eulogy to modesty, beauty, and status:

> Oh! fairest 'mongst a million fair!
> With sunny eyes, and floating hair,
> And sylph-like form, and beauteous face,
> And charm of fascinating grace,
> And stamp of an exalted line,
> That marks each lineament of thine!
> Oh! fairest 'mongst a myriad fair!
> Far *more* than beauty's boast is there,
> Or charm of captivating grace,
> Or pride of a patrician race.
> There lurks the attractive modesty
> That deprecates the admiring eye;
> The ingenuous candour there is seen,
> That, open, smiling, and serene,
> For evermore accompanies
> Sweet Innocence, that scorns disguise:
> And there, too, above all, appears
> The gentleness that most endears,
> That most can win, and most enthrall –
> 'Mid thousand graces, first of all![47]

Yet soon the poem shifts its focus onto Lady Ashley's physical qualities:

> Could ev'n imagination seize
> On beauties more divine than these?
> Eyes – like the sun in morn's young hour,
>
> .   .   .   .
>
> Lips – that like bruised pomegranates blush
> Still with a deep and deepening flush
>
> .   .   .   .
>
> Most glorious hair! that seems to fall,
> Just loosened from some delicate thrall,
> In burnished hyacinthine flow
> The pillar of thy throat of snow,
> And shoulders' sculptured grace below.   (pp. 37–8)

[47] Lady Emmeline Stuart Wortley, 'The Lady Ashley', in *The Book of Beauty*, ed. the Countess of Blessington (London, 1836), pp. 36–8 (p. 36).

Figure 1 Engraving of 'The Lady Ashley', from *The Book of Beauty*, ed. the
Countess of Blessington (London, 1836), facing p. 36. Reproduced with
permission of the British Library.

While the images used are conventional, it is impossible to ignore the
sexual implications of lips which blush 'like bruised pomegranates'
and hair that seems to fall 'Just loosened from some delicate thrall'.
The pomegranate, in particular, associated with Dionysian revel,
suggests a loss of control and sexual ecstasy which are mirrored in

Lady Ashley's tousled tresses.[48] However, by the end of the poem, the eroticism that pervades this description is almost submerged in modesty and virtue:

> Enchantment – yea, Enchantment's there:
> And yet no dangerous Circe thou!
> With those meek eyes, that guileless brow.   (p. 38)

Her beauty, and her sexual allure, then, are blameless, for they are 'guileless' and 'close allied / With sacred virtue's modest pride' (p. 38). Yet the voluptuousness of Wortley's depiction is not fully erased by the end of the poem, for the speaker exclaims, 'Oh! fairest 'mongst a myriad fair! / Can pen rehearse the witcheries there?' (p. 38) suggesting that the speaker remains captive and bewitched.

In 'The Countess of Coventry', Letitia Landon writes in a similar, though less digressive style. Once again the poem faces the engraving in which the Countess, in a reflective pose, her left hand raised to her cheek, sits dressed luxuriously in Turkish fashion. Her breasts are accentuated by the cut of the satin dress, and her neck is adorned with pearls. Landon writes:

> Pause here awhile! if in soft, speaking eye,
>   Or mouth – closed fount of mirth – there lurk a charm,
>   Or neck more fair than pearl, or rounded arm,
> Or tresses that rich autumn's hues outvie,
> Or cheeks near which might roses envying die
>   Yes! this was England's boast – whene'er she came,
>   Like Beauty's watchword ran abroad her name,
> And myriads shouted as her pomp swept by.
>   Pause here. – She was! – and if this pictured face,
> As far as nature doth all art excell,
>   So far is fainter than that living grace
> Which won the sternest with resistless spell –
> Forbear the painter's baffled skill to chide:
> Thou ownest Echo sweet, though Music's self hath died.[49]

Here, once again there is a focus on the woman's body, which is fragmented in order to highlight the sensuous parts – eye, mouth,

---

[48] The plant is said to have sprung from the blood of Dionysus, see Ad de Vries, *Dictionary of Symbols* (Amsterdam, North Holland, 1974), p. 371.
[49] Letitia Landon, 'The Countess of Coventry', in *The Book of Beauty*, ed. the Countess of Blessington (London, 1836), p. 69.

neck, arms, and hair – against the 'whole' presented in the illus-
tration.

Blessington's 'Lines on the portrait of Lady Fanny Cowper' continues
in a now familiar manner. In the illustration opposite the poem, we are
presented with a side view of Lady Cowper who, dressed in white, wears
a dark mantilla which creates the effect of flowing hair (figure 2). She
looks into the distance and holds a fan in her right hand. The pose
accentuates the perfection of her figure. Blessington's poem, like
Landon's, is short. Yet it, too, concentrates on its object's physical
attributes which are listed in the second stanza:

> Thine is England's beauty; –
>   Where, besides, doth rose
> Such a glow of brightness
>   On such a cheek disclose?
> Where, beside, such forehead,
>   Pure as early day –
> Shrine where thought, most holy,
>   Bids the careless pray?[50]

Less erotic than either Wortley's or Landon's poems, Blessington's
nevertheless speaks of the 'glow' of brightness on Lady Cowper's
cheeks. Although such a blush might indicate modesty, it necessarily
acknowledges the desire that elicits that blush, despite the seemingly
religious context of purity and prayer in which it occurs.

Fragments of Fame

These literary portraits of feminine allure appear to adopt certain
conventions common in Petrarchan poetry. It is perhaps unsurprising
that this should be so for, as Nancy J. Vickers has remarked, 'The
import of Petrarch's description of Laura extends well beyond the
confines of his own poetic age; in subsequent times, his portrayal of
feminine beauty became authoritative.'[51] It is important to remember,
however, that such a poetic mode entails the fragmentation of the
female body. Applied by a woman poet, this becomes especially

---

[50] Lady Blessington, 'Lines on the Portrait of the Lady Fanny Cowper', *The
Book of Beauty*, ed. the Countess of Blessington (London, 1839), pp. 129–30.
[51] Nancy J. Vickers, 'Diana Described: Scattered Woman and Scattered
Rhyme', *Critical Inquiry* 8 (Winter 1981), pp. 265–79.

Figure 2 Engraving of 'The Lady Fanny Cowper', from *The Book of Beauty*, ed.
the Countess of Blessington (London, 1839), facing p. 129. Reproduced with
permission of the British Library.

problematic. I suggest that its appropriation compromises the female
poet: it is a 'masculine' masquerade and, simultaneously, an unwitting
identification with the fragmented body that ultimately results in a
form of 'disintegration'. As Mermin has observed, the female poet
already labours under a particular difficulty. Perceived primarily as the
muse, she is generally the object, and not the writer, of poetry: 'The
Victorian woman poet has to be two things at once, or in two places,
whenever she tries to locate herself within the poetic world' for,
traditionally, 'it's not really *poets* that are women, for the Victorians:
poems are women' (p. 68). In contrast, Mermin argues, male poets
writing of women, whether they be self-projections or otherwise,
manage to maintain a distinction between themselves and the
female figures in their poetry. For women, however, things are not so
simple. Mermin points out that, when women write of women, 'the two
[poet and subject] blur into one' (p. 68). I would argue that in the
poems from which I have quoted this blurring is especially evident and
exacerbated by the presence of the illustrated female body. In those of
Hemans and Norton, Sappho as art object merges with their own
identities. When Lady Stuart Wortley writes of Lady Ashley, Letitia
Landon of the Countess of Coventry and Lady Blessington of Lady
Cowper, there is little distinction to be made between the female poet
and the female 'object' depicted in the engravings for both are
essentially 'on display' and eroticised in the process. Both dissolve
into images of desire. In the light of this inevitable dissolution between
subject and object, the poems, like the engravings themselves, form a
palimpsest of female bodies: a process of effacement and replacement
that is repeated perpetually in each edition.

Given these complications, what can the woman poet do? One
option is to fragment her identity and adopt the masculine position.
This is the choice made by Aurora Leigh who distances herself from her
own femininity. As an 'artist woman' she believes she stands outside
'the common sex' and her entry into the public field involves the loss of
her traditional feminine position in society (3: 406–7). This is also
apparently the choice made by the female contributors to *The Book of
Beauty*, for, in the poems cited here, they adopt the recognisable
position of the male lover writing to the female beloved in the amatory
tradition. Yet for the annuals' women poets, this particular strategy of
masculinisation is not entirely successful. Contributing to publications
which play with eroticism and display 'feminine' beauty both in their
covers and their contents, these female poets cannot evade the
implications for their own virtue. Indeed interest in women poets

often centred on their looks. Recollecting the response of Oxford undergraduates to Landon's first appearance on the literary scene, Bulwer Lytton evokes an image of what Brown terms the 'poetess as an eroticised commodity'; he writes:

> there was always, in the reading room of the Union, a rush every Saturday afternoon for the Literary Gazette, and an impatient anxiety to hasten at once to that corner of the sheet which contained the three magical letters of 'L.E.L.' And all of us praised the verse, and all of us guessed at the author. We soon learned it was a female, and our admiration was doubled, and our conjectures tripled. Was she young? Was she pretty?[52]

This sexualised engagement with the body of the author through her poetry raises once more the spectre of prostitution – the selling of one's body in the literary marketplace. Writing of female subjects in the annuals, women poets arguably attempt to deflect attention away from themselves onto the bodies of the women in the illustrations only to find it returned in an endless mirror reflection. Moreover, the amatory style they employ has further implications. If, as Brown suggests, Victorian women poets identified themselves, and were identified by others with Sappho, then the gaze they apply to the 'beloved' in their poems is sexually complicated.[53]

While contemporary accounts of Sappho's poetry emphasised her heterosexuality, there were nevertheless readers of Greek who were aware of the homoerotic nature of many of Sappho's fragments.[54] Among these is 'To a Beloved Girl' in which a woman speaker addresses a female beloved and speaks of the physical dissolution that attends her love:

> If I meet
> You suddenly, I can't
>
> speak – my tongue is broken;
> a thin flame runs under
> my skin; seeing nothing,

[52] Quoted in Brown, pp. 186–7.
[53] Brown, pp. 182–4. Brown observes that women poets, such as Hemans and Landon, empathised with Sappho and saw her both as a source of inspiration and as a symbol of the pain implicit in a negotiation of love and fame.
[54] Catherine Maxwell, *The Female Sublime from Milton to Swinburne: Bearing Blindness* (Manchester, 2001), p. 98.

> hearing only my own ears
> drumming, I drip with sweat;
> trembling shakes my body
>
> and I turn paler than
> dry grass. At such times
> death isn't far from me.[55]

I suggest that, in directing their own words to a female 'beloved', the annuals' women poets employ a 'sapphic' gaze which eroticises the exchange between themselves and the women in the illustrations that elicit their poetry. In addition, the fragmentary poetics that fetishise the beloved for the male poet have a disturbing effect when applied by a woman. If the beloved is a 'reflection' of the poet herself, then the fragmentation of her body through desire results in the 'disintegration' of the poet's body: a dissolution which is figured in Sappho's fragment as death. Interestingly, this disintegration is exacerbated yet further by the choice of Sappho as the female poet who represents an autonomous literary identity for, as Yopie Prins has observed, the Victorians displayed a 'particular fascination with the fragmentation of the Sapphic corpus' that 'culminated in the idealization of Sappho herself as the perfect fragment' (p. 3).

It seems that for the Victorian woman poet there is no escape from the conventions that entrap her. While nineteenth-century perceptions of Sappho appear to legitimise the female writer, they simultaneously blur the line between her body and her work, and problematise her status as a role model for female poets. This is most pertinently exemplified by the fact that even in a poem which paved the way for a new kind of woman poet and a new kind of poetry, these traditional associations could be evaded neither by Barrett Browning, the woman poet who wrote it, nor by her exemplary protagonist, Aurora Leigh. In the text, although Aurora is the poet, Lady Waldemar identifies her as 'the Muse' and it is perhaps only to be expected that Elizabeth Barrett Browning should herself be identified with her creation (3: 363). As Reynolds writes:

> At the heart of *Aurora Leigh* there is a book. It's the book that Aurora sits down to write when she begins her story . . . This

---

[55] 'To a Beloved Girl' was commonly known as Sappho's Second Ode. The translation used here is taken from Mary Barnard, *Sappho* (Berkeley, 1986), p. 39.

imagined book is the pattern for *Aurora Leigh* itself. The real verse-novel published by Elizabeth Barrett Browning at the end of 1856 mirrors the made-up poem written by the fictional Aurora. Both books tell the story of a woman poet that is, and is not, her own story.[56]

The problems I have identified are counteracted, perhaps, by the fact that 'Both books tell the story of a woman poet that is, and is not her own story.' Equally, this story of women poets and the annuals 'is, and is not' their own story. Although the annuals evidently created a feminised world, they also professionalised women's poetry and paved the way for the future publication of significant women poets such as Christina Rossetti, Augusta Webster, Amy Levy, Mary E. Coleridge, and A. Mary F. Robinson. Many of those who began by writing for the annuals attracted readerships that led to the publication of single author volumes of poetry. Others began to take control of their own work and the means of publication; for example, those women poets involved with *Victoria Regia* (1861), edited by Adelaide Anne Procter, which, advertised as a 'Christmas book', became the 'showpiece of an explicitly feminist publishing venture', the Victoria Press.[57] This annual was to be among the last of the gift books. As the century progressed, women would begin to find other outlets for their poetry in magazines and journals such as the *Academy*, the *Westminster Gazette*, and *Macmillan's Magazine*. If, for the Victorians, women were *poems*, and not *poets*, then the fragmented images that often accompany their appearance in the annuals echo obliquely those lyric fragments that brought Sappho her lasting fame.

[56] Reynolds, introduction to Elizabeth Barrett Browning, *Aurora Leigh*, p. vii.
[57] See Brown, pp. 191-2.

Elizabeth Barrett Browning and the Garrisonians: 'The Runaway Slave at Pilgrim's Point', the Boston Female Anti-Slavery Society, and Abolitionist Discourse in the Liberty Bell

MARJORIE STONE

You think I shrieked then? Not a sound!
I hung, as a gourd hangs in the sun;
I only cursed them all around
As softly as I might have done
My very own child; from these sands
Up to the mountains, lift your hands,
O slaves, and end what I begun![1]

'THE RUNAWAY SLAVE AT PILGRIM'S POINT' is not only the most complex of Elizabeth Barrett Browning's dramatic monologues. It is also one of the most surprising works to come from her pen in her fifty-year-long writing career. The speaker is a fugitive slave woman who murders the white-faced child she gives birth to after she is raped, impregnated and flogged. Fleeing north and arriving at Pilgrim's Point, she curses the land the pilgrim fathers blessed 'in freedom's' name, re-lives in memory her history of violation and anguish, and curses the slave hunters who surround her at the poem's close, wishing each 'for his own wife's joy and gift / A little corpse as safely at rest' as her own

I am grateful to John Murray, the English Poetry Collection, Wellesley College Library, the British Library, the Boston Public Library, and the Armstrong Browning Library, Baylor University, Waco, Texas, for permission to examine or cite manuscripts quoted here, and to the Social Sciences and Humanities Research Council of Canada for supporting the costs my research. Also to Alison Chapman for her helpful editorial comments.
[1] *The Complete Works of Elizabeth Barrett Browning*, ed. Charlotte Porter and Helen A. Clarke (New York, 1900; rpt., 1973), 3: 168–9. All subsequent quotations from Barrett Browning's poems are to this edition, identified by stanza number in the text. Throughout this essay, EBB refers, of course, to Barrett Browning, the initials by which she signed herself both after her marriage and before (when she was Elizabeth Barrett Barrett).

murdered child. As she displays the marks on her wrists, where ropes tied her 'up at the flogging place' in 'free America', she identifies the slave hunters as 'born of the Washington-race', connecting the sins of these sons to the sins of the fathers, and the curse on them to the curse on their ancestors. Linking the curses on both to the misbegotten child she murdered to 'save it from [her] curse' (stanza 21), she calls, in the words cited above, for a general slave insurrection.

Neither the chain of curses nor the call for insurrection seemed out of place in the 1848 issue of the Boston *Liberty Bell*, in which 'The Runaway Slave at Pilgrim's Point' first appeared. The *Liberty Bell* was an anti-slavery annual sold each year at the Christmas bazaar organised by the Boston Female Anti-Slavery Society to raise money for the abolitionist cause, in conjunction with William Lloyd Garrison and his co-workers in the American Anti-Slavery Society. In the 1848 issue, prepared for sale at the December 1847 bazaar, EBB's poem was immediately preceded by a lead article, 'The Insurrection and Its Hero', celebrating the heroic black leader of a Southern slave uprising. Other contributions included Benjamin B. Wiffen's encomium on 'Placido, the Cuban Poet', an anti-slavery activist executed after being accused of inciting an 1844 rebellion; Charles K. Whipple's 'Clerical Influence', presenting Moses as a prototype of 'Nat Turner and of Toussaint L'Ouverture'; Frederick Douglass' 'Bibles for the Slaves', a sardonically eloquent denunciation of those who feared black literacy; and Caroline Healey Dall's 'Annie Gray', the story of a fugitive slave on her deathbed in Canada.[2]

If 'The Runaway Slave at Pilgrim's Point' does not seem out of place in the *Liberty Bell*, however, it does seem out of place in the context of its author's life and works up to the time of its publication. As genealogical and historical studies by Jeanette Marks and R. A. Barrett have shown, EBB descended from generations of Jamaican slave-owners. Slave rebellions like the Jamaican 'Christmas' insurrection of 1831–32 – resulting in the torching of many plantations, the destruction of millions of pounds of property, and the summary military executions of hundreds of slaves – were feared by the various branches of the Barrett family in Jamaica by 1800, not advocated.[3] How do we read the 'The Runaway

[2] *The Liberty Bell* by Friends of Freedom (Boston, 1848), pp. 1–28, 60–5, 97–108, 121–7, 184–201.
[3] See 'Torch', in Jeanette Marks, *The Family of the Barrett: A Colonial Romance* (New York, 1938), pp. 381–9; and 'Insurrection: Jamaica 1831–2' in R. A. Barrett, *The Barretts of Jamaica: The Family of Elizabeth Barrett Browning* (Winfield, Kansas, and London, 2000), pp. 83–7.

Slave at Pilgrim's Point' when we realise that its author's great-great-grandfather Samuel Barrett (1689–1760) had personally 'flogged his slaves like a divinity', as she confessed to Robert Browning in June of 1846?[4] And how does one explain the militant abolitionist sentiments of this poem, coming from a writer with little or no history of anti-slavery activism? EBB completed 'The Runaway Slave' in the months immediately following her marriage to Browning in September 1846. She first mentions it on 1 December 1845; on 23 December 1846, she mailed it to James Russell Lowell in America.[5] A bitter anti-slavery poem about rape, infanticide and racial strife is an odd work to issue from a courtship and newly-wed period of legendary happiness.

Critics who have discussed 'The Runaway Slave at Pilgrim's Point' have either not raised these questions, or they have turned chiefly to the Barretts' Jamaican roots and the poet's personal circumstances to answer them. In doing so, most have privileged biographical approaches over historical attention to cultural contexts, and traditional methodologies of source-attribution over theories of intertextuality that foreground the circulation of literary conventions within social and political matrices. To a degree, scholars have acknowledged the poem's wider historical contexts by noting in passing that EBB wrote it in response to an invitation from the 'anti-slavery people at Boston' to contribute a work to their annual (BC, 11: 213). This point is made by Helen Cooper, Dorothy Mermin, Ann Parry, Elizabeth H. Battles, Angela Leighton, Susan Brown and Sarah Brophy in the most substantial analyses of the poem published to date.[6] Yet, apart

---

[4] *The Brownings' Correspondence*, ed. Philip Kelley and Scott Lewis (Winfield, Kansas, 1993), 13: 24. References hereafter appear parenthetically, abbreviated as BC.

[5] See BC, 12: 213, 14: 86. Evidence that EBB actually completed the poem after her marriage is provided by marginal comments in Robert Browning's hand in an initial fair copy; see below, n. 14.

[6] Helen Cooper, *Elizabeth Barrett Browning: Woman and Artist* (Chapel Hill, 1988), p. 111; Dorothy Mermin, *Elizabeth Barrett Browning: The Origins of a New Poetry* (Chicago, 1989), pp. 156–7; Ann Parry, 'Sexual Exploitation and Freedom: Religion, Race and Gender in Elizabeth Barrett Browning's "The Runaway Slave at Pilgrim's Point"', *Studies in Browning and His Circle* 16 (1988), pp. 115–16; Elizabeth H. Battles, 'Slavery Through the Eyes of a Mother: "The Runaway Slave at Pilgrim's Point"', *Studies in Browning and His Circle* 19 (1991), p. 93; Angela Leighton, *Victorian Women Poets: Writing Against the Heart* (Charlottesville and London, 1992), p. 97; Susan Brown, '"Black and White Slave": Discourses of Race and Victorian Feminism', in *Gender and Colonialism*, ed. Timothy P. Foley, Lionel Pilkington, Sean Ryder

from Andrew Stauffer's brief analysis of the textual history of 'The Runaway Slave', the historical contexts and the abolitionist trans-Atlantic networks that led to the invitation, together with their impact on the poem, have remained unexplored.[7] While Parry does seek to locate the poem within its 'contemporary discursive practices', her analysis is inaccurate on several points, as in its questionable inference that the poem is set in the period between the American revolution and 1790, or in its claim that EBB's father 'was all for ending slavery'.[8] The poet herself may have declared in 1833, at the time of the Emancipation Bill, 'I am glad, and always shall be, that the negroes are – virtually – free!' (BC, 3: 81). But the evidence for her father's views is considerably more ambiguous, like the evidence for anti-slavery activism on her own part up to 1846.[9]

Although responses to EBB's dramatic representation of a rebellious fugitive slave have been remarkably diverse, the commonalities in recent criticism are significant. Generally received as a 'noble poem of Passion and Power' in the nineteenth century (by black and white readers alike), 'The Runaway Slave' was neglected for the first half of the twentieth century, then denounced in the 1950s as 'too blunt and shocking to have any enduring worth'; criticised in the 1980s and early 1990s for being too idealised and melodramatic by some, and defended as a radical proto-feminist treatment of sexual politics by others; and denounced again in the late 1990s as an exercise in conservative

and Elizabeth Tilley (Galway, 1995), p. 125; Sarah Brophy, "Elizabeth Barrett Browning's "The Runaway Slave at Pilgrim's Point" and the Politics of Interpretation", *Victorian Poetry* 36 (1998), p. 275. The publication of the poem in the *Liberty Bell* is not mentioned in one of the earliest feminist reinterpretations of EBB published in this period, Angela Leighton's *Elizabeth Barrett Browning* (Brighton, 1986), pp. 40–4.

[7] Andrew M. Stauffer, 'Elizabeth Barrett Browning's (Re)visions of Slavery', *ELN* 34 (1997), pp. 29–48 (p. 29).

[8] Parry, pp. 115, 118. Parry finds an allusion to the Declaration of Independence in undefined lines in stanza 32, leading her to conclude that 'in chronological terms, the poem refers to the period in the North between then and 1790' (p. 116), a conclusion that does not necessarily follow, even if one accepts that the Declaration of Independence is invoked in this stanza.

[9] See EBB's comments on her father's 'consternation' at the Emancipation Bill and its economic effects (BC, 3: 81, 86). Marks observes that in all of the Barrett family 'indentures and wills from 1671 to 1834, except for the will of George Goodin Barrett, who was himself a slave dealer, there is not even a phrase which might be interpreted as an acknowledgement of the injustice of [the family's] "cattle" transactions in slavery' (*The Family of the Barretts*, p. 337).

appropriation of voice.[10] What these contradictory readings have shared, however – with the exception of Brown's nuanced investigation of the poem in relation to Victorian discourses of race and feminism – has been the tendency (at least in the twentieth century) to locate analysis of 'The Runaway Slave' in the context of EBB's personal history. Thus, while several feminist critics have praised the poem's relatively radical gender politics, relating its critique of slavery system to the poet's rebellion against her father, Brophy explains what she sees as its conservative politics by recourse to the poet's supposed submissiveness to her father and male mentors. In these contrasting readings, EBB's personal relationship with her father becomes a primary context for explicating this anti-slavery work.[11]

The focus on biographical contexts is also evident in the reiterated assumption that a primary 'source' for 'The Runaway Slave at Pilgrim's Point' was a story about a fugitive slave given to EBB by a family cousin, Richard Barrett, Speaker of the Jamaican House of Assembly. This assumption is based on EBB's statement in an 1842 letter to Mary Mitford that Richard Barrett (no friend of her father in the family's labyrinthine legal disputes over wills, slaves and cattle) 'gave me a subject for a poem about a run away negro which I still have somewhere, in his handwriting' (BC, 5: 212). However, if one examines the story that the poet seems to have been referring to – identified, on good authority, as the 'Jamaican Story' reprinted in 1983 in *Richard Barrett's Journal* – one finds that it bears little or no resemblance to EBB's anti-slavery poem.[12] Julia Markus rightly notes in passing that this

[10] *National Anti-Slavery Standard*, 20 January, 1848, cited Stauffer, p. 31; Gardner T. Taplin, *The Life of Elizabeth Barrett Browning* (New Haven, 1957), p. 194. The African American educator, Charlotte Forten, thought the poem was 'powerfully', 'earnestly', and 'touchingly' written; see *The Journal of Charlotte L. Forten*, ed. Ray Allen Billington (1953; rpt. New York, 1981), pp. 44–5. Margaret Forster denounces it as 'melodramatic' in *Elizabeth Barrett Browning: A Biography* (London, 1988), p. 204.

[11] Leighton, Cooper, Parry, Battles, and Brown emphasise the poem's progressive sexual politics; Brophy, in contrast, sees the poem as 'inscribing a melodramatic feminine voice within a patriarchal framework of reception' (p. 277).

[12] See BC, 5: 213 and *Richard Barrett's Journal, New York and Canada 1816: A Critique of the Young Nation by an Englishman Abroad*, ed. Thomas Brott and Philip Kelley (Winfield, Kansas, 1983), pp. 121–3. Richard Barrett's story depicts a struggle between a positively represented 'Creole negroe' overseer Austin and 'an African negro' named Copperbottom. I do not have space to detail the history of this misreading, but Gardner T. Taplin first linked the poem to the story in *The Life of Elizabeth Barrett Browning* (New Haven, 1957),

MARJORIE STONE

'Jamaican story' is a 'far cry' from 'The Runaway Slave at Pilgrim's Point'. That said, Markus' own controversial argument that the poem arose from EBB's fear of giving birth to a child of mixed race – based on a highly questionable series of genealogical speculations about the Barrett family's ancestry – merely confirms the tendency to explicate this work within biographical frameworks.[13]

In contrast, this essay emphasises the abolitionist and *Liberty Bell* contexts of 'The Runaway Slave' because evidence suggests these had a much greater formative influence on the poem than the Richard Barrett story, and at least as much impact as EBB's personal life. I focus on what I see as one of the most interesting historical questions raised by 'The Runaway Slave'. How did a British poet and Jamaican slaveholder's daughter, with no evident history of anti-slavery activism prior to 1846, come to write a work that placed her among the ranks of the Boston Garrisonian abolitionists, within the radical wing of the American abolitionist movement – a poem, moreover, that reflects a thorough assimilation of the standard *topoi* and rhetoric of anti-slavery poetry in the *Liberty Bell*? To answer this question, I consider the trans-Atlantic abolitionist networks that led to the commissioning of EBB's poem, in conjunction with the text's surviving manuscripts.

Among these manuscripts, the most interesting is the rough draft now in Wellesley College Library, which reveals a process of composition that is unusually layered and convoluted, even in comparison to the manuscripts of some of EBB's other ballads and dramatic poems from this period. Additional manuscripts include two surviving portions of a subsequent draft (evidently initially intended as a fair copy) with intriguing pencilled comments in Robert Browning's hand, as well as some other fair copies.[14] Neither the manuscripts of 'The Runaway

and the connection between it and 'The Runaway Slave at Pilgrim's Point' has been further confused by subsequent critics. See Cooper, p. 111; Parry, p. 118; Battles, p. 94; and Brophy, p. 276.

[13] *Dared and Done: The Marriage of Elizabeth Barrett and Robert Browning* (New York, 1995), pp. 92–115. I treat some of the problems with Markus' theory in an essay on EBB in the *New Dictionary of National Biography* (forthcoming). For a detailed critique of her genealogical speculations, see Richard S. Kennedy, 'Disposing of a New Myth: A Close Look at Julia Markus's Theory About the Brownings' Ancestry', *Browning Society Notes* 26 (2000), pp. 21–47.

[14] See *The Browning Collections: A Reconstruction With Other Memorabilia*, compiled by Philip Kelley and Betty A. Coley (London and Kansas, 1984), D 799, D800, D801, D802, D803, D804, D805, D806, D807, pp. 324–5. The second and third portions of the fair copy with Browning's marginal comments are located in the British Library and in the Armstrong Browning Library

Slave' nor its *Liberty Bell* contexts have been explored in past studies of the poem. In fact, the manuscripts have been completely neglected in this instance, as in the case of so many other works by EBB, despite the abundance of related archival material.

My approach is thus contrapuntal. I consider compositional phases reflected in the Wellesley draft in light of its wider historical contexts, and I examine these contexts in light of what the manuscript reveals about abolitionist *topoi*. On the one hand, without an understanding of the poem's mid-nineteenth century cultural contexts, it is difficult to appreciate how 'The Runaway Slave' entered into debates that divided the anti-slavery movement, or distinguished English from American positions within it: including conflicts over women's role in political affairs. Nor can one appreciate how the positional complexities and the political rhetoric of the Garrisonian abolitionists and, more specifically, of the Boston Female Anti-Slavery Society, are mirrored in the poem itself. On the other hand, the extraordinarily complex compositional process embedded in the Wellesley manuscript helps to illumine both the characteristic conventions of anti-slavery poetry, and EBB's innovative interweaving of these. The first part of this essay counters misconceptions in literary scholarship concerning the *Liberty Bell* and the Boston Female Anti-Slavery Society by considering the abolitionist conflicts, struggles and networks that the history of each reflects. The second section analyses the manuscript of 'The Runaway Slave' in light of other works in the *Liberty Bell* to suggest how EBB's creative adaptation of anti-slavery *topoi* led to a strikingly original, if politically conflicted, poem. I give particular attention to the 1844 and 1845 issues of the annual since documentary evidence shows that EBB received autographed presentation copies of these, one of them from Maria Weston Chapman, the *Liberty Bell*'s principal editor, most probably at the time she was invited to contribute a poem.[15]

respectively; the third portion (the opening section of the poem), now missing, was entitled 'Black and Mad at Pilgrim's Point'. For a debate about Browning's comments, see Corinne Davies and Marjorie Stone, ' "Singing Song for Song": The Brownings in the Poetic Relation', in *Literary Couplings and the Construction of Authorship: Writing Couples and Collaborators in Historical Context*, ed. Marjorie Stone and Judith Thompson (forthcoming, Madison).

[15] *The Browning Collections*, p. 55.

The Liberty Bell, *the Boston Female Anti-Slavery Society and the Garrisonians*

Historically informed understanding of 'The Runaway Slave's' abolitionist contexts in literary studies has been impeded by constructions of the *Liberty Bell* as a 'domestic and sentimental' or 'fundamentally feminine' annual, to use Karen Sánchez-Eppler's terms. Tricia Lootens reflects a similar view in suggesting that this 'gift book' did not take EBB very far beyond woman's sphere. The *Liberty Bell* may have been 'sold alongside the quilts and jams' at the annual Christmas bazaar of the Boston Female Anti-Slavery Society, and in some respects it might be termed a 'variety of female handiwork', as Sánchez-Eppler suggests and Lootens implies.[16] It is important, however, to see this handiwork within its intellectual and political contexts, as one very effective means of capitalising on female opportunities to 'abolitionize' both America and other countries. As Lee Chambers-Schiller demonstrates, sewing circles organised by New England female abolitionist societies accomplished the double end of educating women about the cause, and producing anti-slavery artefacts, including quills with the motto, 'Weapons for Abolitionists', pen wipers inscribed with 'Wipe out the blot of Slavery', and needle books embroidered with the words, 'May the use of our needles prick the consciences of slaveholders.'[17] It would be more fitting for scholars to situate the *Liberty Bell* among such polemical artefacts than merely among endless 'quilts and jams'.

However one views it, the *Liberty Bell* was no conventional feminine 'annual' and considerably more than an 'abolitionist stocking-stuffer', as Stauffer terms it.[18] Clare Taylor describes it as 'the most significant anti-slavery annual in America', with major British and American abolitionist writers such as Harriet Martineau and Lydia Maria Child among its most regular contributors. Taylor observes that the *Liberty Bell* 'gave a platform to minor literary talent, and attracted major

---

[16] Karen Sánchez-Eppler, 'Bodily Bonds: The Intersecting Rhetorics of Feminism and Abolitionism', *Representations* 24 (1988), pp. 28–59 (p. 34); Tricia Lootens, 'Elizabeth Barrett Browning: The Poet as Heroine of Literary History', Ph.D. dis. (Indiana University, 1988), pp. 188–9, 266.
[17] '"A Good Work among the People": The Political Culture of the Boston Antislavery Fair', in *The Abolitionist Sisterhood: Women's Political Culture in Antebellum America*, ed. Jean Fagan Yellin and John C. Van Horne (Ithaca and London, 1994), p. 260.
[18] Stauffer, p. 30.

writers', while Chambers-Schiller notes that there was often a com-
petition to acquire copies, although the *Liberty Bell* was distributed
without charge to those who worked at the annual December bazaar.[19]
Unlike other annuals too, it ran for nearly twenty years after its first
appearance in 1839; although its publication became less regular in the
1850s, the final issue appeared in 1858.

   While contemporary feminist critics now class the *Liberty Bell* as
'feminine' handiwork, in fact the intellectual and activist work
involved in editing and producing it enabled anti-slavery women like
Maria Weston Chapman, its founder, to move beyond women's sphere,
as the fissures in anti-slavery ranks – in part over the role of women –
testified. Moreover, many of its contributors were male, as well as of
mixed race and nationality. Authors featured in its pages included
several of the most prominent or active abolitionists of the time:
among them, William Lloyd Garrison, Frederick Douglass, Theodore
Parker, James Russell Lowell, Richard D. Webb and Elizabeth Pease.
And in some of its contributions by female authors one discerns the
developing feminist spirit that contributed to the Seneca Fall conven-
tion on women's rights. Witness, for example, a satiric poem entitled
'Idiot Era' published in the same issue of the *Liberty Bell* as 'The
Runaway Slave' purporting to be by a 'backwoods girl' mocking a
'Doctor, of that numerous pack / Who dress their notions, like
themselves, in black'. While the Doctor says 'woman's glory is to
shine unknown', the 'backwoods girl' ripostes, '*I* seek not glory, and
can't shine, I own', then declares: 'let my thoughts through hobbling
verses reel, – / I'll bear the satires that such sat'rists deal.'[20]

   EBB's readiness to respond to the *Liberty Bell* invitation may have
been particularly influenced by the example of Harriet Martineau,
whom she saw as 'the noblest female Intelligence between the seas'
(BC, 7:302). Martineau's trans-Atlantic profile was enhanced by her
travels in America in 1834–36 and close contact with Boston anti-
slavery women at a time when their transgressive initiatives and
association with Garrison subjected them to mobbing and other hostile
attacks. In *The Martyr Age of the United States* she presented a graphic
account of these incidents, casting Garrison and the women aboli-
tionists who defended him, Maria Weston Chapman among them, as

---

[19] Clare Taylor, *Women of the Anti-Slavery Movement: The Weston Sisters*
(Basingstoke, 1995), pp. 87–9; Chambers-Schiller, p. 258.
[20] *The Liberty Bell* (1848), pp. 159–60. The 'backwood' girl' is identified as
'E.C.W.'

heroic martyrs of the age.[21] Throughout the early 1840s, EBB had actively cultivated her own trans-Atlantic reputation through publications in American periodicals and correspondence with American writers and admirers, including Cornelius Mathews and James Russell Lowell. The *Liberty Bell* request evidently came through carefully orchestrated channels: possibly both from Lowell, to whom she mailed the poem on its completion, and also from Chapman and Eliza Follen, whose names are inscribed in the 1844 and 1845 presentation issues EBB was sent. The poem was clearly a solicited submission because, in describing it as 'too ferocious, perhaps, for the Americans to publish' to Hugh Stuart Boyd, she added, ' but they asked for a poem & shall have it' (*BC*, 14: 86).

To appreciate why a poem from EBB was first solicited by the Boston abolitionists, then accepted and given a prominent position in the 1848 *Liberty Bell*, one needs to appreciate the embattled history of this anti-slavery annual and the divisions that had arisen both within the ranks of the American abolitionists and along national lines between America and Britain. Debra Gold Hansen has shown how the *Liberty Bell* was born out of the religious, political and class-based differences that split the Boston Female Anti-Slavery Society in 1839, during the same period when the American abolitionist movement was fractured into two rival factions, in part over the issue of women's proper sphere. As Clare Midgley points out, one of these factions, the 'radical abolitionists,' remained under the leadership of William Lloyd Garrison in the American Anti-Slavery Society, and favoured combining a call for immediate abolition with 'other radical causes, especially women's rights', 'unconventional religious beliefs', and 'anarchistic forms of pacifism'. The other faction, led by Lewis Tappan, seceded to form the American and Foreign Anti-Slavery Society, dominated by clerical and evangelical groups who restricted their focus to specific legislative remedies for slavery. Within the Boston Female Anti-Slavery society, the predominantly upper-class and Unitarian 'Chapmanites' allied themselves with Garrison, while the middle-class evangelical anti-slavery women (dubbed the 'peelers' by the Chapmanites because their abolitionist commitment peeled off

---

[21] Harriet Martineau, *The Martyr Age of the United States of America, with an Appeal on Behalf of the Oberlin Institute in Aid of the Abolition of Slavery*. Repub. from the *London and Westminster Review* by the Newcastle Upon Tyne Emancipation and Aborigines Protection Society. Newcastle Upon Tyne, London, Dublin, and Edinburgh, 1840.

'just like an onion') supported Garrison's more conservative clerical opponents.

When the rivalry between these groups came to a head in 1839 in a 'battle of the fairs', Chapman established the *Liberty Bell*, and used her 'influence, connections, and sheer boldness to procure' contributions for it 'from some of America's premier literary and intellectual figures' and from 'prominent European writers and radicals'. We obtain some sense of Chapman from James Russell Lowell's ambivalent tribute to the woman who was nicknamed 'Captain Chapman' by her opponents. He describes her presiding over the annual fair, an embodiment of the American entrepreneurial spirit, not the virgin but the dynamo, as it were: 'There was Maria Chapman, too, / With her swift eyes of clear steel-blue, / The coiled-up mainspring of the fair, . . . [t]he expansive force, without a sound / That whirls a hundred wheels around'. But he also recognised the charismatic idealism and spirited intelligence that made her, in his words, a 'noble woman, brave and apt', the 'Joan of our arc'.[22] Chapman's success as a 'head-hunter' and the cosmopolitanism of the *Liberty Bell* made it a highly saleable item at the annual fair, where it appeared among the consumer items that Chapman and others procured to make the Boston Anti-Slavery Fair, in Harriet Beecher Stowe's words, 'decidedly the most fashionable shopping resort' of the Christmas holidays: 'Caps and *Fanchons*' from Paris, 'Dresden China of the time of *Louis Quinze*,' 'Chinese envelope boxes, Scotch shawls' and other 'rich' and 'recherché articles of taste and fancy from the old world'.[23]

With some justification, an anti-slavery contribution from a celebrated English poet like Elizabeth Barrett might be viewed as one more such consumer item, catering to a desire for cultural capital. In 1845, when the invitation came, her 1844 *Poems* (published in America as *A Drama of Exile: and Other Poems*) had established her as the leading woman poet of the age. Even the relatively shocking subject matter of 'The Runaway Slave' – rape, infanticide, and black insurrection – can be seen as satisfying this desire because, as Sánchez-Eppler notes, the *Liberty Bell* sold well in part because of the 'allure of bondage' and its

---

[22] Cited by Hansen, pp. 127, 98. Martineau mentions Chapman's nickname (p. 18).
[23] Debra Gold Hansen, *Strained Sisterhood: Gender and Class in the Boston Female Anti-Slavery Society* (Amherst, Mass., 1993), pp. 93, 134, 138–9; Clare Midgley, *Women Against Slavery: The British Campaigns, 1780–1870* (London and New York, 1992), p. 123.

abuses.[24] Nevertheless, it would be a mistake to see the Chapmanites as mere upper-class dabblers in abolitionist philanthropy, purveying cultural capital. As Martineau's account of Chapman and a group of principally female abolitionists in *The Martyr Age of the United States* makes clear, their political acts exposed them to defamatory attacks, along with Garrison and other abolitionists.

Moreover, despite their undoubted social and intellectual elitism, the Chapmanites were more radical in their views on race and gender than many of the middle-class evangelicals who opposed them. For example, they supported and practised the mixing of races as well as genders at abolitionist gatherings, unlike many New England anti-slavery groups, which, as Shirley Yee points out, often maintained seating and social segregation between blacks and whites even when they were 'integrated'.[25] This circumstance may help to explain why, when the Boston Female Anti-Slavery Society split in 1839, the majority of its twenty-five or so African American members supported Garrison and the Chapmanites, despite the growing disillusionment many experienced with the white abolitionist movement.[26]

By the mid-1840s, when EBB was approached, the Chapmanites and Garrisonians who managed the *Liberty Bell* had become more out-spoken in their attacks on slavery, their defences of women's rights, and their critiques of orthodox clericals. Whereas the 1848 issue opened with an article praising black insurrection, the initial 1839 issue had opened with a conciliatory article citing George Thompson's comment that he would not harm a 'hair of a slaveholder's head to liberate every slave in the universe'. In 1839 too, Martineau had used *The Martyr Age of the United States* to praise Garrison as the 'peace-man' among the abolitionists, opposing him to the black (and possibly murdered) insurrectionary activist Walker.[27] But by the mid-1840s, the 'peace-man' had grown more radical himself, though Garrison retained the opposition to direct political action as opposed to moral influence that some viewed as a conservative streak in his stance (and that made

[24] Sánchez-Eppler, p. 35.
[25] Shirley Yee, *Black Women Abolitionists: A Study in Activism, 1828–1860* (Knoxville, Tennessee, 1992), pp. 6, 55, 90. See also Hansen pp. 91–101, and Chambers-Schiller, who notes that the more conservative, evangelical 'peelers' 'objected to the degree to which the fair's managers worked so publicly and in cooperation with men' (p. 261).
[26] Hansen, pp. 64, 122; Yee, pp. 100, 105.
[27] George Bradburn, 'Incendiarism of Abolitionists', *The Liberty Bell* (1839), pp. 2–3; Martineau, *The Martyr Age*, p. 5.

Garrisonian principles compatible with EBB's own view of the poet's political role). In their attempts to exert this moral influence, the Garrisonians turned to increasingly heated rhetoric. The 1845 issue of the *Liberty Bell*, one of those sent to EBB, featured declamatory poems like George S. Burleigh's 'The Work of the Union' crying 'Down with the bloody Union!' and denouncing 'the hungry lash / That ploughs its furrows deep / On Woman's naked flesh' (p. 59); Frederick Douglass' bitter critique of 'The Folly of Our Opponents' (pp. 166–72); and Willliam Lloyd Garrison issuing a volley of 'Accursed's' on America for the sin of slavery (pp. 230–8) – a jeremiad that may later be echoed in the rhetoric of Barrett Browning's 'A Curse for a Nation'. The transformation in rhetoric reflected Garrison's conviction, expressed in an article on 'Hard Language' in the 1848 issue, that '[s]oft phrases and honied accents were tried in vain for years' against 'the leviathan, SLAVERY' (p. 285). Much in 'The Runaway Slave' that seems melodramatic or excessively declamatory to the modern reader seems less so when the poem is read within its *Liberty Bell* contexts. For example, stanza 34, immediately following the slave's call for insurrection in the stanza I began with, is particularly reminiscent of the polemical rhetoric found in the *Liberty Bell* by the mid-1840s:

> Whips, curses; these must answer those!
>   For in this UNION you have set
> Two kinds of men in adverse rows,
>   Each loathing each.

Given her trans-Atlantic fame after the publication of her 1844 *Poems*, enlisting an English author of EBB's stature must have been viewed as a coup by the *Liberty Bell* activists because the majority of English abolitionists did not support the Garrisonians. As Midgley notes, the British and Foreign Anti-Slavery Society aligned itself with Garrison's opponents, the American and Foreign Anti-Slavery Society, when it refused to accept the credentials of the women delegates sent by Garrisonian societies to the first World Anti-Slavery Convention, held in London in 1840. English support for the Garrisonians during the 1840s therefore came mainly from independent abolitionist groups and 'a handful of women', including Martineau and Elizabeth Pease.[28] It is difficult to know how aware EBB may have been of these ideological rifts within the abolitionist ranks. However, she probably

[28] Midgley, pp. 123–4.

had some appreciation of them based on the *Liberty Bell* issues she was
sent, her avid reading of American newspapers and periodicals,
Martineau's writings, and her correspondence with the painter Benja-
min Robert Haydon. Martineau described the splits within the aboli-
tionist movement in a letter published in the 1845 issue of the *Liberty
Bell* (pp. 248–52), and Haydon, of course, did a painting of the
controversial 1840 London Anti-Slavery Conference, at which the
American women delegates were denied admission.[29] Whether or not
EBB fully appreciated the depth of the rifts in the anti-slavery ranks,
the fact remains that, in contributing to the *Liberty Bell*, she was
aligning herself with the Garrisonians and a position on women's rights
that had been explicitly rejected by most official abolitionist organ-
isations in England.

Significantly, given the relatively radical sexual politics that many
contemporary feminist critics have found in 'The Runaway Slave', the
1845 issue of the *Liberty Bell* included a number of essays by anti-slavery
women boldly defending woman's right – indeed, spiritual obligation –
to speak out and act against slavery. In 'The New England Conven-
tion', Susan C. Cabot commented (no doubt with the 1840 London
Anti-Slavery Convention partly in mind), 'I found woman's sphere in
the cause settled by herself, without controversy or argument. She was
gladly welcomed; and . . . there was no need to introduce the question
of her rights. It was esteemed a matter of course, that this cause should
enter into the heart of a woman, as well as a man.' 'Responsibility' by
the English abolitionist Elizabeth Pease opened with an epigraph,
'There are few voices in the world, but many echoes', and the
declaration, 'to all of us belongs the power to determine of what
voices we will be the echo'. And, in 'The Come-Outers of the
Sixteenth and Seventeenth Centuries', Anne Warren Weston invoked
the model of heroic women following the inner light of their
conscience, encouraging young women of the present to withdraw
from Churches sanctioning slavery.[30] Critics have often cited EBB's

[29] Parry, p. 118, cites EBB's reference to reading heaps '"of newspapers and
magazines from America"'. See Midgley, pp. 1–2, on the marginalisation of
women delegates reflected in Haydon's painting, *The Great Meeting of
Delegates, . . . June 1840, for the abolition of slavery and the slave trade throughout
the world.* Haydon included individual portraits of some British women
delegates along one side, but not the American women delegates denied
admission, with the exception of Lucretia Mott, who was 'accorded a tiny
individual portrait in the background'.
[30] Cabot, p. 17; Pease, p. 23; Weston, pp. 91–9.

statement to Anna Jameson in 1853, *à propos* of Harriet Beecher Stowe's *Uncle Tom's Cabin*, 'Oh, and is it possible that you think a woman has no business with questions like the question of slavery? Then she had better use a pen no more. She had better subside into slavery and concubinage herself'.[31] However, it has not been recognised how much EBB's views on this 'question' were influenced by women associated with the Garrisonians and the *Liberty Bell*, well before *Uncle Tom's Cabin*.

The trans-Atlantic networks of the Garrisonians and EBB's exposure to past issues of the *Liberty Bell* also help to explain the striking contrast between 'The Runaway Slave', depicting an insurrectionary and articulate fugitive black woman, and representations of female slaves in the literature of the anti-Garrisonian British 'auxiliary' societies. The literature associated with British female societies generally emphasised the passivity of blacks, their lack of 'ability to speak for themselves,' and their need for the 'maternalistic' intervention of white ladies, Midgley points out. Moreover, whereas the majority of British anti-slavery women 'reinforced evangelical ideology concerning gender relations' in the language of their petitions, EBB chose to portray a female slave who rebels against her double burden of sexual as well as racial oppression ('Wrong, followed by a deeper wrong!' [stanza 15]). British female abolitionists also generally distanced themselves 'from both black resistance to slavery and working-class agitation', as they focused on 'three main aspects of female suffering: flogging, "moral degradation", and separation of mothers from children'.[32] 'The Runaway Slave' reflects all three of these concerns. Yet, in contrast to many British abolitionists, EBB explicitly called attention to the connection between the oppression of slaves and the oppression of Britain's own working-class children by positioning her poem on American slavery next to 'The Cry of the Children' in the 1850 edition of her *Poems*.[33]

It would be a mistake, however, to assume monolithic differences between the Garrisonian abolitionists associated with the Boston societies and the British societies, or to attribute all of the features of 'The Runaway Slave' to its *Liberty Bell* contexts. Midgley notes the image of black passivity created by the widespread reproductions of

---

[31] *The Letters of Elizabeth Barrett Browning*, ed. Frederic G. Kenyon, 2 vols (London and New York, 1897), 2: 110–11.

[32] Midgley, pp. 101–2, 93, 97.

[33] See Kenyon, 1: 462.

female variants on Wedgewood's famous cameo ('Am I not a man and a brother?') disseminated by British anti-slavery women. But Jean Fagan Yellin has shown that such images of a black woman kneeling before the white woman who is her liberator and 'sister' were also very common in America. Analogous verbal and visual images of kneeling or beseeching blacks and standing white women appear in the *Liberty Bell*.[34] Moreover, while many of the essays, poems and stories published in the *Liberty Bell* seem relatively radical by comparison with British mainstream abolitionist discourse, others do not. British writers like the ardent abolitionist Mary Howitt, as well as American writers like Thomas Wentworth Higginson, sometimes contributed innocuous poems with no clear connection to slavery.[35]

As Martineau's 'Incidents of Travel' in the 1848 issue suggests (pp. 80–8), even her regular *Liberty Bell* contributions seem relatively tame in comparison with 'The Runaway Slave', despite her long history of abolitionist activism. In *The Martyr Age of the United States* too, as indicated above, Martineau chose to dwell chiefly on white martyrs to the abolitionist cause like Garrison, not on black ones like the murdered Northern black activist Walker, mentioned only in passing.[36] In contrast, EBB presents a black female martyr to the anti-slavery cause, speaking for her race and articulating the curse that white slaveholders bring upon themselves. 'Your white men', the slave declares in stanza 35, 'Are, after all, not gods indeed / Nor able to make Christs again / Do good with bleeding'. It is blacks who 'bleed', but because their weight of suffering is too heavy for human endurance, they cannot become Christ figures: 'We are too heavy for our cross, / And fall and crush you and your seed'. The phases of composition recorded in the Wellesley manuscript help to reveal how EBB came to write a poem that was relatively radical and innovative, particularly in its representation of a rebel slave mother and slave

[34] Midgley, p. 97; Jean Fagan Yellin, *Women and Sisters: The Anti-Slavery Feminists in America* (New Haven, 1989). In the *Liberty Bell*, see, for example, the illustration accompanying Maria Weston Chapman's 'Sonnet: The Anniversary of Lovejoy's Martyrdom', in the 1839 issue (pp. 69–70), presenting a black man kneeling and a white woman standing against a rising sun.
[35] See Howitt's 'The Blind King' in the 1844 issue (pp. 112–16) and Higginson's 'The Morning Mist' in the 1853 issue (pp. 102–3). Despite the tangential nature of Howitt's particular contribution to the *Liberty Bell* in this instance, she was active in both anti-slavery and labour causes, and a friend of both Garrison and Frederick Douglass (Midgley, p. 163).
[36] Martineau, 'Incidents of Travel', *Liberty Bell* (1848), pp. 80–8; *The Martyr Age*, p. 5.

infanticide. It is not surprising that it was recognised as a 'distinguished work of poetry' by Maria Weston Chapman and her sisters, the editors of the 1848 issue and the majority of other issues of the *Liberty Bell*.[37]

The Wellesley Manuscript and Anti-Slavery Topoi in the Liberty Bell

One of the most startling features of the Wellesley draft of 'The Runaway Slave at Pilgrim's Point' is that it contains a false start: an opening section of approximately 43 lines that EBB drafted then abandoned (but without any indication that she had rejected it, in the form of lines drawn through it, as was her usual practice). Even more intriguingly, this original opening dramatically represents a male, not a female slave. At a relatively early point in composition, however, she evidently decided to switch the gender of her speaker, making 'The Runaway Slave' the most dramatic example of her tendency to shift from male to female perspectives in her works of the 1840s.[38] The Wellesley draft suggests that the Richard Barrett 'Jamaican story' of a physical struggle between a Creole and an African slave may possibly have had a very minor influence on the initial phases of the poem's composition, given that the male speaker in the original opening seems to allude to a physical struggle of some kind. However, the focus in EBB's initial opening is not on this struggle, but on the slave's interior flow of consciousness, as he questions God's purpose and goodness and recalls his black lover's presence.

I have argued elsewhere that both textual parallels and the poem's immediate historical contexts point to a far more significant influence on this abandoned opening featuring a male slave than the vignette given to EBB by her Jamaican cousin. That influence is the 1845 *Narrative of the Life of Frederick Douglass, An American Slave, Written by Himself*, a work intimately associated with the *Liberty Bell* abolitionists, authored by one of the leading lights among them by 1846.[39] While I

---

[37] A. W. Weston to Mrs M. W. Chapman and A. C. Weston, 12 December, dated 1848 in the catalogue, Boston Public Library, ms. A.2., vol. 21, p. 53.
[38] She similarly shifted from a male to a female perspective in working on the Miltonic subject matter of *A Drama of Exile*, abandoning a poem centered on Adam's perspective to write a lyrical drama focused on Eve's. See Marjorie Stone, *Elizabeth Barrett Browning* (Basingstoke and London, 1995), p. 79.
[39] I treat some of the textual and historical evidence for the impact of Douglass' *Narrative* on EBB's poem in section five of 'A Heretic Believer:

have been able to find no documentary evidence that EBB had a copy of Douglass' *Narrative*, however, we do know that she had copies of the 1844 and 1845 issues of the *Liberty Bell*, and 'The Runaway Slave' suggests that she put these to good use.

If the phases in composition reflected in the Wellesley manuscript are analysed in light of these and other *Liberty Bell* issues, one can begin to see how EBB worked her way towards a composition weaving together the principal *topoi* of anti-slavery poetry and resonating with the characteristic rhetoric of the Garrisonian abolitionists. Following the abandoned opening section, the sequence of stanza drafts is as follows: 4–8; 16–28; 32–5; 1–3; 9, 14, 12, 13, 11, 29, 30, 36.[40] In terms of content and convention, this sequence presents a series of abolitionist *topoi*, beginning with the slave theodicy or the slave's questioning of God (in stanzas 4–8 and also in the abandoned opening); the slave mother's anguish (the representation of infanticide in stanzas 16–28); the fugitive slave (stanzas 32–5); the related invocation of Pilgrim's Point as a site of liberty (stanzas 1–3); and the slave romance (stanzas 9–14).

There is nothing in the manuscript versions of stanzas 4 to 8 that follow the abandoned although uncancelled opening lines to indicate the speaker's gender switch. But stanza 8 is then immediately followed by a version of stanza 16, with the opening words, 'I am black, I am black / I wear a child upon my breast'. This point thus dramatically marks EBB's change in course, from portraying a male slave to representing a slave mother. One can infer that she had now settled on this subject because the draft of stanza 8 is followed by the most extended continuous series of stanzas in the Wellesley manuscript (drafts of stanzas 16–28). The slave mother's recollection of impregnation and her act of infanticide rapidly emerges as the focus of this section of the draft, as it does in the published poem (however, stanza 15, describing the rape was not added until EBB made the initial fair

---

Victorian Religious Doubt and New Contexts for Elizabeth Barrett Browning's "A Drama of Exile," "The Virgin Mary to the Child Jesus," and "The Runaway Slave at Pilgrim's Point"', forthcoming, *Studies in Browning and His Circle*.

[40] The stanza numbers are those from the 1850 text of the poem, the basis of subsequent editions. The *Liberty Bell* text lacks stanza 7, although a version of it appears in the Wellesley draft. No version of stanza 15 appears in the Wellesley draft; as indicated below, it was added later; and no clear version of stanza 31 (although lines eventually used in it appear in other contexts in the draft). Evidence indicates that EBB first numbered the stanzas as she was making the initial fair copy.

copy, the one with Browning's marginal comments). The idea of making the slave mother a fugitive and of portraying her at Pilgrim's Point came relatively late in the poem's composition, judging by the manuscript sequence. The final major element to be developed in the poem was the account of the idyllic romance between the slave woman and her black lover portrayed in stanzas 9 to 14 – although some details of this romance reveal the poet returning to and adapting details associated with a romance described from the male slave's perspective in the abandoned opening.

The most dominant of these *topoi*, the slave mother's anguish, was of course a thoroughly conventional subject in abolitionist poetry by women, both inside and outside the pages of the *Liberty Bell*. But EBB departs from convention in 'The Runaway Slave' by integrating this *topos* with others, thereby working against the gendered binaries permeating anti-slavery poetry, even by Garrisonians with their relative respect of women's rights. In the first place, she maintains the motif of the slave theodicy developed in her original opening, despite the fact that this motif was more usually associated with male than with female slaves. Eliza Lee Follen's 'The Melancholy Boy' in the 1844 *Liberty Bell* (pp. 91–5), which may have influenced EBB's poem given its shared concerns with her own 'The Cry of the Children', reflects a variation on this convention in its portrayal of a little black boy who asks, 'Why, if God is good, did He not make me white?' This is a highly sentimental little story, however, and very different from 'The Runaway Slave'. After shifting to a female slave in composing her poem, EBB portrays her speaker engaged in a Blakean questioning of the white male Christian God she has constructed in her brutal master's image, as the slave woman wrestles with her double burden of sexual and racial oppression.

Secondly, EBB departs from convention in representing a slave mother who is also a fugitive and a rebel. Runaway slaves in anti-slavery poetry were typically male rather than female, as they are in John Pierpont's 'The Fugitive Slave's Apostrophe to the North Star' in the 1839 *Liberty Bell* (pp. 75–80). Moreover, in deciding to take her fugitive to Pilgrim's Point, and in portraying her kneeling (in an attitude not of prayer but of bondage) to curse the pilgrim fathers' land, she both invokes and undercuts one of the most common tropes of freedom in the *Liberty Bell*. Boston, the home of the *Liberty Bell*, was portrayed as the 'city of the pilgrim fathers,' as Maria Weston Chapman's sonnet 'Boston' in the 1842 volume suggests (p. 44), and allusions to Pilgrim's Point as a symbol of liberty recur in many issues of the annual. For instance, in the 1845 issue, in a letter addressed to Chapman (pp. 72–6), Fredericka Bremer celebrates the 'Puritans who fled the desert and planted there [in America] the tree of liberty', while in the 1846 issue, Eliza Lee Follen's 'Song, For the Friends of Freedom' (pp. 65–7) invokes 'the Pilgrim spirit true'. Not all references to Pilgrim's Point or the pilgrim fathers in the *Liberty Bell* are straightforward like these. In an extract of a speech in the 1846 issue (pp. 75–6), Samuel J. May noted the frequent allusions to Plymouth Rock in debates about slavery, and commented that the rock was 'actually buried in a wharf', an apt token of the fate of liberty in America. Most allusions to the celebrated 'rock' or to the pilgrim fathers in the *Liberty Bell*, however, lack May's sense of ironic contradiction – in this respect, resembling Felicia Hemans' 'The Landing of the Pilgrim Fathers', another work that EBB may have been ironising in her poem. Like George Burleigh in the 1845 issue, in his poem 'The Worth of the Union' (pp. 52–9), she also counters the conventional invocation of the American eagle as a signifier of liberty: that 'symbol Bird', as Burleigh terms it. While Burleigh inverts the moral value of the eagle, presenting it as a cruel predator snatching away children from unfortunate slaves, she inverts its affiliation with the white master class by portraying the runaway slave casting herself as the 'black eagle' whom the slave hunters have 'killed' (stanza 30).

The idea of presenting a slave mother who is also a runaway may have been suggested to EBB by Martha Hempstead's 'The Fugitive' in the 1845 volume of the *Liberty Bell* (pp. 209–14). But while Hempstead's poem bears more resemblance to 'The Runaway Slave' than Richard Barrett's story, it is a much more conventional work than EBB's. The slave woman Hempstead depicts is not raped; she is the paramour of her master, cast aside and marked out for auction when he takes a northern wife. The 'routinised rape of slave-women by male slave-holders' that was systematically censored in the 'hundreds of slaves' narratives and anti-slavery fictions issued' by anti-bellum Abolitionist presses was also systematically censored in the pages of the *Liberty Bell*.[41] In the context of such systemic censorship, EBB's decision to add the critical stanza 15 at the fair copy stage emerges as a relatively radical act, elliptical as it may seem to the modern reader. This stanza makes it clear that the baby the slave bears is the product

[41] Jon Haus, 'Perilous Passages in Harriet Jacobs' *Incidents in the Life of a Slave Girl*', *The Discourse of Slavery: Aphra Behn to Toni Morrison*, ed. Carl Plasa and Betty J. Ring (London and New York, 1994), p. 145.

not of seduction but of a brutal rape, involving more than one man
('the white men') in detailing 'the shame' (not her shame, note) that
'strangle[s] the sob' of 'agony' following rapidly on the murder of her
black lover. The relationship between the slave mother and her mixed
blood child also differs greatly in Hempstead's 'The Fugitive' and 'The
Runaway Slave'. Hempstead does not develop this relationship, and
her portrayal of the male child privileges the white appearance
inherited from his father: he has father's 'azure eyes' and 'sunny hair'.
As 'The Fugitive' suggests, slave mother poems tend to represent black
women as if they have only one identity: their identity as mothers.
When they become fugitives, their role as mothers and their relation-
ship with their child becomes ancillary. In addition, unlike EBB's
rebellious runaway, Hempstead's 'fugitive' passively weeps in the 'dark
and noisome fen' until 'Her hiding place is found!' by the lover who
hunts her down.

Finally, there is no poetical precedent in the Liberty Bell for the
most striking aspect of Barrett Browning's representation of the slave
mother's anguish: the detailed representation of infanticide that
makes 'The Runaway Slave at Pilgrim's Point' a striking anticipation
of Francis Harper's 'The Slave Mother, a Tale of the Ohio' and Toni
Morrison's Beloved. Infanticide, 'where the female slave murders her
infant that it may never know the horrors of slavery', was one of the
'daily atrocities' of slavery, according to an 1837 Liberator article.[42]
Nevertheless, few anti-slavery poems actually represent slave infanti-
cide, and I have not been able to find an anti-slavery poem in which
a slave woman kills her child out of the mixture of motives portrayed
in 'The Runaway Slave at Pilgrim's Point' – possibly reflecting a state
of temporary madness, the manuscripts suggest, given that an earlier
title for the poem was 'Black and Mad at Pilgrim's Point'.[43] 'I covered
his face in close and tight: / And he moaned and struggled, as well
might be' (stanza 18), the slave mother recalls, as she relives the
experience of the baby striking out with his feet against the shawl he
is bound in, until he 'moaned and trembled from foot to head' then
'after a time, he lay instead / Too suddenly still and mute' (stanzas 19
and 21). In most anti-slavery poems dealing with a slave mother's
relationship to a mixed-blood child, the mother prays that God will
take her female child to save her from sexual violation. Maria
Lowell's 'The Slave Mother' in the 1846 issue of the Liberty Bell

[42] Cited Yee, Black Women Abolitionists, p. 129.
[43] See The Browning Collections, D800.

(pp. 250–2) is representative. Louisa J. Hall's 'Birth in the Slave's Hut' in the 1849 *Liberty Bell* (pp. 42–4) also follows the conventional pattern in depicting a slave mother haunted by the idea of her daughter's sexual vulnerability ('In mercy, say not 'tis a daughter!'), who contemplates the idea of returning 'the *slave's babe* to the sod!' Hall's poem is unusual in portraying the mother praying, 'Oh God, give me leave to destroy / By cord, by sharp knife, or by water, / The thing thou didst mean for my joy!' However, it appeared after 'The Runaway Slave' and may have been influenced by it. And it depicts a mother who only thinks of infanticide. The poem does not show her committing it.

As I have emphasised throughout, none of the abolitionist *topoi* reflected in 'The Runaway Slave' – the slave's questioning of God, the slave mother's anguish, the fugitive slave, Pilgrim's Point as a trope of Liberty, and the slave romance – were new. What is striking in EBB's anti-slavery poem is the poet's innovative modifications of these conventions and her fusion of them in a dramatic monologue in which an insurrectionary female slave moves swiftly through the roles of spiritual questioner, lover, mother, murderer, political rebel, and martyr for her race. Much in the poem – from the polemical denunciation of the fissured American 'UNION', to the ironically layered use of the Pilgrim's Point setting, to the slave's self-description as a 'black eagle', to the images of martyrdom – resonates with the increasingly heated rhetoric characteristic of the *Liberty Bell*, as the Garrisonians intensified their battle against that 'Leviathan', Slavery. Since Garrison and his followers favoured moral suasion over direct political intervention in fighting slavery, what recourse did they have but to ratchet up their rhetoric as the struggle persisted, and divisions in the anti-slavery ranks widened? The Garrisonian reliance on moral suasion, deeply radical in some of its manifestations and conservative in others, is in keeping with the view of the poet's mission that underlies EBB's poem. When 'The Runaway Slave' is read in its *Liberty Bell* contexts, we can better appreciate how the poem both mirrors and contributes to the conflicts within the anti-slavery movement and the trans-Atlantic networks forged by it. We can also better understand how a British Jamaican slave-holder's daughter, with no history of abolitionist activism and a position on sexual politics that was by no means militant in 1845, came to write a poem that so graphically depicts racial and sexual oppression.

If the Chapman sisters saw 'The Runaway Slave at Pilgrim's Point' as a 'distinguished' contribution to the *Liberty Bell*, it is also true that EBB no doubt learned from her exposure to the abolitionists associated with this anti-slavery annual – in particular, some of the dynamic women associated with the Boston Female Anti-Slavery Society. The unguarded references in Scott Lewis' recent edition of *The Letters of Elizabeth Barrett Browning to Her Sister Arabella* indicate that, 'The Runaway Slave' notwithstanding, she did not always burn with ardour for the abolitionist cause, and that, in private life, she retained some of the prejudices and used some of the terms that her class, race and nationality had shaped. When she met Chapman and one of Garrison's fellow 'martyrs', George Thompson, at one of Madame Mohl's social gatherings in Paris in the fall of 1851, she commented to Arabella that 'Mr Thompson, the abolitionist', was 'rather a philanthropical *bore*, it must be confessed – he would insist on talking to me about his flight from Boston from the mob of five thousand, & various circumstances appurtaining. I sympathise with him so utterly, you see, that nothing remains to be said – and he is not eloquent in conversation . . . for an orator!' Then she comments on 'Mrs Chapman, the female mover of the American abolitionist movement . . . a pupil of Dr Channing's – I had had one or two letters from her years ago. She is a clever woman & still pretty, though with two grown up daughters.' Her concluding comment classes Thompson and Chapman with others at that evening's gathering as '[p]eople not of the highest interest, but in their degree, interesting enough'.[44] Nevertheless, despite such comments, one might argue that both her defence of Italian liberty in *Casa Guidi Windows* and her exploration of the rights and wrongs of women in *Aurora Leigh* bear the mark of her historical connection with the Boston anti-slavery societies. Likewise, authors in the *Liberty Bell* continue to reflect the impact of her writing, even before 'A Curse for a Nation' appeared in the 1856 issue. 'O holy knowledge, holy liberty . . . Because my Soul is better for your sake, / Oh Freedom' is one of the epigraphs for a story by Caroline Healey Dall in the 1853 issue of the *Liberty Bell* concerning the situation of blacks who had followed the North Star to an imperfect freedom in Toronto (pp. 26–45). The epigraph comes from *Casa Guidi Windows*, and reflects the trans-Atlantic currents of thought in the mid-nineteenth century that connected Liberty in America and in Canada with Liberty in England and Italy, and the anti-slavery movement with the Risorgimento.

---

[44] *The Letters of Elizabeth Barrett Browning to Her Sister Arabella*, ed. Scott Lewis, 2 vols (Texas, 2002), 2: 420.

The Expatriate Poetess:
Nationhood, Poetics and Politics

ALISON CHAPMAN

. . . a poet's heart
Can swell to a pair of nationalities
However ill-lodged in a woman's breast.
(Elizabeth Barrett Browning, *Aurora Leigh* 6: 50–3)

'WE ARE ALL POETS IN FLORENCE. Not to rhyme would be a distinction.' Thus Barrett Browning humorously writes on 28 August 1854 to her friend and fellow poet Eliza Ogilvy, who had lived in the apartment above the Brownings at Casa Guidi.[1] Women expatriate poets flourished in mid-century Florence, attracted by the lively established Anglo-American community, the low cost of living and, in particular, the Italian struggle for unification. Sandra Gilbert links the Victorian woman poet's attraction to Italian politics with personal rejuvenation: Italy's quest for political liberation mirrors the woman poet's quest for liberation from British patriarchy.[2] Gilbert's association of Italy with a feminine space of rebirth, however, overlooks not only patriarchal Italian society but also the women poet's involvement with the bloody and violent Risorgimento that is a world away from a beneficial symbolically feminised land of plenitude. The British expatriate women poets in Florence that were part of the Browning circle – particularly Eliza Ogilvy, Isa Blagden and Theodosia Garrow Trollope – engage directly with the violent politics of revolutionary Italy in their poetry.[3]

Sincere thanks are owed to Michele Martinez for hunting down a copy of Garrow's 'The Cry of Romagna' and for her astute comments on an earlier version of the essay. The Department of English Literature at the University of Glasgow funded a visit to the British Library that enabled me to research otherwise inaccessible material for the essay.

[1] Peter N. Heydon and Philip Kelley (eds), *Elizabeth Barrett Browning's Letters to Mrs. David Ogilvy 1849–1861, with recollections by Mrs. Ogilvy* (London, 1974), p. 128.
[2] Sandra Gilbert, 'From *Patria* to *Matria*: Elizabeth Barrett Browning's Risorgimento', in Angela Leighton (ed.), *Victorian Women Poets: A Critical Reader* (Oxford, 1996).
[3] Blagden (1817?–1873) and Ogilvy (1822–1912), known mostly to date for their correspondence with the Brownings rather than their poetry, are the

Maura O'Connor has explored how certain British writers founded their professional identities on active support for the Italian nationalists such as Mazzini.[4] Little attention, however, has been given to women poets who were part of Barrett Browning's circle and who shared her commitment to the nationalist cause, if not her precise politics or poetics. This essay addresses why Risorgimento Italy was such a productive subject for women poets, and, in addition, how the identity of the woman expatriate poet, displaced from her own nation and audience, is creatively and professionally enabling. Their work raises the question of the appropriateness of a woman to support revolutionary politics and explores what kind of poetic voice is suitable; indeed, as the poems engage actively in the nationalist struggle, they also call attention to, inscribe or question the limits of their lyric voice.

Eliza Ogilvy, a successful Scottish poet who has received scant critical attention to date, demonstrates the new agency ascribed to women's poetry involved in the Risorgimento. Ogilvy's career as a poetess was initiated with her privately printed volume, dedicated to her recently deceased baby daughter and poignantly entitled *Rose Leaves* (1845). In the following year, Ogilvy published *A Book of Highland Minstrelsy*, which prefaces her lyrical ballads on Scottish legends with short anecdotal and historical essays on Scottish folklore. Her interest in nationhood and poetry is also attested in the companion volume, *Traditions of Tuscany in Verse* of 1851. Like its predecessor, this collection challenges the Anglo-centric conception of the poetess and her sphere, only with more vigour and self-consciousness. In her 1856 *Poems of Ten Years, 1846–1855*, Ogilvy's investment in a political poetics is even more explicit.[5] In the forthright and passionate address 'To the Poets of the New Generation', for example, Ogilvy calls on fellow writers to cease introverted musings on their own 'poetic pain', and to leave their hermitages and solitudes,

subject of informative essays in the *Dictionary of Literary Biography* vol. 199, *Victorian Women Poets*, ed. William B. Thesling (Detroit, 1999). Although Blagden's racial origins are obscure, probably because of illegitimacy, it is thought that she was Anglo-Indian (p. 21).

[4] Maura O'Connor, *The Romance of Italy and the English Political Imagination* (Houndmills, Basingstoke, 1998), chapter 3.

[5] Eliza Ogilvy, *Rose Leaves* (n. p., 1845), *A Book of Highland Minstrelsy* (London, 1846), *Traditions of Tuscany in Verse* (London, 1851), and *Poems of Ten Years, 1846–1855* (London and Edinburgh, 1856). Ogilvy also published *Sunday Acrostics: Selected from Names or Words in the Bible* (London, 1867).

because 'The world is in its throes, / A thousand homesteads of repose / Are shattered as I write' (pp. 268–9). They must instead, the speaker asserts, be part of the revolutionary struggle for nationhood through the act of writing poetry. Her extended rebuke calls for the transcendental Romantic poet to be transformed into an active agent of change: 'Use not, oh poet, priestly rite / In learnèd language dark, /But send your thought a living spark' (p. 270). With the echo of Percy Shelley, Ogilvy's poem insists upon a renewed investment in political poetry that both prophesises and is inter-active, so that it can 'show the loopholes in the prison wall' (p. 271).

These bold political poetics of the expatriate woman poet are not merely transgressing the contemporary constructions of the poetess. The first section of the essay argues that the formation of the poetess in mid-century Britain over-determines her nationality as the epitome of the English character. The newly Anglo-centric poetess, however, is predicated on foreignness: while Felicia Hemans and Joanna Baillie are seen as the epitome of the English poetess, her origins are given as the legendary figures of Sappho and Corinne. Just as the woman poet signifies domestic character and privacy, therefore, she also discloses a repressed national hybridity. The poetess emerges, indeed, as a mobile category, always already in transit, signifying her patriotism paradoxi-cally through devotion to nations not her own. It is poetesses with hybrid nationalities of their own that most blatantly expose the weakness of the Anglo-centric construction of the English poetess. The second section addresses expatriate poetics, focusing on Theodosia Garrow Trollope, in order to suggest not only how the expatriate Florentine poetesses bear an intertextual relationship to Barrett Browning's political poetry, but also how they forge a very different public poetics of agency by manipulating the foreignness embedded in the figure of the English poetess.

The Poetess in Transit

Among Elizabeth Barrett Browning's most quoted pronouncements is the bold and humorous rejection, in a familial metaphor, of her female poetic precursors: 'I look everywhere for Grandmothers & see none.'[6]

---

[6] *The Brownings' Correspondence*, ed. Philip Kelley and Scott Lewis (Winfield, Kansas, 1992), 10: 14. Further references to this edition are given parenthe-tically in the text as BC.

For modern critics, the statement encapsulates her poetic revision of women's poetry and her swerve from a female poetic tradition towards a masculine poetics, something that Linda M. Shires has recently termed 'cross-dwelling', or '[t]he ability to live in incommensurate identities' that is the complex and contradictory foundation of Barrett Browning's authorial identity.[7] Elided in the critical discussion, however, is the wider frame of this remark, which is part of her second letter to Henry Fothergill Chorley written in January 1845 as a response to his essay in the *New Quarterly Review* for that month. Chorley had reviewed Barrett Browning's 1844 *Poems* alongside recent volumes by Frances Anne Butler and Frances Brown and took the opportunity, conventional in reviews of this period, to assess the state of the poetess. The essay begins with a defence of the 'Poetesses of England' who have until now 'been considered a questionable sisterhood'.[8] The 'Sapphos of England' are, however, unfairly ridiculed, for their character and their lives are largely simple, unselfish and sacrificial (p. 78). Furthermore, Britain, Chorley continues, has the highest quality of woman poet: 'No land has a choir of Poetesses like ours' and 'we defy Europe to match our songstresses' (p. 79). Even when examples can be gleaned from the history of poetry on the continent, such as the '*improvvisatrici*' of Italy, they are outdone by English poetesses of the previous century; but even these are surpassed by the present excellence of women's poetry in Britain: 'There are few figures of foreign origin comparable to these; – yet these, as poetical artists, were but very far-off ancestresses of the race which has succeeded them – formal and faded spectres, as compared with living shapes of beauty and power!' (p. 79). For Chorley, the 'English Poetess' is not only the most eminent among nations but also in history: she is a race apart, signifying the contemporary womanly English character in both her work and life.

Barrett Browning responds specifically to Chorley's claims for eminent women poets in England. The first letter sets the terms for her later rejection of earlier female poets:

---

[7] See Linda M. Shires, 'Elizabeth Barrett Browning: Cross-Dwelling and the Reworking of Female Poetic Authority', *Victorian Literature and Culture* 30 (2002), pp. 327–43 (p. 331).

[8] [Henry Fothergill Chorley], *New Critical Quarterly* (January 1845), pp. 77–104 (p. 77). For a discussion of the bad character of the poetess at the end of the eighteenth century, in relation to the demise of the politicised Jacobin woman writer, see Margaret M. Morlier, 'Elizabeth Barrett Browning and Felicia Hemans: The "Poetess" Problem', *Studies in Browning and His Circle* 20 (1993), pp. 70–9 (p. 71).

It is a strong impression with me that previous to Joanna Baillie, there was no such thing in England as a poetess; and that so far from triumphing over the rest of the world in that particular product, we lay until then, under the feet of the world. We hear of a Marie in Brittany, who sang songs worthy to be mixed with Chaucer's for true poetic sweetness – and in Italy a Vittoria Colonna sang her noble sonnets. But in England, where is our poetess before Joanna Baillie? [—] poetess in the true sense? (BC, 10: 4)

This letter repeatedly links the search for a poetess or 'female poet' (terms used interchangeably in this period) with national literature.[9] Barrett Browning casts her eyes about for a 'poetess in the true sense', defined as the letter progresses to be neither talent in epistolary nor wit (with reference to the late seventeenth- and eighteenth-century writers Anne Finch, Margaret Cavendish and Mary Wortley Montagu). Her search is for a specifically *English* 'Grandmother'.

The construction of the poetess as an intrinsic embodiment of nationhood was widespread in this decade. The effort to make equivalent the woman poet and the English national character is part of a more general anxiety about the domestic identity of a nation heavily invested in imperial expansion. The emerging definition of Englishness is fraught with contradictions.[10] In terms of the woman writer, the anxiety emerges as an attempt to Anglicise the poetess, but this is achieved by a repression of the figure's intrinsic foreignness and mobility. The 1840s saw commentators turn to question and define the character of the poetess through constructions of national identity. M. A. Stodart's *Female Writers* (1842), for example, suggests that 'The literature of a country may be considered as the expression of the national mind' and that, for women, this expression is entirely articulated by and through the home: 'Home is and ever must be the true sphere for women, and her domestic duties her first duties.'[11] Poetry's relationship to nationhood does not seem to

---

[9] See Susan Brown, 'The Victorian Poetess', in Joseph Bristow (ed.), *The Cambridge Companion to Victorian Poetry* (Cambridge, 2000), p. 180. Although often held up as the exemplary English poetess in the 1840s, Joanna Baillie is Scottish by birth. Her celticism is silently but widely Anglicised as part of the imperialist project of 'English' national identity.

[10] See, for example, Tricia Lootens, 'Hemans and Home: Victorianism, Feminine "Internal Enemies", and the Domestication of National Identity', in Leighton (ed.), *Victorian Women Poets: A Critical Reader*, pp. 15–20.

[11] M. A. Stodart, *Female Writers: Thoughts on Their Proper Sphere, and on their Powers of Usefulness* (London, 1842), p. 9.

sanction a public poetics, but rather confines the female poet to the domestic sphere ever more securely. While Herbert Tucker suggests that this homely turn, what he calls 'house arrest', is typical of poetry by both sexes in the 1820s, it takes on a potentially pernicious quality in literary criticism in the 1840s for the woman poet.[12] For example, the major review of Felicia Hemans that appeared in *Blackwood's Edinburgh Magazine*, December 1848, associates her work intrinsically with her gender and her nationhood. The essay begins with a toast to 'Felicia Hemans and the poetesses of England!' and asserts that, although Joanna Baillie is the pre-eminent poetess, Hemans 'stands at the head of our poetesses': 'Her piety, her resignation, her love of nature and of home . . . all speak of the cultivated woman bred under English skies, and in English homes.'[13] Several recent critics help to illustrate how these reviews reduce the complexities of women's poetry to a natural expression of gender norms, for Hemans' poetry can be seen to contest the very domestic and nationalist ideology the reviewers claim it upholds.[14] Domesticated by the reviews into a signifier for the English-ness of the paradigmatic woman poet, however, the public agency of Hemans' poetry is entirely displaced.

This underlying formula for a woman's sphere was the template through which many women poets were judged. In September 1840, for example, Henry Nelson Coleridge's unsigned *Quarterly Review* essay 'Modern English Poetesses' exhibits a pride that the authors he reviews 'are our countrywomen'.[15] His essay, whose very title flags up the seemingly natural association between poetess and nation, ends with the conceit of gathering flowers appropriate for each of his nine woman poets (or muses) and weaving them together: 'There's a wreath! Can any other nation show an equal to it?' (p. 417). Anthologies also group together the work of the poetess under her nationality, such as Dyce's *Specimens of British Poetesses* (1827), with the implication that women

[12] Herbert F. Tucker, 'House Arrest: The Domestication of English Poetry in the 1820s', *New Literary History* 25 (1994), pp. 521–48.
[13] [Anonymous], 'Mrs Hemans', *Blackwood's Edinburgh Magazine* (December 1848), pp. 641–58 (p. 641). Chorley's *New Quarterly Review* essay also pairs together Hemans and Baillie in a similar manner.
[14] See, for example, Tucker and Lootens. The relationship between expatriat-ism and English national identity in the 1820s is examined in Lootens' 'Fear of *Corinne*: Anna Jameson, Englishness, and the "Triste Plaisir" of Italy', *Forum* 39 (Spring 2003), pp. 178–89.
[15] [Henry Nelson Coleridge], 'Modern English Poetesses', *Quarterly Review* (September 1840), pp. 374–418 (p. 376).

poets of all periods signify Englishness as a stable and absolute category. Both Dyce and Coleridge illustrate, furthermore, the collapse of the output of the poetess with her very personage: 'poetess' is taken to mean the woman, her figure as poetess, and her poetry. The apparently natural affinity between gender and a nationality that signifies domesticity is not, however, seamless. Within the category of the poetess there is foreignness at work. Furthermore, although the hybrid figure of the 'English Poetess' at this stage presents no threat to British national interests, she prepares the way for an expatriate poetics of revolution that is bloody and violent. The argument Barrett Browning puts to Chorley looks to other nations for examples of the ideal poetess, but reviewers and critics in the 1840s also look abroad for what their exemplary *English* poetess would be. The association between women, poetry and English nationhood is not, then, *a priori*.

Stodart's chapter on the woman poet offers an intriguing example. Her *Female Writers* is partly a conduct book that prescribes women's 'proper sphere' of writing, in response to what she describes as a general and latent prejudice against women's writing (p. 2). The chapter on 'Poetry and Poetesses' begins by describing the sphere of poetry as 'wide', with an 'immense' power over the human heart (p. 83). It encompasses both vastness and minutiae, and Stodart offers many examples of each as she gives poetry a female persona: 'It is the province of poetry to arouse by her trumpet-call to vigorous action, and to melt by her plaintive warblings to gentle and tender emotion' (p. 84). She then asks what women's poetry should and could be in this vast panorama of poetry's field:

> Is the hand of poor weak woman ever permitted to sweep the living lyre, and to elicit its thrilling tones? The notes are varied; it is a lyre of many strings, an instrument of wider range than any constructed by mortal hand; what tones, what notes vibrate most in unison with woman's heart, and will be most likely, when struck by her hand, to speak to the heart of others? (p. 86)

Several assumptions are at work here. Firstly, all poetry is innately lyrical, an association most forcefully disseminated by Mill's 1833 Wordsworthian essay 'What is Poetry', but that was, by the 1840s, increasingly associated with both women and women's poetry.[16]

---

[16] Matthew Rowlinson argues that the Victorian poet's anxieties about the lyric's total appropriation by print culture is represented by the figure of the mute woman, who signifies and memorialises the silent voice. 'The female poet

Secondly, a woman poet's heart matches certain vibrating tones of the lyre. This is a stark and extreme description of women's associative, affective and expressive poetic creation: the belief that women's poetry overflows spontaneously from bodily sensations, by-passing the intellect and spilling out onto the page, an excess of feeling that produces lyrical and somatic writing.[17] Thirdly, in a construction that reminds us of the opening of Coleridge's review, the experience of reading such poetry affects the heart of the reader. Her discussion continues by accepting that, while woman cannot aspire to the poetic power of Homer, Milton or Shakespeare, the sphere of the inner, domestic and emotive is woman's proper domain: 'The true poetic power of women [. . .] is in the heart – over the heart – and especially in the peculiarities of her own heart' (p. 88). The example given is Sappho, 'the earliest and best of the Greek poetesses' (p. 88), who is not only the primordial woman poet, but also the template for women's feeling in poetry, 'the strong but silent emotions of the heart' described 'with delicate correctness of touch': 'we should not feel surprised that critics should hold up Sappho as an example of the beautiful in writing' (p. 89). Her 'few remains' are 'exquisite fragment[s]', 'breathings from the tenderest affections of the heart' (p. 88). Although the discussion moves on to name Hemans as the pre-eminent 'female poet of our own country', 'most emphatically a lady-poet' (p. 91) and 'England's bright daughter of song' (p. 94), the basis of evaluation is Sappho's lyrics.

While the example of Stodart discloses the origins of the poetess's affective effusions in Sappho, tracing this origin as a foreign predicate of the poetess's national character, the foreign body invading her natural Englishness and domesticity, is problematic. In an earlier chapter on 'Women of Ancient Times', Stodart praises both 'burning Sappho' and Corinna as 'specimen[s]' of women's poetry that have vanished almost with the very act of utterance: 'The traces of woman's step are soon effaced from the earth; yet [. . .] some faint marks of her existence in ancient Greece yet remain' (p. 39). This foreign influence, then, is based only on a trace. While critics such as Angela Leighton and Ellen Moers have uncovered Sappho as a dangerous yet seductive

---

writing lyric may experience an identification that makes this muteness in some sense her own.' See 'Lyric' in A Companion to Victorian Poetry, ed. Richard Cronin, Alison Chapman and Antony H. Harrison (Oxford, 2002), p. 73.

[17] For a further discussion of the poetics of expressivity, see Isobel Armstrong, Victorian Poetry: Poetry, Poetics and Politics (London, 1993), chapter 12.

precursor for the Victorian woman poet,[18] Yopie Prins has argued that the figure of the Victorian Sappho is an empty trope and her poetry a decomposing text: 'Sappho becomes an ideal lyric persona, a figure that provokes the desire to reclaim an original, perhaps even an originary, feminine voice' but yet a lyric persona without a personhood.[19] The identification of the poetess with Sappho, Prins comments, associates her with feminine sentiment but also self-effacement, as the lyric voice perpetually postpones the subject of the utterance (p. 175). In an essay co-written with Virginia Jackson, the poetess is further defined as: 'not the content of her own generic representation: not a speaker, not an "I", not a consciousness, not a subjectivity, not a voice, not a persona, not a self.' Furthermore, women poets write within the ideology of the poetess in order 'to imagine the unbearable possibility of lyric outside the terms, or boundaries, of subjectivity'.[20] In such self-conscious disembodiments, 'the presentation of those subjects as already gone reveals their ideal emptiness as well as the lyric's historical function as a vehicle for transporting, and potentially displacing, representative identities' (p. 529). Although the focus on British and American women poets suggests a critical investment in ideologies of nationhood, and although their essay concludes with a call to rethink the 'cultural figures' of 'lyric, woman, nation', their argument does not address the nationalism and mobility that predicates the empty figure of the poetess.

The formulation of the poetess as an endlessly displaced trope of loss fruitfully opens the construction and dynamics of woman's poetic expressivity, but it also overplays the emptiness of the poetic signature. While the displaced lyric voice seems to resist an originary subjectivity and signature, it also signifies, within the somatic logic of sensibility and affect, its fractured and contradictory national public identity. To put it the other way, the poetess is firmly identified with English national character as homely and domestic, but the figure of Sappho that underlies such identifications establishes the lyric voice as not only disturbingly displaced, but also, through its foreign origins and the mobility of the lyric voice, disturbingly in transit. Thus, the trope of the poetess is an unstable and transgressive conceit, signifying both

---

[18] Ellen Moers, *Literary Women* (New York, 1976); Angela Leighton, *Victorian Women Poets: Writing Against the Heart* (Hemel Hempstead, 1992).
[19] Yopie Prins, *Victorian Sappho* (Princeton, New Jersey, 1999), p. 14.
[20] Virginia Jackson and Yopie Prins, 'Lyrical Studies', *Victorian Literature and Culture* 27 (1999), pp. 521–30 (pp. 523, 525).

home and restlessness, stability and flight, the nation and its others. Furthermore, it is the mobility of the figure of the poetess that allows her lyric poetry a political agency.

Sappho's contemporary re-incarnation into the legend of the Anglo-Italian Corinne exemplifies the mobile nationality of the poetess. Madame de Staël's allegorical *Corinne, or Italy* (1807) reworks the myth of Sappho as the tragic precursor of the woman poet into a narrative of both sensibility and nationality. Both the figure of Corinne and her poetry represent 'passionate sensibility', 'natural, involuntary charm', and the nation she has adopted, for she is termed 'the image of our beautiful Italy'.[21] Corinne is a model throughout the nineteenth century for the inspired lyric poet; the identification is most evident in Letitia Landon's translations of Corinne's improvised effusions for Isabel Hill's 1833 English edition and her volume *The Improvisatrice and Other Poems* (1824). In 'Corinne at the Cape of Misena', published in *The Amulet for 1832*, Corinne and her portrait by Gérard is first described and then her improvisation mimicked in the translation of her song at Naples (from Book 13, Ch 4). Corinne is represented as a representative figure for all women poets: 'Corinne / Is but another name for her who wrote, / Who felt, and poured her spirit on her lay' (lines 38–40).'[22] The precursor Corinne sanctions the poetess's invest-ment in nations not her own through the very inspired and spon-taneous lyric voice that also puts poetic identities and subjectivities in question. While it is true that the body of Corinne eventually performs the Sapphic emptiness of her poetic signature – she suffers a romantic disappointment, loses her creative powers, and finally fades away and dies – her improvised lyric poetry performs the complex associations between poetess and national identities. Caroline Gonda remarks that the performance of the improvisatrice was traditionally seen to produce evanescent expressive poetry that was of 'vanishing insubstantiality' and yet was also peculiarly embodied.[23] As text, however, the rhapsodic poetry of Corinne discloses the radical mobility of women's displaced

[21] Madame de Staël, *Corinne, or Italy*, transl. Sylvia Raphael (Oxford, 1998), pp. 25, 27.

[22] Although she does not discuss the foreignness underlying the construction of the English poetess, Susan Brown notes that Victorian women poets often looked to other cultures in order to fashion the 'proper name' for the poetess (p. 184). For more on Corinne and Landon, see Glennis Byron, *Letitia Landon: the Woman Behind L. E. L.* (Manchester, 1995).

[23] Caroline Gonda, 'The Rise and Fall of the Improvisatore, 1753–1845', *Romanticism* 6: 2 (2000), pp. 195–210 (pp. 202–3, 208).

lyric voice, just as it also discloses the complex and contradictory foreignness that was, as we have seen in the reviews and essays from the 1840s, lying all along within the heart of the English poetess.

That commentators should look abroad for the very signifier of the 'English Poetess' is unsurprising in the larger perspective of English national identity. Majorie Morgan argues that travel is fundamental in the construction of national identities in Victorian Britain. The sense of what it means to be British, or English, is founded on discourses of mobility.[24] The result is not only to define Englishness through movement, but also to make mobile and unstable the trope of English national identity. Maura O'Connor, indeed, argues that the British looked specifically to Italy through a wealth of cultural, imaginative and political discourses in order to construct their own sense of nationhood. This is less an appropriation than a crossing of boundaries and identities that renders unstable the very concept of the nation, its integrity and purity.[25] The 'romance of Italy', O'Connor argues, was instrumental 'in the project of imagining a bourgeois, liberal, and, above all, English social order during a critical historical period when class society was being reconfigured and the parameters of national identity were being renegotiated in Britain' (p. 1). Corinne, signifying Sappho's lyric excesses and her foreignness, transposes the figure of the English poetess into Italy and highlights British interest in the Risorgimento. Corinne as a figure for the Anglo-Italian poetess unravels her multiple 'cross dwelling' identities as she also performs the displacement of the lyric affective voice. The 'cross dwelling' is, however, clearly geographic as well as conceptual. The poetess is always already in transit, a mobile trope that signifies multiple and diverse nations and nationalisms. Indeed, the English poetess is, in this sense, always ex-patriated, displaced from her national origins yet signifying the English home.

Expatriate Poetics

The most extended poetic exploration of women's expatriatism is Barrett Browning's *Aurora Leigh*. The eponymous Anglo-Italian heroine-poet is, however, not really at home in England, where she

---

[24] Marjorie Morgan, *National Identities and Travel in Victorian Britain* (Houndmills, Basingstoke, 2001).
[25] O'Connor, *The Romance of Italy*, p. 2.

is forced to live with her aunt after her father dies, nor at home in her
return to Florence in adulthood, where she feels disembodied and
'grown foreign to myself'.[26] Several recent critics have noted the verse
novel's revision of the construction of the poetess and her poetry. As an
Anglo-Italian poetess, Aurora Leigh acknowledges the legacy of
Corinne, but she also rejects Corinne's affective improvised lyricism
as an appropriate model for women's poetics and instead transforms
poetry into public discourse. Angela Leighton, for example, argues that
'Barrett Browning has succeeded in this poem in turning women's lyre
of private feeling into an instrument of public conscience.'[27] The verse
novel accomplishes this transformation by unravelling the conflicted
nationalist logic of the English poetess.

Aurora Leigh was published by Chapman and Hall on 15 November
1856. Although the poem's inception dates from early February 1845,
its composition begins in earnest probably by early 1853.[28] At this time,
Elizabeth Barrett Browning had been resident in Florence for almost six
years and her British expatriate community included several women
poets who were also grappling with issues of women's poetics and
nationhood that would inform *Aurora Leigh*. One associate of Barrett
Browning in particular, Theodosia Garrow Trollope (c. 1820–1865),[29]
exploited the inherent foreignness within the dominant construction
of the English poetess in order to intervene in Italian politics and
address fellow expatriates and her home nation. This expatriate poetess
does not turn to the epic like Aurora Leigh and Barrett Browning;
rather, she illustrates a very different set of responses to the association
between the cultural figures of woman, lyric, and nation.

Barrett Browning had an uneasy and distant friendship with
Theodosia Garrow while they were both resident in Torquay, Devon,
before Garrow's family moved to Florence in the early 1840s. They had
several family friends in common, in particular John Kenyon and
Walter Savage Landor. They even shared a doctor and a diagnosis in

---

[26] Elizabeth Barrett Browning, *Aurora Leigh*, ed. Margaret Reynolds (New
York, 1996), 7: 1210–11, 1215.

[27] Leighton, *Victorian Women Poets: Writing Against the Heart*, p. 108.

[28] On 27 February 1845, Barrett writes to Browning that 'my chief *intention* just
now is the writing of a sort of novel-poem. [. . .] It is not mature enough yet to
be called a plan' (cited in *Aurora Leigh*, p. 330). On 15 March 1853, Barrett
Browning mentions that she is busy with a 'new poem' (cited in Martin Garrett,
A Browning Chronology [Houndmills, Basingstoke, 2000], p. 92).

[29] On the controversy about her year of birth, see Giuliana Artom Treves, *The
Golden Ring: The Anglo-Florentines 1847–1862*, transl. Sylvia Sprigge (London,
1956), p. 335, n. 4.

Torquay: Barrett tells Browning that her doctor 'had never known "a system" approaching mine in excitability . . . except Miss Garrow's . . . a young lady who wrote verses for Lady Blessington's annuals' (BC, 11: 24). While she admired Garrow's various feminine talents as a versifier and musician, and wrote to her with praise for her 'multiform faculty',[30] Barrett complains in her letters to friends such as Mary Russell Mitford that her verse lacks individuality, originality and poetry (BC, 4: 170, 177, 253; 5: 119–20; 6: 149). According to her husband's memoirs, Garrow admired Barrett's 'pure intellectual native power'.[31] Garrow wrote poems from the age of 13 and in the 1840s began to publish in the annuals. In a letter, Robert Browning passed to Barrett the comments of Landor on Garrow's poem in Heath's Book of Beauty for 1847. Landor praises the poem in typically extravagant terms: 'Sappho is far less intense, Pindar is far less animated' (BC, 11: 163). Barrett's response to Browning recalls the terms of her letters to Chorley in 1845 about the poetess and defines her sense of what poetry should be against Garrow's poetics:

> Theodosia Garrow, I have seen face to face, once or twice. She is very clever – very accomplished – with talents & tastes of various kinds – a musician & linguist, in most modern languages I believe – & a writer of fluent graceful melodious verses, . . . you cannot say any more. At least I cannot. [. . .] I might have the modesty to admit besides that I may be wrong & he, right, all through. But . . . 'more intense than Sappho' – more intense than intensity itself! – to think of that! – Also the word 'poetry' has a clear meaning to me, & all the fluency & facility & quick ear-catching of a tune which one can find in the world, do not answer to it – no.[32] (BC, 11: 182–3)

For Barrett, Garrow is not a poetess but a versifier. Together with the charges of affectation and a lack of originality, Barrett's judgement positions Garrow in the tradition of the improvisatrice: the inspired

[30] Cited in Thomas Adolphus Trollope, What I Remember, 2 vols (London, 1887), 2: 181.

[31] Trollope, What I Remember, 2: 171.

[32] Ironically, Landor writes in similar terms about Barrett Browning's poetic genius. In his homage 'To Elizabeth Barrett Browning', he compares her to the Greek poets Sappho and Corinne (the latter also a model for Corinne; see de Staël's note in Corinne p. 420): 'if Sappho and Corinna bore / The prize of beauty, they both waft aside / The crown of laurel, now another's due'. See Walter Savage Landor, To Elizabeth Barrett Browning and Other Verses (London, 1917), p. 8.

lyrical woman, the legacy of excessive sensibility from which Barrett was struggling to break free.[33]

Thomas Adolphus Trollope (the brother of the novelist Anthony) married Garrow in Florence on 3 April 1848, after which they established a rival Casa Guidi in their 'Villino Trollope' in Piazza Maria Antonia.[34] Before and after their marriage, Garrow and Thomas Trollope collaborated on various literary nationalist publications.[35] Theodosia, despite serious invalidism, wrote poetry, translated from Italian and Tuscan into English, published reviews of Italian books in British periodicals and became the Florence correspondent for the *Athenaeum*.[36] Her public commitment to the Risorgimento is, however, closely bound up with her status as an *improvisatrice*. Her husband's autobiography tells of her transformation as an expatriate: 'she was becoming acclimatised to Florentine society. She no longer looked dowdy when entering a room, but very much the reverse; and the little Florentine world began to recognise that they had got something very much like a new Corinne among them' (2: 159). The 'new Corinne', Trollope details, was half Jewish, a quarter Scottish and a quarter Brahmin (2: 157). This complex ethnicity, he suggests, informs not only her exotic appearance and her extreme delicacy and grace (2: 359), but also her highly refined aesthetic sensibilities (2: 358), her extraordinary talent for translation (2: 370) and (paradoxically, one might think) her 'native purity of heart' that guides her conduct above her intellect (2: 372). It is not known what Garrow herself thought of multi-racial identity, but in her husband's representation Garrow's complex background makes her the representative nationalist poetess.

What can been traced of her published poetry, scattered across annuals and periodicals, is a poetic of excess and hyper-sensibility that

---

[33] See, for example, Barrett Browning's 'Felicia Hemans' and 'L.E.L.'s Last Question'.

[34] For more on the Villino Trollope, see Treves, chapter 8. The Brownings, initially appalled by the gossipy and intrusive expatriate life that centred around the Trollopes (especially Garrow's mother-in-law Fanny Trollope), held back from re-establishing a friendship until January 1851. See *The Letters of Elizabeth Barrett Browning*, ed. Frederic G. Kenyon, 2 vols (London, 1897), 1: 476.

[35] For example, Theodosia assisted in Trollope's *Tuscany in 1849 and 1859* (London, 1859). See Treves, p. 142.

[36] See Esther Schor, 'Acts of Union: Theodosia Garrow Trollope and Frances Power Cobbe on the Kingdom of Italy', in Alison Chapman and Jane Stabler (eds), *Unfolding the South: Nineteenth-century British Women Writers and Artists in Italy* (Manchester, 2003).

motivates the figure of the spontaneous lyric woman in order to address political issues.[37] Garrow achieves this by writing within the conventions of the English poetess that Barrett finds so restrictive, and by uncovering and revising the politics of nationalism at the heart of the construction. The poem to which Barrett objected, in her letter to Browning, is 'The Cry of Romagna', a rhapsody that addresses Florence's failure to assist Romagna adequately in its struggle for civic liberty.[38] The ode partly voices the city's anguished 'cry' for the help of the city and sharply chastises Florence for its passivity. The 'cry' is a 'pulse' that 'beats' against the 'turret-gates' of Florence, telling of the abuse of Romagna because Florence slept, luxuriating in its glorious past:

> 'There hath been strife, and thou wast sleep-oppress'd;
> There hath been young warm lifeblood spent in vain,
> And frantic wrestling, as of men possess'd,
> And blind fond patriot-love hath once again
> Dashed 'gainst the flinty walls its hopeless breast,
> While thou, decrepit-hearted! satt'st at home,
> Lulled by old legends of thy withered bloom.'   (stanza 2)

Florence has no ability to act, Romagna's complaint continues: 'We raised the shout of freedom – thy reply / Was but the echo of thy revellers' feet' (stanza 3). The 'cry' of the vanquished city ends by embracing death as a glorious patriotic sacrifice. While the pathos of the abandoned victim might seem suitable for the woman poet to ventriloquise, the denunciation of Florentine politics through the remainder of the poem stretches the appropriate subject matter for the poetess to its limit. The speaker addresses Florence on behalf of the dead, reminding the city of its former glory and power and denouncing the shame that will forever 'stain' its marble (stanza 6).

The contrast between Florence's present and past, the narcoleptic influence of its legendary historical greatness, and the rhythmic pulses

[37] For a list of her poetry contributions to the *Keepsake* and *Book of Beauty*, see Andrew Boyle, An *Index to the Annuals, 1820–1850*, 2 vols (Worcester, 1967), 1: 100.

[38] Miss Garrow, 'The Cry of Romagna', *Heath's Book of Beauty*, ed. the Countess of Blessington (London, 1847), pp. 88–91. The poem seems to refer to 1845 revolts against papal authority in Emilia-Romagna. Barrett Browning had experimented with the trance ode in her spasmodic religious poem 'Rhapsody of Life's Progress', published in *Poems* (1844), although the poem's exuberance and non-referentiality puzzled the critics.

of the dead patriots' cries for help, are repeated in Part One of Barrett
Browning's *Casa Guidi Windows* (published 1851), which tells of
premature celebrations of Tuscan independence from Austrian rule
on 12 September 1847. Despite her attested dislike of Garrow's poem,
Casa Guidi Windows shares its critique of Florence's lethargy under the
weight of its feminised representations. Both poems also share a
performative poetics, addressing public and political issues in order to
precipitate change. Unlike *Casa Guidi Windows*, however, Garrow's
poem works within the ideology of sensibility and affect. The poem's
description of Florence's glorious past, when the city represented
freedom and civic energy, turns into a love poem addressed to Florence
that asks why the city should be content with the adoration of the
'island-wanderer' and not earn the devotion of compatriots: 'Wilt thou
have worship from the stranger's son / And not *one* breath of blessing
from thine own?' (stanza 10). The speaker is explicitly the expatriate
foreigner who is enchanted by Florence: 'we, like thy sons of yore, /
Would garner thee, sweet Witch! In the heart's core!' (stanza 11). By
the final stanza, however, the poem collapses together the 'cry' of
Romagna and the voice of the expatriate in order to rouse Florence to
political action: 'thou hast arm, and voice / And mind, and means, as in
that elder day – / That cold and wanton trifling is thy *choice*'. Florence,
the poem concludes, should be at the heart of the new Italian nation:
'bind the whole Italian race to thee / By the new Sacrament of liberty!'
The mobile voice of the affective expatriate woman poet is overlaid
with the voice of the patriotic Italian nationalist.

  In another rhapsodic poem, 'She is not Dead, but Sleepeth',
published the previous year in *The Keepsake* and dated 14 July 1845,
Garrow describes in detail the feminised representations of Italy that
doom her to passivity.[39] The nation is a 'fair enchanted queen, whom
baleful lore / Would hold in chains of sleep for evermore'. At the end of
the poem, the speaker calls for a revolution instigated by the influence
of the north, once again self-consciously importing her northern
identity into the poem to incite revolutionary action:

> Fling wide the doors! and let the echoing strife,
> The fresh strong current of our northern life
> Rush o'er her brow; this sluggish air is rife
>   With treacherous perfumed rest.

---

[39] Miss Garrow, 'She is not Dead, but Sleepeth', in *The Keepsake for 1846*, ed.
the Countess of Blessington (London, 1846).

Plot no more, or plot *all*. Who may defy
A nation's link in fast conspiracy?
Who shall resist thy sons, O Italy,
If once more freedom-blest?

In the lyrical rhapsodics of the poem's final lines, the speaker blurs the distinction between the reviving northern air exhaled from the affective poetics of the expatriate and the mass action of 'ten thousand hands' of patriotic Italian sons. The blending of the voice of the northern supporter of the Risorgimento with Italian patriots becomes even more explicit after the abolition of press censorship in 1847, when Garrow and Trollope established *The Tuscan Athenaeum*, which ran for thirteen issues between 30 October 1847 and 22 January 1848.[40] The liberal newspaper combines political essays, theatre and book reviews, art history, scientific and medical notices, short stories and poems. Throughout there is an emphasis on the urgent political situation. The newspaper explicitly negotiates between the Anglo-American expatriate community in Florence and the Italian nationalists. The editorial for the first issue makes this clear: 'ought we not to deem ourselves rarely fortunate in this, that the birth of our publication is contemporaneous with that of a new era! – that the regeneration of Italy and our undertaking have been born, and shall grow and ripen to perfection together!' (Number 1, p. 1). The editorial expresses the will of the periodical to publish on the Risorgimento 'in the spirit of earnest sympathy and respectful cooperation', and to advise Italians on Florentine life and politics (p. 2). The editors feel justified not only because of their active sympathy with the nationalist cause, but because, although 'strangers', they are from a free and liberal nation whose institutions have much to offer Italy: they are 'natural' and 'habitual' 'as the air we breathe', and they were partly founded on medieval Italian institutions (p. 2). The liberal history of Britain and Italy is, this editorial suggests, deeply intertwined.

Theodosia Garrow publishes several rhapsodies in *The Tuscan Athenaeum* under the Greek initial theta (Θ), a private reference to her first name and also perhaps to the enigmatic initials of her

[40] The only full series of *The Tuscan Athenaeum* is in the New York Public Library. The British Library holds a microfilm. For a discussion of the politics of the newspaper in relation to *Casa Guidi Windows*, in particular the enthusiasm for Pope Pius IX, see Julia Markus's Introduction to her edition of the poem (New York, 1977), pp. xx–xxv. For further discussion of the Trollopes and the Risorgimento, see Treves, chapters 2 and 8.

precursor L.E.L.[41] These odes utilise the passionate energy of the
rhapsody in order to urge and enact change. They are performative
and excessive poems that call for action and revolution; indeed, they
both prophesy and represent the regeneration of the nation through the
apocalyptic powers of nature. An early poem, 'Song of the Winter
Spirits', from the 1841 *Book of Beauty*, rapturously describes the
destructive power of nature, the 'revelry' and 'frantic mirth' of the
winter spirits.[42] By 1847, nature's agency becomes politicised along
with her poetics. In the 'Morning Song of Tuscany', published in the
first issue of *The Tuscan Athenaeum*, 'The light! the glorious light!' of
the new dawn heralds the new nation free from foreign oppression: 'one
mighty cry / Bursts forth from mountain, plain, and Ocean strand, /
Freedom for Italy!' The revolution, in which 'thousands circle hand in
hand / All ranks, all ages', will be as natural and as inevitable as the
morning light. The poem's voice becomes a part of this process as it
urges action: 'Then Brothers! *all* arise!' Published in Number 11,
8 January 1848, Garrow's appreciative 'Aurora Rugiadosa: Lines on
Gibson's recently finished statue of Aurora' (p. 87), similarly praises
the symbolic figure for the dawn, 'the bearer of the dew' (the traditional
metaphor for Aurora's tears), as a mobile, transient and yet recurring
symbol of 'Aspirations sweet and mild / Blended hopes of Heaven and
Earth'. A direct political address to Rome and the Pope, 'The Meeting
of the Senate' (Number 4, 20 November 1847, p. 28), again uses the
trope of the new dawn to represent the nationalist hope: 'Living birth
of thought sublime! – / Issue into day!' The lyricism has an explicit
performative function as the woman poet appropriates the energy of
the Italian patriots. The speaker urges quiet in St Peter's to be replaced
by the living voice of freedom, which her song both captures and
effects:

> Fill, and rush, and overflow
>   With a song, a living glow,
>   A strong pulse of striving men;
>   For the Senate meets again.

[41] Treves states that these poems are translations of popular Tuscan Italian
patriotic songs (p. 137). Whereas she certainly did translate such songs in her
letters to the London *Athenaeum* about the Tuscan Revolution, there is no
evidence that the poems in *The Tuscan Athenaeum* are translations. Although
they may be inspired by patriotic songs, they bear the same rhapsodic
characteristics and themes of her earlier annual poems.
[42] *Heath's Book of Beauty*, ed. the Countess of Blessington (London, 1841),
pp. 249–50.

This lyric is prefaced in this issue by another homage to the Pope that
makes explicit Garrow's expatriatism. Although from a 'distant land'
with different religious affiliations, the northerner's support of the
Pope's role in the Risorgimento will increase his power and help to
effect change:[43]

> Though we kneel at different altars,
>   Island children of the sea –
> Yet with eager kindred feeling,
> Thousand hands for combat thrilling
>   Turn, Promethean soul! to thee –
>   Speak! And we will swell thy hand
> Own one banner floating o'er us
> Charge amid one thundering chorus,
>   'Progress! Light! for every land.'

This poem bears both the expatriate voice of difference and also the
voice of the symbolic Italian patriot. Through her very national
difference from the Italians, Garrow's support of the Pope in this
rhapsodic poetics helps to unite Italy's own differences.

   The ability of nature to destroy and regenerate is a familiar symbol of
the Risorgimento poetry. Barrett Browning's imagery of the resurrec-
tion of dead Italian patriots to fight for the cause, in her controversial
1860 volume *Poems before Congress* (especially 'Napoleon III in Italy'),
suggests that the representations of Italy as a doomed tragic woman
(condemned at the start of *Casa Guidi Windows*) can be undone
through both the Italian soldier's heroism and her own poetry.[44] Eliza
Ogilvy represents revolutionary energies metaphorically in Rome's
flooding in the ode 'On an Overflow of the Tiber in March, 1848'.[45]
Isa Blagden's 'Rome from the Ripetta' (which begins with an epigraph
from *Casa Guidi Windows* and seems to be addressed to Barrett
Browning) similarly links the flooding of the Tiber to 'symptoms of a
mighty birth' and 'signs of travail in this pausing earth' as 'A people
rise, where once knelt slaves supine'.[46] Garrow's use of similar tropes

---

[43] As Part Two of *Casa Guidi Windows* documents, however, the nationalists'
enthusiasm for the Pope was to be bitterly disappointed.
[44] See Alison Chapman, 'Risorgimenti: Spiritualism, Politics and Elizabeth
Barrett Browning', in *Unfolding the South*.
[45] Ogilvy, *Traditions of Tuscany*, pp. 275–80.
[46] Isa Blagden, *Poems, with a Memoir by Alfred Austin* (Edinburgh, 1873),
pp. 77–82.

pre-dates these examples and draws its poetic lineage implicitly from
Shelley, in particular his 'Ode to the West Wind' composed around 25
October 1819 and written in woods skirting the Arno in Florence,
which insists that poetic utterance has a performative function and a
tangible and radical effect on the world. Garrow's intertextual relation-
ship with Shelley is most obvious in an extraordinary poem, 'October
Singeth to the Earth', which appeared in the third issue of *The Tuscan
Athenaeum* (13 November 1847, pp. 20–1). This is a rhapsodic lullaby.
Personified October sings of the decay of Autumn in order to lull the
earth to sleep. Shelley's powerful west wind is transformed in Garrow's
ode into a maternal figure: 'Like a patient nurse I sit / Hushing thee
with ancient song'. Even at night, when stormy 'bolder numbers' makes
the earth quake with fear, the energy of the personified month makes
the earth forget about the ease and pleasures of summer: 'Hush! Hush!
the first frost cometh, / Soft as slumber – calm as death', 'Feelst thou
Earth! the coolness cast / O'er thy veins which throb and heave'.
October sings her 'tales of dread December / Gliding forth in coffin
dress', an 'awful rhyme' that instils terror in the earth. The end of the
poem turns to 'Human hearts' and 'Mortal hands' that work and suffer
and are now at rest: 'Life can never ebb too fleet.' Positioned after a
notice abridged and translated from the patriotic newspaper the *Patria*,
which narrates a procession marking the unity of Tuscan nationalist
purpose with that of Sardinia, 'October Singeth to the Earth' represents
the revolutionary potential of the season to destroy the old order. As a
lullaby, furthermore, the poem brings about what it describes: it
ventriloquises the 'ancient song' that decays and destroys, but also
eventually promises peace.

Landor's poem 'To Theodosia Garrow' describes her as 'wakening
Italy with song / Deeper than Filicaia's'.[47] Barrett Browning's *Casa
Guidi Windows* terms Vincenzo da Filicaia, the seventeenth-century
Italian patriotic poet, as leading a school of nationalist poets char-
acterised as 'Bewailers for their Italy enchained' (1: 21). Barrett
Browning condemns their representations of Italy as 'Some personating
image' (1: 30) that dooms the nation to over-aestheticism and
passivity. Garrow, however, for whom Italy is 'a fair enchanted
queen' and Florence a 'sweet Witch', works within this very tradition.
Drawing on the construction of the nationalised English poetess, she

---

[47] The poem is cited in Kate Field, 'English Authors in Florence', *Atlantic
Monthly* (December 1864), pp. 660–71 (p. 663). See also his comment to
Robert Browning in *BC*, 11: 163.

addresses both Italy and Britain from Florence, giving a new destructive and vengeful agency to the trope of the feminised nation. Tricia Lootens comments that, for the mid-century women poets, 'no British struggle provoked such ambitious patriotic poetry as did the Risorgimento'.[48] The Italian unification gave women poets, Lootens argues, the opportunity to write patriotic poems of triumph that reimagines England and Englishness (p. 260). The license to write patriotic poems about another nation, however, is granted by the foreignness underlying the construction of the English poetess, which expects the woman poet to uphold the private sphere of the hearth and the family, as 'naturally' feminine, and yet also defines her lyrical sensibility through the ancient Greek and modern Italian precursor poetesses Sappho and Corinne. Furthermore, Garrow's patriotic poems for Italy are not simply another way of inscribing English national identity or character. Although Garrow draws on the feminine poetics of sensibility and affect, her poems also figure the poetic voice as retributive, destructive and apocalyptical, often implicitly (and explicitly in her journalism) condemning the British political complicity with the Austrian occupation of Tuscany. As the 'new Corinne', Garrow's poetic identity as improvisatrice does not doom her to unhappiness and self-deletion; rather, it enables a revised poetics from within the tradition of sensibility every bit as performative as Barrett Browning's newly public poetic discourse.

---

[48] Tricia Lootens, 'Victorian Poetry and Patriotism', in *The Cambridge Companion to Victorian Poetry*, p. 259.

Rethinking the Dramatic Monologue: Victorian Women Poets and Social Critique

GLENNIS BYRON

WOMEN'S DRAMATIC MONOLOGUES have rarely been included in the general theoretical discourse on the form. While this is understandable in the case of such early critics as Robert Langbaum,[1] it is surprising how often they continue to be ignored by those who have benefited from the historical recovery and scholarly reconstruction of women's poetry that has taken place over the past few decades. In her 1996 monograph, for example, Elizabeth Howe mentions only one pre-twentieth-century woman poet, Christina Rossetti, who barely manages a page of her own.[2] W. David Shaw's 1999 study on the genre similarly focuses on male writers, bringing Barrett Browning into his discussion but remaining strangely silent on that key Victorian woman writer of monologues, Augusta Webster.[3]

Articles discussing the monologues of women poets are, however, beginning to appear and to qualify or challenge many of our previously accepted ideas.[4] Kate Flint, for example, has demonstrated that, despite the association of women poets with the personal and confessional, 'a major distinguishing feature in their writing is a readiness to inhabit the voices, the subject positions of others'.[5] Augusta Webster's poetry, in particular 'A Castaway', has begun to attract much critical interest, with Christine Sutphin and Susan Brown considering her use of this monologue to engage with the question of women's sexuality and the

---

[1] Robert Langbaum, *The Poetry of Experience: The Dramatic Monologue in Modern Literary Tradition* (London, 1957).
[2] Elizabeth Howe, *The Dramatic Monologue* (New York, 1996).
[3] W. David Shaw, *Origins of the Monologue. The Hidden God* (Toronto, 1999).
[4] Many of these monologues are also starting to be reprinted in anthologies, see in particular Virginia Blain (ed.), *Victorian Women Poets* (Harlow, 2001) and Angela Leighton and Margaret Reynolds (eds), *Victorian Women Poets* (Oxford, 1995).
[5] Kate Flint, '". . . As a rule, I does not mean I". Personal Identity and the Victorian Woman Poet', in Roy Porter (ed.), *Rewriting the Self: Histories from the Renaissance to the Present* (London, 1996), pp. 156–66.

debates over prostitution.[6] Cynthia Scheinberg has challenged the
exclusion of women poets from theoretical discussions of the dramatic
monologue and exposed the problematic nature of Langbaum's influ-
ential reader-centred definitions; her work on Amy Levy has been
particularly illuminating in drawing attention to the problems of
interpretation inherent within this generic form.[7]

Cornelia Pearsall's essay in *The Cambridge Companion to Victorian
Poetry* (2000) suggests one way in which our perspective might well
begin to shift now that we have recuperated many women's mono-
logues and can start to incorporate them into our more general
discussions of the form. Pearsall, who considers a wide variety of
monologues by both men and women, persuasively argues that, far
from being characterised by unintentional revelation, the traditional
position on the monologue, 'a major feature of this poetic genre is its
assumption of rhetorical efficacy'.[8] All this recent work clearly
confirms that generic grouping is simply a matter of historical process
and not fixed categories. Both the grouping and the form itself have
now become subject to redefinition. In this essay I am going to look at
women's dramatic monologues in order to consider two general
questions. First, and quite briefly, should we also be adjusting our
perspective on the dramatic monologue to the extent of revising our
theories about its origins? Second, and in more detail, do men and
women conceptualise and exploit the form differently?

Today, the generally accepted position is that the dramatic mono-
logue was developed simultaneously but independently by Tennyson
and Browning during the 1830s,[9] and the first published examples of

[6] Christine Sutphin, 'The Representation of Women's Heterosexual Desire in
Augusta Webster's "Circe" and "Medea in Athens"', *Women's Writing* 5: 3
(1998), pp. 373–92; 'Human Tigresses, Fractious Angels, and Nursery Saints:
Augusta Webster's *A Castaway* and Victorian Discourses on Prostitution and
Women's Sexuality', *Victorian Poetry* 38: 4 (2000), pp. 511–31; also her recent
edition of Webster's work, *Portraits and Other Poems* (Peterborough, 2000).
Susan Brown, 'Economical Representations: Dante Gabriel Rossetti's "Jenny",
Augusta Webster's "A Castaway", and the Campaign Against the Contagious
Diseases Acts', *Victorian Review* 17: 1 (1991), pp. 78–95.
[7] Cynthia Scheinberg, 'Canonizing the Jew: Amy Levy's Challenge to Victor-
ian Poetic Identity', *Victorian Studies* 39: 2 (1996), pp. 173–200; 'Recasting
"sympathy and judgement": Amy Levy, Women Poets, and the Victorian
Dramatic Monologue', *Victorian Poetry* 35: 2 (1997), pp. 173–92.
[8] Cornelia Pearsall, 'The Dramatic Monologue', in Joseph Bristow (ed.), *The
Cambridge Companion to Victorian Poetry* (Cambridge, 2000), p. 68.
[9] The arguments of Herbert F. Tucker in this respect have been particularly
convincing. See 'From Monomania to Monologue: "St Simeon Stylites" and

the genre are considered to be Tennyson's 'St Simeon Stylites', written in 1833 and published in 1842, and Browning's paired poems of 1836, 'Johannes Agricola in Meditation' and 'Porphyria's Lover'. The emergence of these dramatic monologues is now usually seen in terms of a cultural critique of contemporary theories about poetry and a challenge to Romantic representations of the self. This challenge, as Herbert Tucker and Isobel Armstrong have convincingly shown, is effected primarily by putting the self into context, and thereby putting into question the authority, integrity and autonomy of the isolated lyric voice.[10] The poetic 'I' is shown to be, in Joseph Bristow's words, not 'a subject guiding language at will but a speaker who was, instead, subjected to language'.[11] The result is more complex, fragmented, and contextualised representation of the subject.

Over the last ten years, however, a number of critics have instead suggested that it might be such women poets as Letitia Landon and Felicia Hemans, writing during that transitional period of the 1820s, who 'invented' the dramatic monologue.[12] This is a position I would hesitate to endorse completely, and while this is not the place for a full scale engagement with the argument,[13] I would like to suggest one possible problem with respect to the dramatic monologue's characteristic dynamic of self and context.

The dramatic monologue would certainly appear to be a useful form for early women poets given the traditional gendering of the speaking subject as male and the tendency to associate women writers with the personal and self-representational. Speaking in the voice of a dramatised 'I' allows women to assume the position of the authoritative speaking subject while insisting that the voice is not to be identified as her own. Why, however, Isobel Armstrong has asked, if the use of the dramatised speaker is simply a distancing strategy, is there such an emphasis on 'speaking in another *woman*'s voice'? (p. 325). Armstrong suggests the use of the mask allows the woman writer to be 'in control of her objectification and at the same time anticipates the strategy of

the Rise of the Victorian Dramatic Monologue', *Victorian Poetry* 22: 2 (1984), pp. 121–37; 'Dramatic Monologue and the Overhearing of Lyric', in C. Hosek and P. Parker (eds), *Lyric Poetry: Beyond New Criticism* (Ithaca, 1985).

[10] Ibid., and Isobel Armstong, *Victorian Poetry: Poetry, Poetics and Politics* (London, 1993).

[11] Joseph Bristow, *The Victorian Poet: Poetics and Persona* (London, 1987), p. 5.

[12] See, most persuasively perhaps, Isobel Armstrong, pp. 318–32.

[13] For a more detailed assessment of this argument, see the chapter on Origins in my forthcoming *Dramatic Monologue* (Routledge).

objectifying women by being beforehand with it and circumventing masculine representations' (p. 326). If the form does offer women the chance of 'circumventing masculine representations', however, why do such early poets as Hemans frequently appear to use their dramatised speakers to reproduce and confirm, rather than challenge, these representations? Hemans's speakers seem to have thoroughly internal- ised the conventional gender ideology which effaces any sense of themselves as individual subjects. The speaker of 'The Chamois Hunter's Love', for example, is no more than what the title states. Hemans's celebration of woman as subject in such volumes as *Records of Woman* generally seems paradoxically achieved through the erasure of woman as subject: they are reduced to strangely depersonalised types of heroic wife or lover, mother or daughter.[14]

Furthermore, while Hemans may distance herself from her speakers through time and place, she nevertheless identifies herself with these speakers by working from within, as Anne Mellor has shown, the very constructions of female subjectivity she seems to be investigat- ing. She draws upon lyric and narrative voice to write herself as the icon of female domesticity and at the same time she reproduces variations on this self in the poems which might be considered early dramatic monologues. Linguistic connections are repeatedly made between the poet and her speakers, establishing similarity in differ- ence and linking women of all times and places in a vision of universal womanhood.

To give one example of these connections, consider the unidentified quotation that serves as epigraph to 'Properzia Rossi' (1828):

> Tell me no more, no more
> Of my soul's lofty gifts! Are they not vain
> To quench its haunting thirst for happiness?
> Have I not loved, and striven, and fail'd to bind
> One true heart unto me, whereon my own
> Might find a resting-place, a home for all
> Its burden of affections?

The voice of the explanatory paragraph which precedes these lines, identifying Rossi for the reader, can be associated with Hemans; the voice in the subsequent monologue is clearly that of Rossi. But who speaks here? It could be one of Rossi's own poems, because it

---

[14] See Felicia Hemans, *Records of Women, with Other Poems* (London, 1828).

anticipates both the sentiments and the images she goes on to express
in such lines as

> . . . give the reed
> From storms a shelter – give the drooping vine
> Something round which its tendrils may entwine –
> Give the parch'd flower a rain-drop, and the meed
> Of love's kind words to woman! Worthless Fame!
>
> (lines 88–92)

But it may equally be associated with the lyric voice of Hemans, since
sentiments and images also match those reproduced in such lyric poems
as 'Woman and Fame' (1839):

> Thou has a charmed cup, O Fame!
> A draught that mantles high,
> And seems to lift this earthly frame
> Above mortality.
> Away! To me – a woman – bring
> Sweet waters from affection's spring.   (lines 1–6)

And just to complicate things further, not only does Hemans use lines
from her 'Corinne at the Capitol' (1830) for her epigraph to 'Woman
and Fame', but she also uses these lines from 'Woman and Fame' as her
epigraph to the narrative poem 'Joan of Arc, in Rheims' (1828). So
with whom do we associate these lines: Rossi the sixteenth-century
Italian artist, Joan the fifteenth-century French heroine, Mme de
Staël's fictional Corinne, or the nineteenth-century English poet
herself, Felicia Hemans. Or, to expand the possibilities to a ridiculous
degree, perhaps they should be associated with the tragic Ariadne of
classical myth; after all, this is the woman whom Rossi is sculpting and
to whom she gives her 'form' and 'lineaments' (line 49).

Hemans may cross boundaries of time, race, and culture in present-
ing her speakers, but she nevertheless emphasises the links between
these individual subjects as women. The dramatised speakers echo the
sentiments held by the women described by the poet in her narrative
poems and the sentiments which, through their expression in lyric
form, Hemans encourages us to believe she shares. The speakers serve,
then, a key role in Hemans's establishment of similarity in difference. It
is not just the poet who defines and interprets women in this way; her
opinions are validated by the distinct voices of women from other times
and places. And by echoing Hemans, these dramatised voices speak

directly to the validity of the sentiments of early nineteenth-century domestic ideology. They consolidate the authority of the dominant model of femininity.

Context is crucial to the dramatic monologue as we now understand it since it is precisely the dynamic of self and context which reveals the fixed and essential self to be in fact fragmented, composite, and the product of a particular set of socio-cultural conditions. With Hemans, however, context appears to be used primarily as a means of reinforcing the idea that, in all times and all places, the essential nature of woman is fixed. The poems are, I think, crucial predecessors of the dramatic monologue, but they exploit the dynamic of the self in context in a manner diametrically opposite to the way now considered character-istic of the form.

Critics are certainly beginning to find evidence that Hemans's poems contain not only a celebration of a particular notion of female subjectivity but also a critique of its assumptions. As Mellor convin-cingly observes, 'having accepted her culture's hegemonic inscription of the woman within the domestic sphere, Hemans's poetry subtly and painfully explored the ways in which that construction of gender finally collapses upon itself, bringing nothing but suffering, and the void of nothingness, to both women and men'.[15] It is not, however, the specific form and conventions of the dramatic monologue that seem to effect this critique; Hemans's use of dramatised speakers instead appears to function in the service of the celebration of the hegemonic inscription of woman. I have, consequently, some reservations about the position that women 'invented' the form, primarily because while they may indeed ultimately critique the hegemonic inscription of woman, the monologue's crucial dynamic of self and context is not exploited in the service of this critique. Putting the self into context, in the case of poets like Hemans, is not a means of putting the self into question; rather, it is a means of reinforcing the idea that the nature of woman is universally stable and fixed.

What I would argue, however, is that even if women poets did not invent the form, they did play a primary role in establishing and refining that line of development which has proven most enduring: the use of the monologue for the purposes of social critique. Once Browning and Tennyson have used the monologue to challenge Romantic representations of the self, they and other poets then go on to exploit the form's central dynamic of self and context in various

---

[15] Anne Mellor, *Romanticism and Gender* (London, 1993), p. 142.

diverse ways. They offer different models of the self and different strategic approaches to that self, but always propose and explore a complex, fragmented, and contextualised representation of the subject. In one of the most important lines of development, this dynamic of self and context is appropriated for the purposes of social critique.

Does this mean that Victorian male and female poets conceptualise and exploit the form of the dramatic monologue differently? In 1986, when the work of recuperating forgotten and marginalised women poets was still in its early stages, Dorothy Mermin suggested that perhaps they did. With respect to the work of Elizabeth Barrett Browning and Christina Rossetti, Mermin observed that, surprisingly given the opportunities it offers for exploring the problematic nature of the gendered speaking subject, neither poet appeared to make much use of the form. And when they did,

> the women's dramatic monologues are different from the men's . . . The women seem usually to sympathise with their protagonists, and neither frame them with irony as Browning does nor at least partly objectify them like Tennyson by using characters with an independent literary existence. The women did not find figures in literature or mythology or history . . . Nor do they show off their own virtuosity the way Browning does in 'My Last Duchess', for instance: we are not made aware of the poet signalling to us from behind the speaker's back . . . where men's poems have two sharply differentiated figures – in dramatic monologues, the poet and the dramatised speaker – in women's poems the two blur together.[16]

The subsequent recuperation of the work of such poets as Augusta Webster and Amy Levy has demonstrated that even if the dramatic monologue was not the preferred form of Barrett Browning or Rossetti, it was frequently used by many other women poets. Nevertheless, a number of Mermin's observations are, with some qualifications, remarkably percipient in many ways. Initially, she may seem to be setting out on a dangerous path here, perhaps suggesting there might be, to echo one editor's unfortunate choice of words when introducing Webster, something we might call the 'womanly dramatic monologue'.[17] In fact, however, a reconsideration of Mermin's observations

---

[16] Dorothy Mermin, 'The Damsel, the Knight, and the Victorian Woman Poet', *Critical Inquiry* 13 (1986), pp. 64–80 (pp. 75–6).
[17] Valentine Cunningham (ed.), *The Victorians: An Anthology of Poetry and Poetics* (Oxford, 2000), p. 768.

about women poets and their dramatised speakers does not suggest that the work of male and female poets within the genre constitute different traditions. Rather, as I hope to show in the remainder of this essay, the characteristics Mermin observes appear primarily to be the result of the women working within that line of development which focuses on social critique.

Since 1986, a significant sub-group of monologues has been recovered in which women do use figures from literature, history, or myth. Adah Isaacs Menken's 'Judith' (1868), Webster's 'Circe' (1870) and 'Medea in Athens' (1870), Amy Levy's 'Xantippe' (1881) and Catherine Dawson's 'Sappho' (1889) provide some of the most notable examples. Such speakers are usually appropriated in order to demonstrate how cultural beliefs and traditions, particularly with respect to gender, have been fixed and formalised. Nevertheless, on the whole, women poets do prefer using fictionalised speakers placed within contemporary society. And this is mainly, it would seem, because they wish to focus attention more directly on the problems and concerns of their own worlds. While it would be possible to claim that Robert Browning is drawing attention to the problematic nature of gender ideology in such monologues as 'My Last Duchess' (1842), for example, Elizabeth Barrett Browning is surely engaging with this issue in a far more direct and complex manner in her 'Bertha in the Lane' (1844).

A similar point can be made by comparing the work of Browning, as the primary male writer of monologues, with the work of Webster, the primary female writer of monologues. As a number of critics have suggested, with Browning the speaking 'I' is explored primarily as subject to forces within itself, even though these forces are always socially or historically determined. With Webster, on the other hand, the focus is on the 'I' as subject to forces outside itself. Comparing his 'Andrea del Sarto' (1855) with her later 'A Painter' (1870) demonstrates the point. Webster invites the comparison from her unnamed Victorian speaker's opening lines: 'So, 'tis completed – not an added touch / But would do mischief – and, though so far short / Of what I aimed at, I can praise my work' (lines 1–3). The lines resonate with echoes of both Andrea's meddling with the Rafael and his doctrine of the imperfect: 'Ah, but a man's reach should exceed his grasp, / Or what's a heaven for' (lines 97–8). The links between the two speakers serve only to emphasise the differences. Browning's Andrea has clearly had much to do with fashioning those fetters he believes constrain him; Webster's significantly unnamed Victorian painter, however, is primarily at the mercy of social and economic conditions. The monologue's dynamic of self and context remains firmly in place, but the emphasis varies: Browning looks to the past, Webster to the present; Browning's concerns are primarily psychological, Webster's are social and economic.

Mermin's observation that Barrett Browning and Rossetti tend to sympathise more with their speakers also remains applicable to many women whose monologues have been recently recovered. It is a statement, however, which needs some qualification. There is, to begin with, the problematic nature of 'sympathy' and its dependence on reader response, something which becomes intensified in the dramatic monologue where the poets themselves step back, offering none of the 'guidance' we would associate with the Romantic lyric. As many earlier readings of dramatic monologues have demonstrated, most notoriously perhaps Robert Langbaum on 'My Last Duchess', different readers are quite likely to respond to speakers in dramatically different ways. Adah Menken's 'Judith' might provide an extreme example of how responses could vary. There are, clearly, some disturbing elements to this castrating female: she anticipates taking the head of Holofernes and revels in the 'wild unspeakable joy' (line 50) she will have when his blood 'courses down my bare body and dabble my cold feet' (line 51). Nevertheless, a feminist reader may well respond with some satisfaction to Judith, embodying as she does the powerful and authoritative voice of female defiance. Indeed, the feminist reader might even be tempted to paraphrase Langbaum's startling assessment of the duke: what interests us more than Judith's wickedness is her immense attractiveness, and we suspend moral judgement because we prefer to participate in her power and freedom, in her hard core of character fiercely loyal to itself.[18]

Even if, however, we put aside the problematic question of reader response and concede that, on the whole, women *do* seem to sympathise more with their speakers, this does not necessarily mean that they do not objectify them or frame them with irony. Rather, what it means is that their target is more usually the systems that produce the speakers than the speakers themselves. This is surely the case with Barrett Browning's 'Bertha in the Lane'. Manipulative as she may be, the speaker is nevertheless shown to be the almost inevitable product of a repressive gender ideology.

It is perhaps because women are more concerned to target the system

18 See Langbaum, p. 83.

than the speaker that they frequently exploit the strategy of inhabiting
the conventional in order to expose it. Examples of this can be found in
such monologues as 'Bertha in the Lane', Levy's 'Christopher Found'
(1884), Webster's 'The Happiest Girl in the World' (1870) and 'Sister
Annunciata' (1866), Constance Naden's 'The Carmelite Nun' (1894)
and 'The Sister of Mercy' (1894). The doubleness or discursive splitting
that is considered characteristic of the dramatic monologue is produced
here not only through the split between poet and speaker but more
importantly through the speaker's internalisation of the ideology that
defines her. To draw upon Isobel Armstrong's analysis of what she calls
the 'double poem', as the speaker gives a subjective account of her own
situation, that account is simultaneously offered to us for objective
analysis. This leads to both a demonstration and a critique of the
cultural conditions that have produced the speaker.

Naden's 'The Carmelite Nun', for example, begins with this
apparently confident pronouncement from the speaker:

> Silence is mine, and everlasting peace
> My heart is empty, waiting for its Lord;
> All hope, all passion, all desire shall cease,
> And loss of self shall be my last reward.   (lines 1–4)

What the monologue then goes on to show, however, is precisely how
little peace this woman has. Instead of being blessed by silence, she
seems haunted by the sounds of the world and longs only for death, for
that time when the 'music of the heavenly throng' (line 32) might
drown out these other voices. Her heart is not empty, but full of old
emotions; loss of self might well be seen as a 'last reward', since it is an
intense consciousness of self that so torments her. Naden, perhaps not
surprisingly an atheist, suggests the comforts of religion to be no more
than illusions, and the dedication of one's life to religion a simple waste
of potential.

Inhabiting the conventional does not always involve speaking in the
voices of mainstream society, as the frequent choice of nuns, models,
and prostitutes variously suggests. The more clearly the speaker is
situated in mainstream society, however, the more we begin to see what
Mermin means when she observes that while in men's monologues poet
and speaker are sharply differentiated, in women's dramatic mono-
logues the two blur together. The women's tendency to use figures from
contemporary society as their speakers may at least partly account for
this sense. The dramatic monologue always contains signals that we

should not conflate poet and speaker, but they are not always as obvious as in, say, Browning's 'My Last Duchess', where the speaking subject is clearly distinguished by time, place, and culture from the writing poet. With the cross-gendered monologue 'A Woman's Last Word' (1855), for example, the fact that we know it was written by Robert Browning plays a significant part in our definition of the poem as dramatic monologue since the speaker is only vaguely particularised. When Adelaide Anne Procter responds with her version of 'A Woman's Last Word' (1858), we are on less certain ground. Since the speaker is again only vaguely particularised, and there is no cross-gendering to alert us, it is far easier for poet to merge into speaker and become the lyric 'I'. The definition of this poem as dramatic mono-logue relies heavily on the reader being aware of Browning's previous poem and recognising this as a dramatised response.

A similar point might be made concerning Dinah Craik's 'Only a Woman' (1866). There is little here to signal the voice as a dramatised 'I', and some readers may well conclude the speaker to be the lyric 'I' of the poet herself. What does signal that this is a dramatised speaker, however, is the highly textualised nature of the speaking voice, the various references to and echoes of other poems which offer or comment upon conventional representations of women. Most directly, familiar lines from Patmore's *The Angel in the House* (1854–63) are used as the epigraph:

> She loves with love that cannot tire:
>   And if, ah, woe! She loves alone,
> Through passionate duty love flames higher,
>   As grass grows taller round a stone.[19]

In addition, both the language used and the dramatic situation set up repeatedly echo Browning's 'James Lee's Wife' (1864) and Barrett Browning's 'Bertha in the Lane', rewriting the former, along with Patmore's *Angel*, and subtly emphasising that surfaces may not tell the whole story with the latter. Once the web of references has been established, it is far easier to see that this is a dramatised persona that is being used to rewrite or expose various representations of women. The references tend to subvert the sense of any 'real' character and instead establish the speaker as a literary construct. Context becomes as much a matter of other literary texts as it is of the Victorian social world that

---

[19] Text from Dinah Maria Craik, *Poems* (Boston, 1866), p. 228.

is recreated. What the betrayed woman says and does may suggest to the man that duty makes love flame higher, but this façade is no more than the product of combined pride and necessity. Underneath this wife has simply become indifferent; she may appear the same smiling happy woman in love with her husband, but as she ironically observes, 'When the ship's gone down, I trow, / We little reck whatever wind may blow' (lines 56–7). A poetic form intricately involved in role playing, therefore, becomes appropriated to expose gender ideology and to critique the social conditions that force women into assuming their assigned roles.

In spite of signals that we should distinguish poet from speaker, there is, nevertheless, a kind of merging which occurs in many women's monologues. It is not, however, the kind to which Augusta Webster so energetically objects in her essay on 'Poets and Personal Pronouns'. Taking issue with those readers who assume the experiences and feelings described in a poem are necessarily those of the poet, in this essay Webster makes the whole notion appear ridiculous. 'Turn over the pages of any dozen poets now living, men and women', she observes, and 'suppose the first personal pronoun not artistically vicarious but standing for the writer's substantive self; what an appalling dozen of persons!' With all the love affairs, the 'miscellaneous tragedies and idylls . . . how do they preserve their reason through such a conflicting variety of emotions'. The very fact these poets manage to cope with the process of getting their books into print, she wryly observes, is 'consoling evidence that, as a rule, I does not mean I'.[20]

But in the case of the dramatic monologues, and perhaps particularly women's dramatic monologues, that opposition between speaking subject and writing poet is neither as stable nor as clear cut as Webster seems to suggest. In order to consider the question further, it might first be useful to consider advances in critical thinking on the question of voice and the relationship between poet and speaker in the dramatic monologue. For Robert Langbaum, 'the meaning of the dramatic monologue is in disequilibrium with what the speaker reveals and understands . . . we understand, if not more, at least something other than the speaker understands' (p. 146). The implication here is that the monologue is characterised by dramatic irony and there is a distinct split between poet and speaker: we can distinguish the voices of two distinct subjects for a single discourse.

[20] Augusta Webster, 'Poets and Personal Pronouns', in *Portraits and Other Poems*, pp. 369–70.

As the canon has expanded, however, it has become evident that such a clear split is not always a feature of the genre, and the form is now considered to allow for various positionings of the speaking subject with respect to the writing poet. Certainly in many dramatic mono-logues, and not just those by women, readers are left with the sense that the basic proposition offered by the speaker is fully endorsed by the poet. In this respect, Loy D. Martin offers a useful point of clarification. 'The division between the voice of the poet and the voice of the imaginary speaker', he observes,

> is based on a reader's willingness to construe them both equally as 'persons'. If these persons are imagined to be corporeal, then they must be discrete, mutually excluding entities. But if they are voices and merely voices, can they not in some sense be both different and the same?[21]

This is certainly the case with many monologues concerned with social critique, particularly such overtly political monologues as Barrett Browning's 'The Runaway Slave at Pilgrim's Point' (1848), Webster's 'A Castaway' and Levy's 'Xantippe'. When Barrett Browning's slave asserts with reference to the infanticide, 'I am not mad, I am black' (line 218), for example, both speaker and poet are simultaneously challenging the dominant definitions of both madness and blackness, and in this respect the voices merge.[22] This is not to say, however, that poet and speaker share the same experiences or even precisely the same views. The speaker, unlike the poet, has clearly internalised much of the racist ideology even as she speaks against it, and part of Barrett Browning's critique is to demonstrate precisely this point through the monologue; in this respect, the voices remain quite distinct.

In the case of the revisionist monologues, the connection between the voice of the poet and the voice of the speaker is primarily made through context. Even as they use historical or mythical speakers to distance their monologues, the poets usually still, at least indirectly, call forth their own Victorian world. With Webster's 'Circe', the speaker's boredom, her desire for something to break the 'sickly sweet monotony' (line 32) of her restricted life on the island, often appears more evocative of middle-class Victorian women's existence

---

[21] Loy D. Martin, *Browning's Dramatic Monologue and the Post-Romantic Subject* (Baltimore, 1985), p. 110.
[22] Text from Elizabeth Barrett Browning, *Poems* (London, 1850).

than of the life of the powerful sorceress of myth.[23] The figure has been revised for the purposes of social critique, and the target of that critique is the Victorian, not the classical world. Similarly, when Levy sets the spinning room of Xantippe and her maids against the leafy arbour in which Socrates and his friends discuss philosophy, she appears to be reproducing the gendered Victorian spheres of private and public. While context is the main issue here, it inevitably has implications for the identity of the speaking subject. The historical or mythical speaker does not have the same relationship with the poet as is found in Hemans when she has the various voices situated in different contexts all reproduce the same sentiments. Rather context here problematises identity by drawing attention to the controlling hand of the poet and to questions of representation. The speaker does not merge with the poet; she is shown to be the construct of that poet.

A sense of the poet's controlling mind, as Alan Sinfield's concept of the feint indicates,[24] is something characteristic of all dramatic monologues; even 'My Last Duchess' gestures towards the poet's world through its rhyming couplets. Nevertheless, it is something that is particularly well developed and intensified by women poets as the dramatic monologue evolves, and primarily for the purposes of social critique. What begins to happen in many revisionist monologues is an increasing problematisation of the identity of the speaking subject precisely in order to explore questions of representation.

This problematising of the speaker is something which, as Cynthia Scheinberg has shown, is particularly evident in Amy Levy's 'Magdalen' (1884). With the choice of the 'culturally loaded icon Magdalen', Scheinberg argues, Levy plays with and questions the assumptions of her readers. 'Is that subject,' she asks, 'the historical figure Mary Magdalen – the first witness to Christ's Resurrection, . . . – or the voice of a fallen woman, a contemporary Victorian "Magdalen"?' If the former, Magdalen is speaking to Christ after the Resurrection, 'condemning him for having abandoned an earthly romance for his divine mission'. If the latter, the Victorian woman is addressing the man who betrayed and abandoned her.[25] Scheinberg suggests Levy's point is to address the difficulties of communication and interpretation and to challenge the practice of Christian symbol-making. It also, however,

---

[23] Text from Webster, *Portraits and Other Poems.*
[24] Alan Sinfield, *Dramatic Monologue* (London, 1977). See particularly Chapter 3, 'Manners of Speaking', pp. 23–34.
[25] Scheinberg, 'Canonizing the Jew', p. 191.

draws attention to questions of representation. In Levy's monologue there are various details that encourage us to see the speaker as the biblical Magdalen, but for readers like myself who do not have any specialised knowledge of Jewish tradition, far more details which place her as a Victorian woman. The result for such readers is that the speaker seems to belong to the poet's world, but the language nevertheless intermittently works to destabilise this identification of voice and gesture towards the original Magdalen. It is surely extremely coincidental that this Victorian fallen woman, now apparently in a Magdalen home, should recall a past moment with her lover which involves such heavily weighted detail as is found here:

> And once my hand, on a summer's morn,
> I stretched to pluck a rose; a thorn
> Struck through the flesh and made it bleed
> (A little drop of blood indeed!)
> Pale grew your cheek; you stoopt and bound
> Your handkerchief about the wound;
> Your voice came with a broken sound;
> With the deep breath your breast was riven;
> I wonder, did God laugh in Heaven?   (lines 25–33)[26]

Scheinberg suggests that Magdalen believes she was participating in a lover's meeting and for her, the rose was a romantic image. Now, at the moment of speaking, she realises that he 'understood the moment from within Christian symbology: the moment the rose is connected with images of the "thorn" and "bleed[ing]" . . . the entire weight of Christian narrative is galvanised, calling up, for a predominately Christian reading audience – the crown of thorns and stigmata'.[27] That which from one perspective was a romantic moment is transformed into a symbol of Christ's future suffering. While Scheinberg reads this primarily in the context of Levy's challenge to the practice of Christian symbol-making, it also serves to remind us how dependent the Victorian construct of the fallen woman is upon a Christian ideology which emerges out of a far more ancient world. In this respect, the problematising of the identity of the speaking subject through the insertion of Scriptural language and images into a modern speaker's monologue works to foreground questions of representation generally. It begins to expose the conflicting and multiple positions through

[26] Text from Amy Levy, A Minor Poet and Other Verse (London, 1891).
[27] Scheinberg, 'Canonizing the Jew', p. 193.

which the self can be situated, and to show this self as the product of various socio-economic and linguistic systems. It also anticipates the strategy of many later women poets.

The Modernist poet Charlotte Mew, for example, similarly proble-matises identity through language in 'Ne Me Tangito' (1929), a monologue spoken by another Magdalen figure.[28] The title refers to the command given by Christ to Mary Magdalene in the garden after the resurrection, 'do not touch me', and this, along with the epigraph, establishes the speaker as the biblical Magdalene and the auditor as Christ. And yet the very opening line, 'Odd, *You* should fear the touch' (line 1), makes the speaker sound strangely modern. This effect is intensified throughout with references, for example, to the 'whole gay, unbearable, amazing show' (line 7), and the 'early evening mackerel sky' (line 15) which similarly signal towards a more modern world. Mew, then, simultaneously gestures towards the worlds of both speaker and poet and consequently again draws attention to the issue of representation. This in turn draws attention to the culture that has produced the construct, the world of the poet, and allows for social critique. In the case of 'Ne Me Tangito', it seems to be a critique of both religious and social attitudes towards female sexuality.

The speaker recognises Christ's fear of the sexual and consequently of her. She sees the 'ugly doubt' hidden behind a 'hurried puzzled little smile' (line 9) when he believes he glimpses in her the 'shade of something vile' (line 10), and relates to him the dream she had the night before. As she walked through the 'April fields',

> Someone stood by and it was you:
> About us both a great wind blew.
> My breast was bared
> But sheltered by my hair
> I found you, suddenly, lying there,
> Tugging with tiny fingers at my heart, no more afraid:
> The weakest thing, the most divine
> That ever yet was mine,
> Something that I had strangely made,
> So then it seemed –
> The child for which I had not looked or ever cared,
> Of whom, before, I had never dreamed.   (lines 16–27)

---

[28] Text from Charlotte Mew, *Collected Poems and Prose*, ed. Val Warner (London, 1982).

The lines seem to invite a number of possible readings and it is difficult to decide whether this dream is wish-fulfilment or whether its images simply make concrete the more abstract problem. The resurrection scene is rewritten so that Christ no longer fears her touch but is instead physically dependent upon her; he is reborn not in the manner of the biblical story, but as a child at her breast, no longer fearing her sexuality as the 'shade of something vile'. In some ways she merges into the other Mary, the virgin mother, but her sexuality is not eliminated: the eroticism of the scene remains intact.[29] Furthermore, she assumes new power and control in the relationship, along with Christ's love. On the other hand, this child is 'the weakest thing' and something she, or at least her sexuality, seems to have 'made' or produced. And whether she wants this weak thing is debatable; it does not seem to be something she has ever dreamed of or cared for. The dream child may then simply be an externalised representation of his immaturity in being unable to accept female sexuality. Either way, what this Magdalen comes to recognise is not that she is flawed, but that the belief system that defines her as sinner is flawed.

In the ways they problematise the speaker poet relationship in order to draw attention to questions of representation and allow for social critique, the Magdalen poems of Levy and Mew initiate many of the strategies of contemporary women poets, particularly those who are continuing to write revisionist monologues today. With the monologues in such works as U. A. Fanthorpe's *Standing To* (1982), Rita Ann Higgins's *Sunny Side Plucked* (1996) and Carol Ann Duffy's *The World's Wife* (1999), the poet speaker relationship is increasingly complicated. No attempt is made to provide a language recognisably specific to their historical or mythical figures, and instead they self-consciously use language associated with their own world. The result is frequently quite jarring. To provide just one example, consider how modern idioms invade the monologue of Carol Ann Duffy's 'Mrs Aesop' (1999):

---

[29] As Linda Mizejewski points out in her analysis of another of Mew's fallen women poems, 'Madeleine in Church', Mary Magdalene had become the 'archetype of the tragic but redeemable woman' and 'the model of female sexuality extinguished by Christianity'. See Linda Mizejewski, 'Charlotte Mew and the Unrepentant Magdalene: A Myth in Transition', *Texas Studies in Language and Literature* 26 (1984), pp. 282–303 (p. 283).

> By Christ, he could bore for Purgatory. He was small,
> Didn't prepossess. So he tried to impress. *Dead men,*
> Mrs Aesop, he say, *tell no tales.* Well, let me tell you now
> That the bird in his hand shat on his sleeve,
> Never mind the two worth less in the bush. Tedious.
>
> (lines 1–5)[30]

These opening lines reproduce many of the characteristics associated with the Victorian dramatic monologue generally; there is the abrupt beginning that places us in the middle of a situation, the presence of an auditor, and the use of colloquial language. But colloquial as it may be, Mrs Aesop's chatty voice hardly sounds like the voice of a woman who lived around 600 BC. There is no attempt here to create the illusion of a 'real' Mrs Aesop: we can never forget this is the poet's representation of that speaking subject, and, once again, the social critique can be directed towards male-female relationships within the poet's own world.

Although this essay has focused primarily on gender, social critique in women's dramatic monologues is not confined to this issue. Women frequently use the form to give a voice to marginalised and silenced figures in society. Ellen Johnston's 'The Last Sark' (1859), May Kendall's 'Legend of the Crossing-Sweeper' (1894) and 'Underground. The Porter Speaks' (1894) use many of the same strategies previously described while providing examples of monologues which draw attention to class and economic issues. This emphasis on social critique is perhaps not so surprising, given that so many of the women who used the form, including Emily Pfeiffer, Constance Naden, May Kendall and Augusta Webster, were to varying degrees social activists. Expanding the grouping of the dramatic monologue to include women poets suggests that polemic was a much more important part of the development of the monologue than traditional criticism has allowed.

I do not mean to suggest, however, that it was only women poets who exploited the form in this way. Swinburne, for example, is just as polemical as Webster, even if he tends to distance his critique through his historical and mythical speakers. Contemporary criticism has revitalised Tennyson scholarship generally by demonstrating how frequently his poetry, including his monologues, becomes the site of debates over such issues as masculinity, sexual politics, empire, nationalism, and capitalism. The importance of social critique to the dramatic

---

[30] Text from Carol Ann Duffy, *The World's Wife* (London, 1999).

monologue generally, however, becomes even clearer if we expand the grouping of dramatic monologues to include 'minor' male poets too. Robert Buchanan, for example, frequently uses dramatic monologue to explore the condition of the urban working class in *London Poems* (1866). Later in the century, Kipling also used the form for social critique. It is quite telling to compare, for example, his 'The "Mary Gloster"' (1894) with its Browning model, 'The Bishop Orders His Tomb at St Praxed's Church' (1845). While heavily influenced by Browning in terms of colloquial language and rhetorical strategies, Kipling updates his model to suggest the corruption and disorder of the modern capitalist present rather than a distant historical past. Once the monologues of the women poets have been incorporated into the canon, these other polemical monologues no longer seem quite as marginal to the form. Our attention is directed away from Robert Browning; indeed, to an interesting degree Browning seems strangely decentered, and his historical monologues representative of only one of various ways in which the genre's dynamic of self and context was developed. Furthermore, to conclude with some brief comments on the post-Victorian use of the form, monologues written today frequently have little in common with that Browning line of development. Those that do, most notably the monologues of Richard Howard, are frequently considered to be rather anachronistic.

The usual position on the fate of the monologue is that Modernist poets who admired Browning's work and appropriated the form were responsible for its decline. They used it to cultivate an 'elusive and impersonal voice' which could both suggest the 'mysterious and incalculable nature of the human psyche'[31] and transcend 'historical and individual particularity'.[32] In the hands of Pound and Eliot, then, the monologue is considered to become redundant. Such a voice, however, does not appear to have been particularly congenial to those poets for whom identity was still something which needed to be claimed, established or contested. In the hands of such poets as, to give just a few examples, Charlotte Mew, Langston Hughes, and Gwendolyn Brooks, the monologue survived, and the twentieth-century form evolved primarily as an instrument of polemic. These were mainly poets considered 'minor' or marginal to the canon, however, and the form was frequently only one of many used. Consequently, it at least appeared that the form's overall popularity diminished.

---

[31] Sinfield, p. 71.
[32] Carol Christ, *Victorian and Modern Poetics* (Chicago, 1984), p. 32.

Christina Rossetti's Petrarca

MICHELE MARTINEZ

CHRISTINA ROSSETTI's *Monna Innominata* ['Unnamed Woman'] (1881), a sonnet sequence published in her third collection of poetry and often seen as her valediction to secular verse, has received much critical attention and acclaim in the late twentieth century, especially for its brief, quasi-historical preface on medieval and Victorian sonnet traditions.[1] After decades of immersion in the commentaries and translations of Dante and Petrarch by close family members and friends, Rossetti uses the preface, fourteen sonnets, and twenty-eight mottoes culled from *Divina Commedia* and *Rime Sparse* to incorporate the sequence into Italian and English literary history.[2] Rossetti's own critics have been attracted to the preface of *Monna Innominata* as a place to begin exploring the poet's engagement with Dante, Elizabeth Barrett Browning, and Petrarch.[3] This essay will turn to the beginning

---

[1] *Monna Innominata* was first published in *A Pageant and Other Poems* (London, 1881). See *The Complete Poems of Christina Rossetti: A Variorum Edition*, ed. R. W. Crump, 3 vols (Baton Rouge and London, 1979–93), 2: 86. All citations of Rossetti's poetry will be taken from this edition.

[2] Between 1825 and 1842, Rossetti's father Gabriele published Italian-language commentaries on Dante's *Commedia*, the 'anti-papal' spirit of the Reformation, and the mysteries of Neoplatonism represented by Dante's Beatrice. Rossetti's siblings respectfully dissented from their father's strict allegorical interpretations, insisting especially on the historical identity of Beatrice. See Dante Gabriel Rossetti's *The Early Italian Poets, from Ciullo d'Alcamo to Dante Alighieri* (1861), revised as *Dante and His Circle* (1874), for his biographical notes on Beatrice. In 1865, William Michael Rossetti published a translation of Dante's *Inferno* in blank verse and later *Dante and His Convito: A Study with Translations* (1910). Eldest sister Maria Francesca Rossetti's *A Shadow of Dante: Being An Essay Toward Studying Himself, His World, and His Pilgrimage* (1871) most radically opposes her father's secular interpretation of Dante and expounds the *Commedia* 'as a discourse of the most elevated Christian faith and morals'. See Christina Rossetti's comments on her siblings' works in 'Dante. The Poet Illustrated Out of the Poem', *The Century* (Feb. 1884), p. 566. Christina's scholar friend and one-time suitor translated the entire *Commedia* into English *terza rima* and was the first Englishman to translate all of Petrarch's vernacular poetry. Christina assisted Cayley with the translations of Petrarch. See *Dante's Divine Comedy* (1851–55) and *The Songs and Stanzas of Petrarch* (1879).

[3] For the most comprehensive analysis of Rossetti's Petrarchism, see William

of Rossetti's career and show how her biographical article 'Francesco Petrarca', published in John F. Waller's *Imperial Dictionary of Universal Biography* (1857–63), makes another kind of intervention, entering quietly into Victorian debates about Petrarch's lyric poetry and the historical identity of his beloved Laura.[4] 'Francesco Petrarca' is significant because most critical accounts of Rossetti's career locate a later engagement with Petrarch and overlook his influence on her early poetry.[5]

Recent studies by Alison Milbank, Mary Arseneau, and Marjorie Stone have usefully explored Rossetti's careful balance between allegorical and biographical interpretation with respect to Dante's Beatrice and her dissatisfaction with the secular rather than spiritual love favoured by Barrett Browning in her famous sonnet sequence.[6] Yet only Rossetti's biographer Jan Marsh has suggested looking critically at Rossetti's formative exercise in biographical commentary – a three-thousand word biographical dictionary article on Petrarch begun in

Whitla, 'Questioning the Convention: Christina Rossetti's Sonnet Sequence *Monna Innominata*', in *The Achievement of Christina Rossetti*, ed. David A. Kent (Ithaca and London, 1987), pp. 82–131; and Antony H. Harrison, *Christina Rossetti in Context* (Chapel Hill and London, 1988), pp. 142–85. Others that have written on the intertextuality of the sequence include: Linda Schofield, 'Displaced and Absent Texts as Contexts for Christina Rossetti's *Monna Innominata*', *Journal of Pre-Raphaelite Studies* n.s. 6 (Spring 1997), pp. 38–52; and Marjorie Stone, '*Monna Innominata* and *Sonnets from the Portuguese*: Sonnet Traditions and Spiritual Trajectories', in *The Culture of Christina Rossetti: Female Poetics and Victorian Contexts*, ed. Mary Arseneau, Antony H. Harrison, and Lorraine Janzen Kooistra (Manchester and New York, 1999), pp. 46–74.

[4] C.G.R., 'Francesco Petrarca', *Imperial Dictionary of Universal Biography: a series of original memoirs of distinguished men of all ages and all nations. By writers of eminence in the various branches of literature, science, and art*, ed. John Francis Waller, 3 vols (London, 1857–63), 2: 542–4.

[5] The biographical article also foreshadows Rossetti's devotional prose. Between 1874 and 1892 Rossetti published six widely read devotional commentaries, written from the perspective of a devout High Anglican. The work most clearly anticipated by 'Francesco Petrarca' is *Called To Be Saints: The Minor Festivals Devotionally Studied* (1881), an archive of history, biography, legends, and verse on the apostolic saints remembered in *The Book of Common Prayer* and on the feast days of the Anglican calendar.

[6] See Alison Milbank, *Dante and the Victorians* (Manchester and New York, 1998), pp. 131–49; Marjorie Stone, op cit.; and Mary Arseneau, '"May My Great Love Avail Me": Christina Rossetti and Dante', in *The Culture of Christina Rossetti*, pp. 22–45.

1857 and finished by 1863.[7] 'Francesco Petrarca' is formative not only because Rossetti deploys rhetorical and hermeneutic strategies to reject secular interpretations of Petrarch's poetry but also because Rossetti researched and composed it while filling notebooks with poems that would eventually appear in her first two collections of poetry. Moreover, Rossetti concludes the article with an anecdote that reflects upon lyric strategies in her own verse, especially 'Memory', which was published in her second collection, *The Prince's Progress and Other Poems* (1866).

Part one of this essay will address Rossetti's implicit rejection of two Victorian critical traditions: one which treated Petrarch as a political allegorist and Laura as a symbol, and the other which regarded him as a sexually frustrated courtier with a real Laura as his love object. Neither of these traditions emphasise what for the devoutly Anglo-Catholic Rossetti is Petrarch's real achievement: the use of Italian lyric forms – the sonnet, canzone, and sestina – to represent the soul's struggle to transform *cupiditas* into *caritas*.[8] Although Rossetti as biographer casts doubt on most documented evidence of an historical Laura, she does not want to deny her existence entirely. For the poet Rossetti, Petrarch's 366-poem sequence memorialises Laura just as Dante's *Vita Nuova* and *Commedia* commemorate a real Beatrice.[9] Thus, in her limited but creative capacity as biographer, Rossetti devises two solutions: one, to cite well-known sources that posit opposing identities for Laura; and two, to find evidence in the visual arts for her portrait or memorial.

[7] See *Christina Rossetti: A Literary Biography* (London, 1994), pp. 211–12. Rossetti's letters reveal that she was working on 'Francesco Petrarca' as late as 1858 and that she had completed it by January 1863. A letter dated 5 January 1863, to family friend Dr Adolph Heimann, who had been closely following her progress on the piece, conveys her feelings about the endeavour:

> Here, in a dislocated form, is my Petrarca article, about which you enquired the other day. After telling you that we do not take in the Dictionary, I recollected that William possesses, in an ungainly shape, most of our own articles: and from his store I have borrowed the life in question. May you not detect in it a tissue of blunders!

See *The Letters of Christina Rossetti*, ed. Antony H. Harrison, 4 vols (Charlottesville and London, 1997–), 1: 172.

[8] For a more detailed account of the Augustinian struggle to renounce earthly desire in Rossetti's poetry, see Harrison, *Christina Rossetti in Context*, pp. 96–101.

[9] Both Dante Gabriel in his notes to *Vita Nuova* in *The Early Italian Poets*, and Christina in 'Dante. The Poet Illustrated Out of the Poem' affirm their view that Beatrice Portinari (c. 1266–90) was Dante Alighieri's beloved.

While the writer of a biographical entry might not typically have the space or inclination to engage in intense critical debate, Rossetti's citation of biographical studies constitutes a challenge to her father, the Neapolitan exile and poet-commentator Gabriele Rossetti, who argued that both Laura and Beatrice were allegorical figures. By the mid-nineteenth century, most Italian and English authorities, including Rossetti's siblings, believed that they had verified the existence of a real Beatrice in Dante's Florence. Petrarch's Laura, however, was a different story. Her identity was (and remains) impossible to establish, and in the lyric sequence *Rime Sparse* she appears uncommunicative and iconic – a fusion of nature, myth, and art. Yet some Victorian critics, such as Thomas Macaulay, Thomas Campbell, and Walter Savage Landor, believed that unlike Dante, whose love in *Vita Nuova* and *Divina Commedia* was interpreted as philosophical rather than erotic, Petrarch in *Rime Sparse* expresses his desire for an illicit affair. Moreover, he was thought to eschew spiritual for material goals in pursuit of the laurel crown and to use overly elaborate conceits and wordplay in order to flatter Laura.[10]

In response to these secular readings, Rossetti adopts a Christian interpretative framework not only to claim that Petrarch had struggled to be devout in his life and poetry, but also to suggest that Laura had been an ideal Christian in a proto-Anglican mold. She speculates that Laura had possessed 'piety' and 'reserve', the latter being a practice associated specifically with Tractarianism, the High Anglican movement to which Rossetti and her mother were adherents. 'Reserve' is a Tractarian social attribute and religious doctrine, characterised by verbal restraint and based on the concept that God and religious truth are never fully disclosed.[11] Thus, in Rossetti's account Petrarch's

---

[10] For an overview of Romantic and Victorian criticism, see Beatrice Corrigan, *Italian Poets and English Critics, 1755–1859* (Chicago, 1969), pp. 1–31. See Thomas Macaulay, *Criticisms on the Principal Italian Writers* (1824), Thomas Campbell, *The Life of Petrarch* (1841), and Landor's 1841 review of Campbell's *Life and Letters of Petrarch*, quoted in Corrigan, pp. 169–70.

[11] On the doctrine of reserve, see G. B. Tennyson, *Victorian Devotional Poetry: The Tractarian Mode* (Cambridge and London, 1981), pp. 44–50. Tractarianism was a product of the High Anglican Oxford Movement, led by John Henry Newman and Edward Pusey between 1833–45, and its theological ideas were advanced in the publication *The Tract of the Times*. Poet Isaac Williams wrote Tracts 80 and 87, titled 'On Reserve in Communicating Religious Knowledge' (1838 and 1840), in which he explains the practice to be a form of reticence and the 'indirection necessary in speaking of religious matters' (Tennyson, p. 143). With her mother and sister, Rossetti attended the sermons of the

poetry is not solely the record of an unconsummated love affair, as many Victorian readers had seen it. Rather she suggests that *Rime Sparse* is a memorial for a woman, whose beauty and reticence represents religious truth that will someday be fully revealed to the poet. Rossetti tacitly suggests that Laura's inaccessibility and mystery is a function of her reserve, not her marital status, which finds support in at least one source cited in a moment of scholarly enthusiasm in the article.[12]

Rossetti's second strategy for confirming Laura's existence, though not her exact identity, is to find the record of a portrait or monument. At the conclusion of the article, she reveals the contents of a pamphlet dated 1821, which contains an apocryphal anecdote about Petrarch and a 'sculptured image' of Laura. In part two of the essay I will argue that Rossetti's few sentences on the pamphlet suggest a parable about Laura's true significance in Petrarch's life and poetry. Richard Wendorf has used the term 'iconicism' to describe the way literary biographers preface or conclude their narratives with visual analogies, creating portraits of their subjects in digressions that express a biographer's wish to inspire the reader's admiration or devotion to his subject, and I would identify Rossetti's conclusion as a prime example of this strategy.[13]

Iconicist moments are also sometimes accompanied by poetry, and the final words of Rossetti's entry are the words of a quatrain allegedly written by Petrarch and inscribed upon the sculpture of Laura. While the quatrain suggests that Laura was ultimately a spiritual guide to

---

Reverend William Dodsworth at Christ Church Albany Street, who was a chief exponent of the movement.

[12] Dolores Rosenblum relates Rossetti's stony and vigilant female poetic personae to her experience as an artist's model to members of the Pre-Raphaelite Brotherhood. While my view of Rossetti's early poetry does not discount this reading, I suggest that Petrarch's lyric speakers may have inspired her to find solace in this pose. See *Christina Rossetti: The Poetry of Endurance* (Carbondale, 1986), pp. 109–44. I think Petrarch also serves as a precedent for Alison Chapman's account of Rossetti's lyric subjectivity, which 'vacillates between presence and absence [. . .] and seems to have erased its own historical context'. See *The Afterlife of Christina Rossetti* (London, 2000), p. 8; and Mary B. Moore, *Desiring Voices: Women Sonneteers and Petrarchism* (Carbondale and Edwardsville, 2000).

[13] Richard Wendorf, *The Elements of Life: Biography and Portrait-Painting in Stuart and Georgian England* (Oxford, 1995), p. 20. Wendorf begins his discussion of 'iconicism' with Izaak Walton's biography of John Donne in the series called *Lives* (1675).

Petrarch (much as Beatrice was for Dante in the *Vita Nuova* and *Commedia*), Rossetti ultimately leaves the question of Laura's identity open-ended. She defers to Petrarch's own putative words and leaves the reader with an aporia only to be filled by a devotional lyric. In part three of the essay, I will relate the conclusion of 'Francesco Petrarca' to Rossetti's poem 'Memory', composed between 1857–65 and frequently interpreted to be one of Rossetti's most enigmatic poems. To a certain extent, 'Memory' provides a Rossettian gloss on the conclusion of 'Francesco Petrarca' as well as on the conceits of Laura in *Rime Sparse* that Rossetti so admired.

Rossetti's 'Petrarca'

Studies of Christina Rossetti and Italian culture in recent years have focused on Dante Alighieri, whose vernacular poetry Christina's family members translated and commentated upon for English readers in various ways.[14] Except for Rossetti's father, who claimed that Petrarch was (like Dante) a political allegorist and member of a Neoplatonic brotherhood, none of the other family members published a translation or a particular view of Petrarch.[15] Family friend and biographer Mackenzie Bell (citing William Michael Rossetti) claims that as a young woman Christina 'never cared much for Petrarch' and that her interest developed much later in life.[16] Yet in researching her biographical entry, Rossetti clearly mined her father's library, which contained various editions, commentaries, and biographies of Petrarch, and produced a narrative of spiritual progress to represent the life of 'Petrarca' and to give some insight into Laura's. In fact, Gabriele Rossetti's death in 1854 may have freed his daughter (and eventually her brothers and sister) to challenge in print his strictly secular approach to the works of Petrarch and Dante.

[14] On the commentaries and translations of Gabriele and other family members, see R. D. Waller, *The Rossetti Family, 1824–54* (Manchester, 1932); Milbank, pp. 117–49; Stone, pp. 46–74; and Arseneau, pp. 22–45.
[15] See Gabriele Rossetti, *La Divina Commedia di Dante Alighieri con Comento Analitico* (London, 1826); *Lo Spirito Antipapale che produsse la Riforma* (London, 1832), translated into English by Caroline Ward as *Disquisitions on the Antipapal Spirit Which Produced the Reformation: Its Secret Influence on the Literature of Europe* (London, 1834); and *La Beatrice di Dante* (London, 1842).
[16] MacKenzie Bell, *Christina Rossetti: A Biographical and Critical Study* (London, 1898), p. 355.

According to William Whitla, the first person to examine closely Christina Rossetti's access to and knowledge of Italian literature, the Rossetti family library contained at least two sixteenth-century editions of Petrarch, including a 1560 edition of Alessandro Vellutello's *Le volgari opere del Petrarcha* (1525).[17] Vellutello was a Venetian commercial publisher, who had little interest in the monarchist or republican interpretations of Petrarch that had been introduced by earlier editors.[18] Instead, Vellutello portrayed Petrarch as a lover rather than as a political or Christian allegorist and focused solely on textual scholarship and historical evidence that would produce a real Laura as the object of his desire.

Vellutello's edition includes two prefatory essays, 'The Life of Petrarch' and 'The Life of Laura', and using Petrarch's epistles, prose works, and marginalia, he explains that *Rime Sparse* is a record of the poet's infatuation with a real woman. In order to support his claim, Vellutello went further than most editors of his day and visited Avignon, where he talked with descendants of people who had known the poet and possibly Laura. Vellutello's meeting with Gabriel de Sade, a very old man claiming to be a descendant of Laura's husband, Hughues de Sade, prompted the scholarly sleuth to investigate baptismal and death records in local villages. Vellutello found that Laura (or Laurette) de Sade's dates did not correlate with the purported youth of Petrarch's Laura (a conclusion that eighteenth-century biographer the Abbé de Sade would later refute). Searching parish registers in the neighbourhood of Vaucluse, however, Vellutello found an entry for Laura, daughter of Arrigo di Chiabau, signor of Cabrières, born 4 June 1314. He also discovered that she died an unmarried woman and was buried at the Franciscan Church of Lisle in 1348. These birth and death years are congruent with Petrarch's famous marginalia inscribed on the flyleaf of his copy of Virgil, which record the poet's first sight of a young Laura on 6 April 1327 and the report of her death on that same date in 1348.[19] Vellutello could not identify Laura beyond these records, and his conjecture left her identity open to speculation by later commentators. Nonetheless, Vellutello's *Le volgari*

[17] Whitla, pp. 109–10 n. 36.
[18] William J. Kennedy, *Authorizing Petrarch* (Ithaca, 1995), pp. 2 and 45–52. Thomas P. Roche argues that Vellutello's edition struck a blow to the tradition of reading Petrarch's poetry structurally and allegorically. See Thomas P. Roche, *Petrarch and English Sonnet Sequences* (New York, 1989), p. 74.
[19] For the flyleaf inscription, see Robert M. Durling, 'Introduction', *Petrarch's Lyric Poems* (Cambridge, MA, and London, 1976), pp. 5–6.

opere was the edition most influential on later French and English biographers, especially the two that Rossetti names in her article: the Abbé de Sade and Lord Woodhouselee. Both writers use Vellutello to identify a real Laura, but to very different ends: while the former hopes to redeem his family name, the latter initiates the making of a saint-like woman.

Before turning to Sade and Woodhouselee, I will discuss how Rossetti situates their debate within her article, which is essentially a narrative of spiritual progress that transforms Petrarch from a courtly lover and patriot into a tormented soul.[20] Rossetti's essay falls roughly into four sections: (1) a narrative of Petrarch's early life, especially his scholarly and diplomatic career, which is peppered with facts about his family and excerpts from his poetry; (2) Rossetti's speculation about Laura's historical identity; (3) an account of the poet's persecutions and humility in later life which make him an exemplary Christian worthy of admiration; and (4) two iconic analogies, epitomising the transformations of Petrarch and Laura from worldly to spiritual beings. I will discuss the first and second sections presently and address sections three and four in part two.

Rossetti's first authoritative gesture appears in the title of the entry, 'Francesco Petrarca', which retains the Italian rather than Anglicised spelling, and she begins with a brief account of his family. Francesco was born at Arezzo in Tuscany on 20 July 1304 to Eletta Canigiani and Pietro Petracco, a Florentine Guelph who had gone into exile in 1302, 'the year when Dante and many of the Bianchi faction were banished from Florence' (p. 542).[21] Without the hope of returning to his native city, Petrarch's father in 1312 took the family to a town near Avignon, the seat of the hotly contested papal court of Clement V. Rossetti relates that Petrarch was educated near Avignon in Carpentras and that 'the born poet pored far more willingly over Latin classics than over legal documents'. The death of his father allowed him to pursue his true 'calling', which involved assuming the habit of a secular clergyman and continuing his classical studies. Rossetti notes that Francesco was a serious scholar, and thus was shielded from the 'corrupt gaieties' of the court of Pope John XXII, and that he formed loyal friendships with the sons of the powerful Colonna family of Rome.

---

[20] Rossetti appears to follow a biographical narrative that Richard Wendorf has identified in Izaak Walton's *Life of John Donne*. See Wendorf, pp. 26–52.

[21] The White Guelphs were opposed to the imperialist powers of the German emperors and sought the restoration of the papacy to Rome.

Overshadowing his humanist endeavours and political allegiances, however, is the event that in 1327 marked the turning-point in Petrarch's life. Recalling 'one of the most popular narratives', Rossetti cites Petrarch's own account of having beheld Laura in the church of St Clara in Avignon on the 6th of April, Good Friday.

While one might expect Rossetti to delve into the question of Laura's identity at this point in the narrative, she resists attributing Petrarch's fame solely to love poetry. Her account defers the subject of Laura to the end of the essay and turns instead to Petrarch's 'appeals, poetic and epistolary, [which were] addressed to the popes and temporal powers, urging the restitution of the papal court to Rome, and the deliverance of Italy' (p. 543). Rossetti conceives of a republican Petrarch, who chose Rome rather than Paris to be crowned poet-laureate and whose friendship with the failed revolutionary Cola di Rienzo, or Rienzi, evoked Petrarch's sympathy and allegedly a canzone: 'Spirto gentil che quelle membra reggi'. Rienzi (c. 1313–54) was an Italian patriot, who led several campaigns to bring the papal court back to Rome and unify the Italian states. He was eventually murdered by imperial soldiers upon making one last triumphal entry into Rome. In fact, the three poems from *Rime Sparse* named in the article are not at all about Laura: the first is a sonnet for the patriarch of the Colonna family; the second, also a sonnet, commemorates the death of a woman beloved by his brother Gherardo, who eventually became a Carthusian monk; and third is the Rienzi canzone.[22] Rossetti's emphasis on Petrarch's republican sympathies would have struck a chord with her father's community of Italian exiles and English supporters of Italian liberty, and her account reminds her readers that Petrarch's writings include political poetry and many Latin and vernacular works besides 'in prose and verse'.[23]

---

[22] Rossetti cites '"Glorioso Colonna in cui s'appoggia" (Glorious Colonna, *i.e.*, Column, on which leans)', p. 542. She explains that the sonnet is addressed to Stefano Colonna the Elder, head of one of Rome's most powerful families, and the father of Petrarch's close friends, the Cardinal Giovanni Colonna and his brother Giacomo, Bishop of Lombes. Rossetti reiterates the claim of earlier critics that the sonnet '"La bella donna che cotanto amavi" (The beautiful lady whom thou lovedst so much)' is addressed to Petrarch's brother Gherardo, who 'abandoned the world for a monastic life, being moved thereto, it is said, by the death of a woman whom he loved' (p. 543). Petrarch himself was a secular clergyman and never took monastic orders.

[23] On the English revival of interest in early Italian poets and patriots during the Risorgimento, see Hilary Fraser, *The Victorians and Renaissance Italy* (Oxford, 1992), pp. 134–78.

Yet Rossetti's attempt to portray Petrarch as a public poet comes under strain, particularly when she claims that he suffered from a 'disastrous passion', which he sought to alleviate in his 'sundry short journeys' to various courts. After noting Petrarch's first glimpse of Laura and the 'untiring minuteness' with which he records his every sighting of her, Rossetti states: 'To read these elegant Tuscan strains, one might imagine that this veritable slave of love had few cares or interests or occupations but what sprang from the master passion' (pp. 542–3). Although she tries to suggest that Petrarch's master passion was Italy by citing his various canzoni and sonnets to his patrons and heroes, Rossetti cannot help but raise above all others the mysterious Laura, who for 'twenty-one years swayed the current of his life' and whose 'eyes and voice, habitual reserve and exceptional pi[e]ty, inspired poem after poem' [my emendation]. Rossetti does not try to explain the reasons for Laura's 'habitual reserve' and 'exceptional piety', but her choice of words is enormously suggestive of an opinion about her character.

Vellutello's 1525 'Life of Laura' asserts that Laura di Chiabau was a chaste woman and neither part of the Sade family nor ever married. The biggest challenge to this claim was made by an eighteenth-century *abbé* and aristocrat, Jacques François Paul Alphonse de Sade (1705–77), uncle of the infamous Marquis. The Abbé de Sade's *Mémoires pour la vie de François Pétrarque* (1764–67) was a scholarly and eccentric compilation of materials, which synthesised three centuries of French and Italian commentary and included family documents proving Laura to be his own direct ancestor and the mother of eleven children. So sensational was this claim that long before Petrarch's own complete *Rime Sparse* had been translated into English, Sade's memoir was translated by Susannah Dobson, whose 1775 *The Life of Petrarch. Collected from Mémoires pour la vie de Petrarch* [sic] was widely read and cited as authoritative, reaching a sixth edition in 1805.[24] Nearly all nineteenth-century English commentary addressed either Dobson's translation or Sade's *Mémoires* in some way, either accepting it as gospel or vehemently refuting its claims.

---

[24] If for centuries commentators had moralised Petrarch's poetry, then Susannah Dobson's *Life* attempted to moralise Sade's *Mémoires*. As Julie Hayes has observed, Dobson's preface to the heavily condensed two-volume work 'warns anyone tempted by adulterous affections "to check every unhappy inclination in its birth"'. See Julie Candler Hayes, 'Petrarch/Sade: Writing the Life', *Representations of the Self from the Renaissance to Romanticism*, ed. Patrick Coleman, et al. (Cambridge, 2000), p. 132 n. 27.

In 'Francesco Petrarca', Rossetti cites the Abbé de Sade as providing a credible answer to the question of Laura's identity:

The question remains – Who was Laura? and is answered by the Abbé de Sade: She was the daughter of Audebert de Noves, syndic of Avignon, and the wife of Hugh, son of Paul de Sade; and was in fact, my own ancestress as family documents prove. This assertion has been endorsed by common opinion. (p. 544)

Rossetti's citation of Sade takes into account recent authorities, including Ugo Foscolo's *Essays on Petrarch* (1823) and Thomas Campbell's *The Life of Petrarch* (1841), who both accepted Sade's ancestral claim. Her attraction to the Abbé's assertion may come from his insistence that Petrarch became a great poet by virtue of his love for Laura:

In a word, without Laura, without the desire to please her that spurred him on, not only would Petrarch never have written the poems that have made his name immortal, but he also would perhaps have sunk into debauchery, never to achieve the fame that we shall see him enjoy with such distinction, setting so to speak the tone for his age.[25]

In an act of biographical speculation that I suspect Rossetti favoured, Sade suggests that Laura had possessed the power of moral influence and artistic inspiration: a veritable muse and angel of the house, whose goodness enabled the man tortured by love and tempted by sin to stay respectable.[26]

The most controversial aspect of Sade's memoir, however, concerns the question of whether or not Laura was married. Since Dante also commemorated his love for a married woman in the *Commedia*, Sade perceives little scandal in claiming that Petrarch loved a married woman and mother. Yet Sade's English translator Susannah Dobson finds the emphasis on Petrarch's love for a married woman offensive: 'it is not possible on the principles of religion and morality to clear them

[25] Hayes, p. 121, citing [Abbé de Sade], *Mémoires pour la vie de François Petrarque, etc.*, 3 vols (Amsterdam, 1764–67), 1: 114–15.
[26] We hear the echo of Sade's claim in Rossetti's 1884 essay, in which she proposes that Beatrice took an active role in edifying Dante: 'Beatrice must apparently have gone far to mold her lover; to make him what he was, to withhold him from becoming such as he became not' ('Dante. The Poet Illustrated Out of the Poem', p. 571).

from that just censure which is due to every defection of the mind, from those laws which are the foundation of order and peace in civil society, and which are stamped with the sacred mark of divine authority'.[27] Dobson can only think literally about Petrarch's adoration of Laura, which she interprets as adulterous. Arthur Henry Hallam, a more astute but no less sentimental critic than Dobson, accepted Sade's claim because if Laura was unwed then her inaccessibility must reflect either a frigid or a coquettish disposition: 'the coldness of Laura towards so passionate and deserving a lover, if no insurmountable obstacle intervened during his twenty years of devotion, would be at least a mark that his attachment was misplaced, and show him in rather a ridiculous light'.[28] For Hallam, Laura's inaccessibility, if not due to her status as a married woman, makes Petrarch look like a fool rather than an adulterer. Both Dobson and Hallam suggest that Sade's claim greatly affected their perceptions of Petrarch, and it is clear that other nineteenth-century critics were also prompted to sentimentalise his poetry.[29]

Of Sade's most ardent detractors, Rossetti's essay names the 'recusant' Scottish jurist, Alexander Tytler, Lord Woodhouselee, and his illustrated study *An Historical and Critical Essay on the Life and Character of Petrarch* (1810).[30] Although she does not quote from the essay, it is the only full citation that Rossetti gives in her article, suggesting there may be something to it. Ostensibly a study of Petrarch, the essay closely refutes Sade's direct ancestral tie to Laura and attempts to claim that she was a chaste young woman, who may have suffered in her refusal of Petrarch. Woodhouselee revives Vellutello's conclusion that Laura di Chiabau lived her whole life in Cabrières near Petrarch's residence in Vaucluse and affirms that she died 'an unmarried woman'.[31]

---

[27] Susannah Dobson, 'Preface', *The Life of Petrarch. Collected from Mémoires pour la vie de Petrarch [sic]*, 2 vols (London, 1805), 1: xvi.

[28] Arthur Henry Hallam, *View of the State of Europe During the Middle Ages* (1818), 3 vols (New York and Boston, 1862), 3: 454.

[29] Thomas Macaulay blames Laura's love of flattery for Petrarch's elaborate metaphorical conceits: 'I cannot but suspect also that the perverted taste, which is the blemish of his amatory verses, was to be attributed to the influence of Laura, who, probably, like most critics of her sex, preferred a gaudy to a majestic style' (Corrigan, p. 140). The more gallant Walter Savage Landor states that 'Laura loved admiration, as the most retired and diffident of women do' (Corrigan, p. 158).

[30] *An Historical and Critical Essay on the Life and Character of Petrarch* (Edinburgh, 1810). Rossetti cites the 1812 edition.

[31] Woodhouselee, pp. 210–11.

At a critical moment in his study, Woodhouselee refutes the Abbé's interpretation of a passage from *Secretum*, Petrarch's dialogue with St Augustine, in which the poet describes Laura as having suffered from much '*ptubs*', an abbreviated Latin word that could indicate either *perturbatio* ('mental inquietude') or *partus* ('child-bearing') (pp. 166–77). Woodhouselee defends his interpretation of '*ptubs*' as 'mental inquietude' and sympathetically asks: 'How many women of prudence and of modesty, are, from unavoidable circumstances of situation, the victims of mental inquietude; and experience, even in a life of the utmost privacy and retirement, the keenest anguish, from the turbulent passions, the malevolence or the caprice, of those with whom they are connected' (pp. 176–7).[32] Thus, Woodhouselee argues that Laura's reserve comes from her 'privacy and retirement', which was not without its mental torments, or even some form of domestic abuse.

Rossetti never affirms the theories of either Woodhouselee or Sade, and after mentioning them continues to treat Laura's identity as open to question.[33] She observes 'with astonishment that the elder biographers of Petrarca give no adequate account of this lady, whom he himself depicts as altering the tenor his life. Boccaccio, indeed the contemporary of Petrarca, in one place where he mentions Laura, explains her as a symbol of the laurel crown' (p. 544). Much to Rossetti's frustration, not even Petrarch's famous flyleaf record in the Virgil is reliable: 'for discrepancies have been noted', she writes, 'and special stress has been laid on the fact that in the year 1327 the 6th of April was indeed Monday in Holy Week, but certainly not Good Friday, in spite of Petrarca's distinct statement that so it was' (p. 544). With such unreliable evidence, Rossetti leaves the historical question unresolved and instead turns from documentary to monumental evidence for proof that Laura existed.

---

[32] Rossetti family friend Charles Tomlinson reiterates this argument and goes so far as to transform Laura into a saint: 'Laura's character as we are repeatedly assured by the poet, had in it something that belonged rather to heaven than to earth; and in the dialogue with St Augustin [*sic*] already referred to, she is described as having her mind disengaged from the cares of this world, burning as she is with heavenly desires.' See *The sonnet, its origin and place in poetry* (London, 1874), pp. 221–2.

[33] While Rossetti writes in the first person plural in a moment of conjecture near the end of the essay, recent critics have assumed that in quoting Sade's statement Rossetti claims Laura as her own ancestress. I think that Rossetti is too meticulous a writer to make such an unsupportable statement and that Sade's documented evidence helps to validate her general sense that a real Laura existed. See Marsh, p. 212, and Arseneau, p. 43 n. 36.

Rossetti's Iconicism

To prepare the reader for her introduction of an unnamed pamphlet at
the end of the biographical article, Rossetti summarises the spiritual
aspect of Petrarch's progress. After describing Petrarch's career as
scholar and poet and noting nineteenth-century debates about Laura's
historical identity, Rossetti transforms the poet into an exemplary
Christian. Although Rossetti spends most of her article portraying the
public Petrarch, near the conclusion she describes the poet's mental
torments, his 'temptations of the flesh', and chastisement of body and
mind: 'we read of his systematic fasts, his masses put up for the soul of
Laura, his social habits, contempt of riches, and pious practices'
(p. 543). The next sentence describes the grandeur of Petrarch's
funeral, which

> was attended by Francesca da Carrara, with the bishop and chapter
> of Parma, and a throng of nobles and clergy, doctors and students;
> the body, laid on a bier covered with cloth of gold and over-
> shadowed by a golden canopy lined with ermine, was carried to the
> church of Arquà, and there deposited in a ladye [sic] chapel built by
> Petrarca; and Francesco da Brossano had raised to his memory a
> monument, supported by four columns and approached by two steps,
> all alike of red marble. (p. 543)

Rossetti's description of the princely funeral procession and public
monument suggests that Petrarch's 'eminently [C]hristian, though
harassed' life was worthy of commemoration in a site of prayer and
pilgrimage. The monument within the lady chapel (built by Petrarch
himself, as she notes) provides the opportunity for pilgrims to pay
homage to a poet whose work and life, she believed, ultimately served
God.

In his account of iconicism in literary biography, Richard Wendorf
refers primarily to verbal descriptions of painted portraits, in which a
poet is presented as an icon worthy of devotion (p. 69). Rossetti's
emphasis on the architecture of Petrarch's memorial, however, recalls
the monumental and sculptural analogies often used to describe the
poet's body of work or even the biographer's own narrative. Rossetti
appears to reject Petrarch's claim that his lyrics are merely *rime sparse*
(or 'scattered rhyme'), but instead represents Petrarch's tomb as a
monument to his art and faith. Thus, da Brossano's stately monument
and the lady chapel built by the poet himself commemorate Petrarch's

lyric speaker and each poem that enshrines the memory of Laura. Moreover, the tomb's placement within the church of Arquà makes a house of God in Italy the wandering poet's final resting place.

In seeking a conclusion to her article with a monument dedicated specifically to Laura, however, Rossetti produces another questionable record:

> To those who still prefer a flesh and blood Laura to a mysterious impersonation, it may be interesting to know that a pamphlet published in 1821 tells how in the Casa Peruzzi at Florence was preserved the alleged veritable effigy of Laura, sculptured by the painter Simone Memmi, and carried from place to place by the poet-lover in his frequent wanderings. On the back of the marble is inscribed the following quatrain attributed to Petrarca: – 'Splendida luce in cui chiaro si vede / Quel bel che può mostrar nel mondo Amore, / O vero exemplo del Sopran Valore / E d'ogni meraviglia intiera fede' ['Splendid light in which one may clearly see that beauty which Love shows in the world, O true example of the Supreme Worth and complete faith of every marvel'].[34]

Rossetti makes no further comment beyond this passage, leaving the reader to determine the significance of the anecdote and quatrain. The pamphlet published in 1821 is an Italian letter written by a Florentine gentleman Signor Bindo Peruzzi, which was published in 1753.[35] Woodhouselee's *Life and Character of Petrarch* also gives the contents of this letter but cites a different source: a 1753 Venetian edition of *Il Rime del Petrarca*.[36] Woodhouselee relates the discovery of a *basso rilievo* in the house of Signor Peruzzi and gives a description of two marble effigies.[37]

---

[34] The translation comes from *The Selected Prose of Christina Rossetti*, ed. David A. Kent and P. G. Stanwood (New York, 1998), p. 168.

[35] *Notizie sopra due piccoli ritratti in bassorilievo rappresentanti il Petrarca e Madonna Laura, che esistono in Casa Peruzzi di Firenze, con delle iscrizioni del XIV. secolo.* (Lettera dell'illustrissimo Signor Cav. Bindo Peruzzi ai Signori compilatori del Magazzino di Livorno, letta all'Accademia della Crusca l'anno, Parigi, 1753). I must thank Alison Chapman for helping me locate the reference. The British Library no longer possesses the pamphlet which was destroyed in a fire.

[36] For the engraving of the *basso rilievo* and an account of the letter, see Woodhouselee, p. 177 and pp. 225–7.

[37] The two portraits were inscribed with the names *F. Petrarca* and *Diva Laura*. The back of one bore the inscription *Simion de Senis me fecit, sub Anno Domini 1344* and the other the verses cited above. Woodhouselee's text renders the

I have tried to confirm the authenticity of these sculptures attributed to the Elder Simone (known correctly now as Martini rather than Memmi), but have found no recent reference to them. A portrait, usually assumed to be a painting or miniature of Laura, is attributed to Simone by Petrarch himself in two sonnets, but that image is now lost.[38] Giorgio Vasari in volume one of *The Lives of the Painters, Sculptors and Architects* wrongly attributes the identity of Petrarch and Laura to many frescoes and paintings located in the vicinity of Florence, most of which have now been correctly identified by modern art historians, but none in the Casa Peruzzi.[39]

My intention, however, is not to materialise the artwork that Rossetti herself describes as the 'alleged veritable effigy of Laura'. In fact, Rossetti stands aloof from scholarly pursuit, reiterating the fact that there are two camps on the question of Laura's identity: 'those who might prefer a flesh-and-blood Laura' and others who believe she was 'a mysterious impersonation'. The anecdote neither resolves the disputes among biographers nor discounts them, yet Rossetti leaves her reader with a potent picture of Petrarch as a wandering devotee, carrying a stony icon and one of his own devotional quatrains from place to place. The word 'effigy' evokes the sculpted image of a martyr or saint, preserved in a place of worship or sanctuary, and the quatrain suggests how Petrarch might have transformed his *idée fixe* into a subject of devotional meditation.

The sculpted effigy and the quatrain recall one of the ways that Petrarch represents Laura in *Rime Sparse*, as 'l'idolo mio scolpito in vivo lauro' ('my idol carved in living laurel').[40] The image comes from Petrarch's famous sestina 'Giovene donna sotto un verde lauro' ('A youthful lady under a green laurel'), an anniversary poem in which the speaker subsumes Laura's name in his devotion to the laurel tree. In this Ovidian conceit, Petrarch employs the myth of Apollo and Daphne to represent his attempt to capture Laura's vitality and beauty in verse as well as to obtain the reward of the poet's laurels. The sestina concludes

engravings of these sculptured images from the Venice edition and notes with some disappointment that the woman's portrait 'gives no high idea of the personal charms of Madonna Laura'.
[38] See Poems 77 ('Per mirar Policleto a prova fiso') and 78 ('Quando giunse a Simon l'alto concetto') (Durling, pp. 176-9). See also Andrew Martindale, *Simone Martini: Complete Edition* (New York, 1988), pp. 183-4.
[39] Giorgio Vasari, *The Lives of the Painters, Sculptors and Architects*, 4 vols, trans. A. B. Hinds (New York and London, 1927), 1: 128-34, 295-6.
[40] Poem 30 (Durling, pp. 86-9, line 27).

with the speaker's claim to have been wandering 'from shore to shore' for seven years and seeking pity from those who 'a thousand years from now' might see his 'well-tended laurel'.[41]

Yet the anecdote about Petrarch wandering with a sculpted image of Laura also recalls Ovid's myth of Pygmalion, the Greek sculptor who creates an ideally beautiful statue and falls in love with it. In Poem 78, a sonnet in which the speaker regrets that the painter Simone could not give Laura a voice when he painted her portrait, Petrarch apostrophises Pygmalion with much self-directed irony.[42] Rossetti's anecdote verges on parody in its representation of Petrarch as a love-sick idol-worshipper, an image that some Victorian critics would affirm, but the quatrain saves the poet from this fate.

In its invocation of a 'Splendida luce' ('Splendid light') and apostrophe to 'O vero exemplo del Sopran Valore' ('Splendid example of Supreme Worth'), the quatrain inscribed on the back of Laura's effigy suggests that in life she may have been a *donna angelicata*, a figure of the female beloved celebrated by Petrarch's Provençal and Italian lyric precursors. Dante's Beatrice is generally regarded as the epitome of the *donna angelicata*, who appears in the *Vita Nuova* and *Commedia* as 'a kind of messenger of grace and wisdom sent from God to the human spirit to raise it up to him'.[43] Thus, the quatrain and the effigy serve as aids to devotion, which the poet uses to create a tabernacle or sanctuary wherever he goes. The quatrain ostensibly reminds Petrarch that Laura's beauty was a revelation of *Amore* ('Divine Love') and her life a true example of *Sopran Valore* (which means 'Supreme Worth' but also 'Courage') and of *intiera fede* ('complete faith'). In effect, Rossetti's choice to conclude the biographical article with a lyric not only turns the reader's thoughts away from the figure of the historical Laura but also toward Petrarch's poetic achievement.

The pamphlet's anonymity in the article and the fact that 'the veritable effigy of Laura' is both alleged and untraced (at present) contribute to an air of mystery at the conclusion of Rossetti's

[41] Rossetti takes line 32 of this sestina for the motto of sonnet 14 in *Monna Innominata*: 'sol con questi pensier, con altre chiome' ('alone with these thoughts, with changed locks'), lines that contrast the speaker's unwavering obsession with Laura to his aging body (Crump 2: 93).
[42] The sonnet begins 'Quando giunse a Simon l'alto concetto' ('When Simon received the high idea') (Durling, pp. 178–9).
[43] See Michael R. G. Spiller, *The Development of the Sonnet: An Introduction* (London and New York, 1992), p. 30.

biographical memoir.[44] Moreover, in delivering this parable-like con-
clusion, Rossetti uses the phrase 'mysterious impersonation' in opposi-
tion to 'a flesh-and-blood Laura'. 'Impersonation' might be either an
allegorical personification or a person whose life exemplifies one
principle or idea. Rossetti suggests that Laura's 'habitual reserve' in
life has enabled her to hover between personification and personhood
in death and that the *Rime Sparse* is above all else a record of Petrarch's
memory of a woman who inspired him to seek and to reveal *Amore* in
his lyrics. Yet the anecdote also renders the poignant image of a man
relentlessly haunted and frustrated by the memory of his beloved. In
part three of this essay, I will discuss the relation between Rossetti's
anecdotal conclusion and a lyric contemporary with the article, called
'Memory', which reveals her early poetic debt to Petrarch and attempts
to allay Petrarchan restlessness with reserve.

Rossetti's 'Memory'

Of the many lyrics written in the 1850s that have proven provocative
to biographer-critics, 'Memory' has been interpreted mostly as a
confessional poem about Rossetti's broken marriage engagement with
Pre-Raphaelite painter James Collinson.[45] The engagement lasted from
1848 to 1850, and most biographers speculate that Rossetti ended the
relationship because Collinson was a Catholic convert. Yet part one of
'Memory' was written seven years after the Collinson affair, and while
it may be a reflection on the act of renouncing love, one can hardly
attribute the poem's creation solely to that incident. Rather 'Memory'
(written in two parts both during and after the composition of the
Petrarch article) is a riddle-like account of a self, caught in a fallen
world and seeking an aesthetic redemption.[46] While part one (com-

[44] On mystery in Rossetti's poetry, see W. David Shaw, 'Poet of Mystery: The
Art of Christina Rossetti', pp. 23–56.
[45] Crump 1: 147–8. For biographical readings of 'Memory', see Lona Mosk
Packer, *Christina Rossetti* (Berkeley and Los Angeles, 1963), pp. 113–14 and
196–7; Harrison, *Christina Rossetti in Context*, p. 125; Katherine J. Mayberry,
Christina Rossetti and the Poetry of Discovery (Baton Rouge and London, 1989),
pp. 60–3; and Marsh, p. 197. For readings that contest literal interpretation, see
Rosenblum, pp. 82–98; and Jerome J. McGann, 'Introduction', *The Achievement
of Christina Rossetti*, pp. 14–16.
[46] In this interpretation of 'Memory', I echo Giuseppe Mazzotta's analysis of
Petrarch in 'The *Canzoniere* and the Language of the Self', *The Worlds of*

posed in 1857) explores the Petrarchan obsession with memory, part two (written in 1865) reflects Rossetti's own solution as represented in the conclusion of her biographical article. Moreover, I will suggest that Rossetti deliberately makes a mystery of the event or person constituting the memory in her poem and resists the autobiographical impulse notable in Petrarch's vernacular and Latin prose. In practising reserve about the relationship between her life and art, Rossetti anticipates the secular reader's temptation to sentimentalise or to seek scandal in her lyrics.

Rossetti chose not to publish part one of 'Memory' in her first collection *Goblin Market and Other Poems* (1862), but while preparing her next collection *The Prince's Progress and Other Poems* (1866), added a second part in order to include it. In part one of the poem, composed around the time she began the Petrarch article in 1857, the speaker metaphorically describes the destruction of an 'it', presumably the memory of a person, idea, or event, and the feelings of considerable grief that accompany this act. In five quatrains, the speaker recounts the decision to destroy the 'it', portraying his/her mind as a 'room' in which the speaker has faced the 'naked truth' (line 5). Even more than the memory itself, the decision to destroy it is what seems to haunt the speaker.

Although Rossetti relies on the pronoun 'it' for most of part one, the speaker becomes more specific in line 15, calling 'it' an 'idol'. In the third stanza the speaker's metaphor of using balances to weigh her decision about destroying it echoes Daniel's injunction to King Belshazzar.[47]

> I took the perfect balances and weighed;
> No shaking of my hand disturbed the poise;
> Weighed, found it wanting: not a word I said,
> But silent made my choice. (lines 9–12)

Rossetti's scriptural source points toward God's demand that a king renounce his wealth and power, and her speaker has apparently imposed a similar judgement upon him/herself and the subject of the memory. Using anaphora in the fourth stanza to emphasise the 'choice

Petrarch (Durham and London, 1993), p. 59. I must also acknowledge the insights of Christopher R. Miller on early versions of this essay.
[47] Daniel translates God's handwriting on the wall during Belshazzar's feast: 'TEKEL, you have been weighed in the balances and found wanting' (Daniel 5.27).

made', the speaker describes his/her solemn decision to destroy the
memory as a tremendous act of will:

> None know the choice I made; I make it still.
>   None know the choice I made and broke my heart,
> Breaking mine idol: I have braced my will
>   Once, chosen for once my part.   (lines 13–16)

This iconoclastic decision is so imposing that in the fifth stanza the
speaker draws on Old Testament imagery of destroying idols: 'I broke it
at a blow, I laid it cold, / Crushed in my deep heart where it used to
live' (lines 17–18).[48] So crushing is the blow that the speaker's heart
'dies inch by inch' as 'the time grows old' (line 19). The expression of
despair reflects the difficulty of living with the severest form of
Christian piety: renunciation of the heart's desire. Moreover, in an
attempt to practice the utmost reserve, Rossetti's speaker discovers that
his/her grieving heart is dying because he/she is unable to speak openly
about it. The poem's original title 'A Blank' suggests that the idol's
destruction leaves the speaker in a death-like state without words to
express his/her anguish.

Part two, composed in 1865, two years after the completion of the
Petrarch article, reflects a new approach to the problem of the speaker's
afflicted self as well as a form of consolation derived from Petrarch and
Dante. Rossetti alerts the reader to a change of heart by changing the
structure of the quatrains and describing the speaker's mind-set in more
positive terms.[49]

> I have a room whereinto no one enters
>   Save I myself alone:
> There sits a blessed memory on a throne,
>   There my life centres.   (lines 1–4)

This penetralia in which the speaker spends his/her life no longer
contains an 'idol' but a 'blessed memory' that 'sits' like royalty 'on a
throne'. Recalling Petrarch's stately bier in Rossetti's biographical
article, the speaker has created a tomb-like shrine in which to spend

---

[48] See, for example, Numbers 33.52, Ezekial 30.14, and 2 Chronicles 34.4.
[49] The *abab* end-rhymes in part one are changed to an *abba* scheme in the four
stanzas of part two. The metrical pattern is altered from three iambic
pentameter lines and one trimeter in part one to alternating iambic pentameter
and trimeter lines in part two.

the rest of his/her days with the former idol. In stanza two, the speaker describes sitting with the memory through all the seasons, and like Petrarch's speaker in the anniversary poem, 'Giovene donna sotto un verde lauro', explains that his/her thoughts have not altered despite the passing of time.

The resemblance between Rossetti's speaker and Petrarch's from 'Giovene donna sotto un verde lauro' becomes even more striking in the last two stanzas of the poem. Shifting focus from the room to the memory, the speaker describes it as though it were an 'idol carved in living laurel':

> If any should force entrance he might see there
>   One buried not yet dead,
>   Before whose face I no more bow my head
> Or bend my knee there.   (lines 29–32)

No longer a worshipper of the idol, the speaker still finds him/herself with a living memory. The 'one buried not yet dead' also possesses a 'face', which contributes to a personification of the 'idol' but does not give a sense of his/her identity. John Freccero has argued that unlike Dante's *Commedia*, which represents Beatrice's face as a source of divine revelation, Petrarch's poetry resists that unveiling, using the pun Laura/lauro to indicate that language only obscures it.[50] Rossetti's speaker appears to take the Petrarchan view of his/her own idol, but in the last stanza shows that his/her own face may one day be a source of revelation:

> But often in my worn life's autumn weather
>   I watch there with clear eyes
>   And think how it will be in Paradise
> When we're together.   (lines 33–6)

Rossetti's concluding stanza directs the reader away from the idol and toward the heavenly vision for which the clear-eyed speaker watches. In Dante's *Commedia*, Beatrice, the *donna angelicata*, already possesses perfected vision and helps to prepare the poet for his view of the Empyrean at the conclusion. Rossetti's Anglicised *Paradiso* in the penultimate line of 'Memory' recalls both Dante's visionary poet-

[50] John Freccero, 'The Fig Tree and the Laurel: Petrarch's Poetics', in Patricia Parker and David Quint (eds), *Literary Theory/Renaissance Texts* (Baltimore and London, 1986), pp. 28–30.

speaker and his female heavenly guide. Moreover, the reader is left with the picture of Petrarch and Laura at the conclusion of the biographical article: the idolator who no longer worships the idol but keeps it as a reminder that a heavenly reunion awaits himself and his beloved.

The speaker's move from isolation in the temporal world to the conception of a divine reality that will make amends for life's sacrifices is a formula found in many of Rossetti's devotional lyrics.[51] The emphasis in 'Memory' on the speaker's idolatry and redemption through reserve and vigilance makes this poem an acutely Tractarian enterprise. But 'Memory' is also Petrarchan, particularly in its demands on the reader, whom Rossetti expects to sympathise with the lyric speaker's distressed psychological state. Petrarch's introductory sonnet of *Rime Sparse* begins with 'Voi' ('You') and appeals to the reader's ear and heart, hoping 'to find pity, not only pardon'.[52]

Rossetti's speaker in part one of 'Memory' also appears to take the reader into his/her confidence, but in part two exercises a prickly reserve, suggesting that 'he' who 'should force entrance' (i.e. read the poem) violates the speaker's privacy (line 29). Distinguishing her speaker from Petrarch's doleful wanderer even more, Rossetti positions him/her sitting in a 'room', where emotions are distilled from life experience and soothed through contemplation. Both the conclusion of 'Memory' and the Petrarch article suggest that a resourceful poet is capable of exercising the highest form of Christian reserve through verbal and formal economy, Biblical allusion and typology, and 'mysterious impersonation'. Thus, Rossetti chose not to leave behind the equivalent of Petrarch's flyleaf marginalia to confirm the identity of the 'idol' and emphasises instead its transformation into a 'blessed memory', representing the lyric speaker's turn from *cupiditas* to *caritas*.

'Francesco Petrarca' sheds light on Rossetti's late poetry and prose, especially I think her method of introducing Dante and Petrarch through their female muses in the preface to *Monna Innominata*: 'Beatrice, immortalised by "altissimo poeta . . . cotanto amante"; Laura, celebrated by a great tho' an inferior bard'.[53] By inferior, Rossetti I think alludes to the fact that Petrarch never progressed from lyric to

---

[51] See Linda Schofield, 'Being and Understanding: Devotional Poetry of Christina Rossetti and the Tractarians', *The Achievement of Christina Rossetti*, pp. 301–21; and Harrison, *Victorian Poets and the Politics of Culture*, pp. 125–44.
[52] Durling, p. 36.
[53] Crump 2: 86. Rossetti quotes from *Inferno* 4.80 and 5.134 ('The highest poet . . . with such a lover' [Rossetti's ellipsis]) to praise Dante.

epic, an expansive poetic form in which allegory and autobiography had more successfully deterred nineteenth-century critics from sentimentalising and misconstruing Dante's devotional mode. In its restraint and indirection, Rossetti's 'Francesco Petrarca' is a remarkable work of spiritual biography and literary criticism, in which the author saves Petrarch and Laura from Victorian secularism.

'A still and mute-born vision':
Locating Mathilde Blind's
Reproductive Poetics

SUSAN BROWN

MATHILDE BLIND SUFFERED A FATE common to many Victorian women
poets when a strong reputation in her lifetime evaporated after her
death. Her somewhat oblique relationship to English intellectual
tradition and national identity may partly explain this, but she was
ill served by her literary executor Arthur Symons' dubious praise of her
as one to whom 'all life was an emotion; and thought, to her, was of the
same substance as feeling'. He proclaims 'She was a poet, almost in
spite of herself.'[1] This familiar reduction of poetic achievement to a
spontaneous effusion of emotion sits particularly oddly with Blind's
work, which her contemporaries praised for boldness, mastery, and
artistry.[2] She was ambitiously innovative in genres ranging from the
ostensibly feminine lyric to the scientific epic. This essay explores one
facet of her achievement by considering the poetics Blind evolved for
her political poetry, particularly *The Heather on Fire: A Tale of the
Highland Clearances*.

Blind was primed to write political poetry. Born in Germany in
1841, she moved to England with her mother and her step-father, Karl
Blind, who eventually took political refuge in England after leading an
uprising during the 1848–49 insurrections in Baden.[3] Blind's early
poetry attests to a strong transnational commitment to nineteenth-
century democratic movements. Her first volume, published as 'Claude
Lake' in 1867,[4] is dedicated to her intellectual mentor, Italian

I would like to thank Ananda Pellerin, Robyn Read, and Laura Stenberg for
research assistance, and Charles Davidson, Jennifer Schacker, and Janice
Schroeder for helpful advice in connection with this essay.

[1] 'Introduction', *A Selection from the Poems of Mathilde Blind*, Symons ed.
(London, 1897), pp. v, vi; 'Preface', *The Poetical Works of Mathilde Blind*
(London, 1900), p. ix.
[2] 'Opinions of the Press', in Mathilde Blind, *The Ascent of Man* (London,
1889), pp. 1, 3.
[3] Richard Garnett, 'Memoir', *The Poetical Works of Mathilde Blind* (London,
1900), p. 2.
[4] Mathilde Blind as Claude Lake, *Poems* (London, 1867).

nationalist Joseph (Guiseppe) Mazzini. Mazzini advised her on her
studies and, she recollected, helped with his 'essentially spiritual
doctrine to bridge over' the void of despair resulting from her
consciousness of 'the preponderance of evil and sorrow, the poor
pittance of happiness doled out to the individual'.[5]

The opening poem, 'The Torrent', one of a pair of 'Poems to J.M.',
introduces some characteristics of Blind's verse: bold diction, vivid
natural imagery, conceptual ambition, wide-ranging allusion, and
unusual yet effective verbal patterns. An initial waterfall image is
offered as a handy 'material symbol' (p. 10) for Mazzini, giving way to
other liquid imagery:

> Thou hero! for through prejudice's walls,
>   That lock up earth against the quick'ning floods,
> And 'gainst the fresh regenerating falls
>   Of young ideas, that in sprouting mood
> Seethe like new wine, stirred by the grape's hot blood,
>   In the old bottles; thou, oh, brave and bold!
> Didst force thy way.   (p. 10)

Elizabeth Barrett Browning, a major influence on Blind, had employed
the image of new wine cracking old wine skins in advocating new
poetic forms in Aurora Leigh.[6] Blind's version fuses artistic preoccupa-
tions to political endeavour as represented both by Mazzini and by her
own poetic enterprise, since the poem concludes: 'I will heroic deeds,
prophetic words, proclaim' (p. 13). With unflinching self-assertion she
aligns herself with the male political revolutionary whom her ded-
ication characterises as a 'Prophet, Martyr and Hero' (prelims). This
constitutes a significant proclamation of agency by the female poet,
albeit muted by the pseudonymous mode of publication. Blind
perceived Mazzini as deeply invested in gender differentiation, recall-
ing his criticism of her scepticism[7] and his dismay that 'women, even
women, who should be all compact of faith and devotion, are

[5] Mathilde Blind, 'Recollections of Mazzini', Fortnightly Review 3078 (May
1891), p. 703.
[6] Elizabeth Barrett Browning, Aurora Leigh, ed. Margaret Reynolds (Athens,
Ohio, 1992), 1: 998–1002, p. 202. Compare also her Poems before Congress
(1860).
[7] Her evocation of George Eliot's own youthful inquiry suggests that Blind
revelled in possibilities opened up by scepticism and critique. Mathilde Blind,
George Eliot (London, 1883), p. 22.

beginning to question and to analyse!'[8] Yet her poem subtly feminises him by yoking him to fluid images associated with reproductive processes – quickening, regeneration, fermentation – and the fruitful if apparently destructive liberation of the earth from the trammels of prejudice.[9]

Reproductive imagery recurs elsewhere in the volume with positive connotations. 'Invocation, June 1866' invites the 'Spirit of the time! / Pregnant with the future' to 'Breathe thro' me in music' as the speaker applauds resistance in Venice, Rome, Poland, and Germany to 'imperial chains' and 'tyranny' (pp. 79–80). 'Ode To a Child' argues that genius receives the greatest gift of nature: participation in 'creation', the highest of activities. Human reproduction represents a kind of poetic fulcrum for Blind, balanced between the present and a fragile and uncertain set of possibilities, which the poet strives to discern and articulate:

> At times, perchance, I seem to see
> The hid existence of far off events,
> Trailing their slumb'rous shadows silently.
> For in the dusky deeps
> Of thy large eyes
> Sometime the veilèd outline of a still
> And mute-born vision sleeps
> As in the hollows of a hill,
> With dim and darksome rents
> The dreamful shadow of the morning lies,
> And softly, slowly, ever down doth roll,
> Till lost in mystic deeps it flees our watchful eyes.   (p. 84)

This prophet discerns, dimly and fleetingly in the eyes of an existing child, a kind of proto-embryo, an obscure possibility for the future in a very tenuous form: that of a sleeping, inarticulate 'vision', an object of the gaze discernible only in a sketchy outline. Perception here is as troubled as the syntax. Even as it asserts that the vision is merely sleeping, the passage suggests through the enjambment which places 'still' prominently at the end of the line, that it may be still-born as well as mute. The poet's role is the more critical, since her glimpse of this

---

[8] Blind, 'Mazzini', p. 706.
[9] On the role of gender politics in English middle-class support for Italian nationalism, see Maura O'Connor, *The Romance of Italy and the English Political Imagination* (New York, 1998).

evanescent possibility may be all that survives. Reproductive risk is bound up with the difficulty of attaining and sustaining poetic inspiration, while the melding of vision and voice is perhaps an ironic reflection on her own name.

Blind's first collection thus conveys the difficulties of the kind of politically-engaged poetry she desires to produce, a prophetic aesthetic addressing a fervently anticipated but uncertain futurity. Because she was not a Christian who could read in history the gradual unfolding of God's plan but was instead susceptible to the bleak perspective that 'we are ephemeral creatures here to-day and gone to-morrow, that the life in us is as the flame of a candle which burns down to the socket and goes out',[10] she was forced to contemplate the possibility that the changes she envisioned might not come to pass.

In 1886 Mathilde Blind published *The Heather on Fire: A Tale of the Highland Clearances*.[11] Blind herself had no connection to Scotland before visiting there, which she did first in 1873 when she was in her early thirties, when she was deeply impressed by the grandeur of the landscape, particularly in the Hebrides, and the history of the people.[12] And it was a topical subject. The forcible eviction of tenant farmers from their lands in the highlands and islands of Scotland had begun in the late eighteenth century as a result of factors including the suppression of the clans and the desire to increase the profitability of estates. Following the decade of famine which began in 1846, there had been a new wave of Clearances. A growth in radical journalism and cultural nationalism, continued economic strain in crofting regions, and awareness of the militant land struggles in Ireland culminated in 1881 in agitation that marked the beginning of the 'Crofters' War'. A Royal Commission was established to investigate crofters' grievances. Its failure to devise a solution provoked renewed agitation and civil disobedience by crofters and their urban allies, which met with military intervention on the Isle of Skye late in 1884. Legislation was finally passed in 1886, following the election to Parliament of five Crofters MPs in the wake of the Third Reform

---

[10] Blind, 'Mazzini', p. 703.

[11] Mathilde Blind, *The Heather on Fire: A Tale of the Highland Clearances* (London, 1886). Many of Blind's works are available at the Victorian Women Writers Project, Perry Willett general editor, Indiana University: http://www.indiana.edu/~letrs/vwwp/index.html.

[12] Garnett, pp. 27–30. Scotland also inspired Blind's *The Prophecy of St Oran* (1881).

Bill.[13] Blind's poem was published just as the Crofters' Holdings (Scotland) Act, modelled on the 1881 Irish Land Act, received royal assent.[14]

The diversity of form and address in *The Heather on Fire* is immediately striking. The framing materials engage directly with contemporary political controversy. They consist of a dedication to Captain Cameron, 'Whose glory it is to have thrown up his place rather than proceed in command of the steamer "Lochiel", which was to convey the police expedition against the Skye crofters in the winter of 1884', a preface which claims a factual basis for the 'atrocities' (p. 1) the poem describes, and notes which excerpt memoirs, analyses, and condemnations of the Clearances.[15] While footnotes to poems were hardly unknown in the context of historical or topical poetry, what is noteworthy here is a sharp disjunction in tone and style (most striking at the beginning) between the poem proper and its apparatus. The poem seems a formally and historically distanced historical artifact telling a universalised or at least decontextualised story of human experience.

On a new page, following a woodblock-style floral illustration that signals a break in the text, are the poem's title and a heading also with decorated capital, 'Duan First'. 'Duan', from Gaelic, was first used in English in 1765 by James MacPherson to designate parts of an epic poem in his alleged translation of the legendary Scots bard Ossian.[16] It aligns Blind's work at once with a highly romanticised and primitivist (if partly manufactured) tradition of poetic discourse. The poem's opening view of a solitary figure reinforces this sense:

> High on a granite boulder, huge in girth,
> Primæval waif that owned a different birth
> From all the rocks on that wild coast, alone,
> Like some grey heron on as grey a stone,
> And full as motionless, there stood a maid,

[13] See Ewan A. Cameron, *Land for the People: The British Government and the Scottish Highlands, c. 1880–1925* (East Linton, 1996); Eric Richards, *The Highland Clearances* (Edinburgh, 2000).

[14] The Act received royal assent on 25 June 1886; the *Newcastle Daily Chronicle* reviewed Blind's poem on 3 July. Cameron, *Land*, pp. 37–8; 'Opinions', p. 4.

[15] On the conflict in Skye see I. M. M. MacPhail, 'The Skye Military Expedition of 1884–5,' *Transactions of the Gaelic Society of Inverness* 48 (1972–74): 1, pp. 62–94.

[16] *The Oxford English Dictionary*, ed. J. A. Simpson and E. S. C. Weiner, 2nd edn (Oxford, 1989), 'Duan'.

Whose sun-browned hand her seaward eyes did shade
Flinching, as now the sun's auroral motion
Twinkled in milky ways on the grey heaving ocean.

(I.i, p. 5)

The imagery, coupled with the ambiguity in the apposition of the
initial descriptive phrases, creates a link between the female figure,
nature, and a fecundity suggested by the girth of the rock and the
heaving sea.

Allusions to the primeval, to the immensely slow processes of
geological creation that have produced the landscape, and to the
vast operations of the cosmos, along with the extended description,
relaxed pace of the metre, and length of the vowels in the rhymes, all
contribute to the impression of universality and timelessness, rather
than specificity and topicality. The sense of the poem as an archaic
account of a timeless people is sustained as the reader proceeds.
Although some characters have names, the main figures, Michael
and Mary, feel more iconic than individual, and Mary is compared to
the Virgin mother. We learn that Rory, the family patriarch, served in
the Napoleonic Wars, but only by way of explanation of his infirmity.
Familial and social relations, narrowly defined, are the focus of the
poem until into the third Duan of four.

Yet *The Heather on Fire* is surrounded by historical precision. The
preface recounts how Blind heard from a Scottish woman on a visit to
Arran in the summer of 1884 an account of the expulsion of the Glen
Sannox people in 1832 by the Duke of Hamilton. The notes detail
actual incidents in relation to particular stanzas, although the notes
themselves are not signalled in the body of the poem. The poetry, in
other words, seems to strive exclusively for what Blind terms the
'thrilling pathos' of the old woman's account, the 'idyll' of her
evocation of the lives of the crofters prior to the Clearances (p. 3).
An emerging sense of the poem as an elegy for what was, by the time
of its publication, understood by many to be the vanishing culture of
a people succumbing to the inevitable march of civilization, is
apparently confirmed by extended descriptions of nature, the
rhythm of Highland life, and of exotic cultural practices such as
ceilidhs. In other words, while the preface roundly condemns the way
the crofters were 'ruthlessly expelled [from] their native land to make
way for sporting grounds rented by merchant princes and American
millionaires' (p. 3), economic analysis and political critique intially
seem to have been expelled from the body of the poem, which instead

offers a generalised Scottish landscape inhabited by representative Crofters.

What is at stake in the negotiation in *The Heather on Fire* between two clusters of associations, the universal, primitive, natural and domestic or familial, on the one hand, and the historically specific, civilised, cultural, and political on the other? The tension between them, I will argue, is closely connected to the poem's linguistic and narrative preoccupation, evident in its opening stanzas, with reproduction, and together they are crucial to Blind's attempt to articulate her vision of the political.

Creation in nature and reproduction in human society are paralleled from the outset of the poem, as its opening illustrates. The narrative is simple: Mary, the maid of the rock, has been affianced for nine years to Michael, a crofter and fisher. The first Duan portrays their meeting upon his return from sea, and their love of the land as they walk to the cottage which shelters his parents. This section concludes with Mary's return to her job – her waged labour an early sign that this is not a nostalgic pastoral idyl – as head of the dairy of 'The lordly mansion of the lord of all that land' (I.xlv, p. 27). Here the simple stanza scheme of four sets of rhyming couplets, which Blind has varied admirably in the preceeding stanzas, becomes inexorably repetitive as she details his property – the glens, pastures, hills, forests, and the birds, wildlife, and fish in stream – culminating in the fact that the lord effectively owns not just the land but the the labour of his tenants:

> For him the hind's interminable toil:
> For him he ploughed and sowed and broke the soil,
> For him the golden harvests would he reap,
> For him would tend the flocks of woolly sheep,
>
> For him would thin the iron-hearted woods,
> For him track deer in snow-blocked solitudes;
> For him the back was bent, and hard the hand,
> For was he not his lord, and lord of all that land?
>
> (I.xlvii, p. 28)

This invocation of greed and a one-way relationship between landlord and tenant follows oppressively, at the conclusion of the first Duan, on the catalogue of nature's bounty and variety.

The second Duan describes in twenty-four stanzas the couple's wedding day and the ceilidh that follows it. There are strong echoes of the egalitarian union of lovers at the conclusion of *Aurora Leigh* (9: 910ff.) in Blind's portrait of Mary's expectations as a bride:

> Ah! dear to her that narrow, grey-thatched home,
> Where she would bide through all the years to come;
> Round which her hopes and memories would entwine
> With fondness, as the tendrilled eglantine
> Clings round a cottage porch; where work and love,
> Like the twin orbs that share the heavens above,
> Would round their lives, and make the days and nights
> Glad with the steady flame of those best household lights.
>
> (II.vi, p. 32)

The first half of the poem, then, represents in pastoral mode the lives of paragons of rural thrift, virtue, and domestic affection; in the second half, political forces intrude to destroy them.

Duan Third takes up the story in the stormy autumn nine years later (this second use of the number nine reinforcing the emphasis on gestation), with a pregnant Mary nursing a sick child, one of four, while Michael is again away fishing. Her daily occupations are interrupted by frantic neighbours announcing fire in the glen from thatched cottages kindled by the agent of the absentee lord. This duan depicts the family precipitously forced from their home, so that Michael's bedridden mother is burning in her bed by the time she is removed, only to die, and the sick child expires that night as they sleep in the open air. The question of a benign providence is raised, in language that parodies that of Biblical parable, as the passivity of these brave stalwarts of the British empire is explained:

> They fly and turn not on the hireling band,
> That unresisting drives them from their land.
> Dowered with the lion's strength, like lambs they go,
> For saith the preacher: 'God will have it so.'
>
> (III.lxiii, p. 73)

The fourth and final Duan describes the horrific aftermath of the firing: the family's refuge in a ruined keep on the cliffs, during a furious storm in which Mary labours, births, and then expires shortly after her newborn; their discovery by the landlord's men; the truncated funeral at which the eldest child dies; the hounding of the crofters to boats. Rory is so overcome by his wife's horrific fate that 'like a village Lear / His eyes rolled maddening' (III.xlvi, p. 65); in his delirium he is

(echoing another Shakespearean tragedy) taken for a ghost by Michael
in the gale outside the ruined castle. Rory evades the emigration vessel,
only to witness the ship containing the remnants of his family wrecked
on rocks in the Sound of Sleat. The poem follows this literal
miscarriage of the vessel with a final image of death as a form of
nurturing and, ironically, of safety from further pain of separation from
their beloved land:

> Safe in the deep,
> With their own seas to rock their hearts to sleep,
> The crofters lay: but faithful Rory gave
> His body to the land that had begrudged a grave.
>
> (IV.xlviii; p. 97)

The Heather on Fire is permeated by images of reproduction and
miscarriage, nurturing and predation. It thus employs the trope, by then
standard in British poetry of famine and protest, of depicting social ills
through the sufferings of pregnant or lactating women, helpless
children, and the aged or infirm. Speranza's 'The Famine Year', for
example, answers the question, 'Pale mothers, wherefore weeping?'
with 'Would to God that we were dead – / Our children swoon before
us, and we cannot give them bread.'[17] Blind's stress on motherhood
exceeds the function of provoking pity and outrage, however. In many
respects, it belongs to the tradition in British women's political poetry
of articulating a poetic voice out of an emphasis on the generative
female body.[18] Mothering permeates Eliza Ogilvy's early work, includ-
ing *A Book of Highland Minstrelsy* (1846),[19] and informs her call in
Poems of Ten Years (1854) for a newly politicised poetics. Elizabeth
Barrett Browning had incorporated her own reproductive body into the
political commentary of *Casa Guidi Windows* (1851), and used the

[17] Jane Francesca Wilde, *Poems by Speranza*, 2nd edn (Glasgow, n.d.), p. 10.
Compare *Tuath is Tighearna: Tenants and Landlords, An Anthology of Gaelic
Poetry of Social and Political Protest from the Clearances to the Land Agitation
(1800–1890)*, ed. Donald E. Meek (Edinburgh, 1995).
[18] Recent important work on women's political poetry includes Isobel Arm-
strong's *Victorian Poetry: Poetry, Poetics and Politics* (London, 1993); Tricia
Lootens, 'Victorian Poetry and Patriotism', in Joseph Bristow (ed.), *The
Cambridge Companion to Victorian Poetry* (Cambridge, 2000), pp. 255–79; plus
work on individual poets by critics including Leigh Coral Harris, Antony
H. Harrison, Lootens, Esther Schor, and Marjorie Stone.
[19] See A. A. Markley, 'Eliza Ogilvy, Highland Minstrelsy, and the Perils of
Victorian Motherhood', *Studies in Scottish Literature* 32 (2001): pp. 180–94.

figure of Anita Garibaldi to establish a poetics, both perilous and inspiring, of female political engagement in the maternal body. Yet, indebted as she may be to such predecessors, Blind's emphasis on reproductive processes is more tightly interwoven with contemporary political debate.

As its opening's reference to geological process suggests, the poem stages a dialogue between the human and natural worlds in a decidedly scientific context. Blind's studies of geology had led her at an early age to atheism, for which she was expelled from school,[20] and her framework for understanding the Clearances was decidedly materialist. Blind noted elsewhere that 'the poet's attitude toward, and interpretation of, Nature may be said to undergo continual modification in harmony with the development of religious and scientific thought'.[21] The ascendent theory in her day for explicating the course of human history was the theory of evolution, according to which the reproduction of a species produces random variations in organisms; the processes of competition which result in either survival or death ensure that, as a consequence of 'natural selection', only those variations adapted to their environments are preserved. The centrality of reproduction to both evolutionary theory and *The Heather on Fire* suggests that Blind exploits the former as an interpretive rubric for the Highland Clearances.

The night following Mary's expulsion from her home, her attention is focused on her sick infant held against her pregnant body:

> Mary's care
> Was centered on the child upon her knee,
> Who gasped, convulsed, in his last agony,
> Close to the burden of the life beneath
> Her heart – that battle-field of wrestling life and death.
>
> (III.liv, p. 69)

This is the struggle for survival in relation to environment at its baldest, but its dimensions are not merely physical. The battle-field is ambiguous: the body of the unborn child and perhaps also the mother's womb and her heart are caught up in the struggle. This suggests that the application of theories of nature to the complexities of human culture is hardly a straight-forward matter, and indeed Blind's project in *The Heather on Fire* hinges on the difficulty of that relationship. For

[20] Garnett, 'Memoir', p. 8.
[21] Mathilde Blind, *Shelley's View of Nature Contrasted with Darwin's* (London, 1886), p. 9.

as surely as she mocks the notion of the Clearances as the working out of a divinely ordained providence, she describes the events as a travesty rather than a fulfillment of evolutionary process.

Mary has acted according to the dictates of natural selection in choosing to marry and reproduce with a man well adapted to his natural environment. Both she and Michael are handsome, stately, fitted to their habitat and occupations. The vicious factor, whom she spurned as a lover, is by contrast 'A little limping man' (III.xxiv, p. 54). His disability reflects not only the penchant in Victorian literature to associate moral failing with physical deformity, but in the context of Darwinism suggests unfitness. However, he thrives on injustice, and, through him, the inverted social order punishes Mary for her choice, killing the offspring produced by her union with Michael (two of whom are named after their parents, stressing reproduction). The poem throughout draws on traditional Christian imagery, but reverses its values. The eviction of the crofters is represented as the transformation by human agency of paradise into hell; but the angel at the gates is a deformed factor with a burning brand and those burned in hell are innocents like Rory's wife, whose 'fall' cannot be attributed to moral or spiritual failing.

The relationship between poetic text and paratexts strengthens as the narrative develops. The first note attaches to a point in the second Duan which offers a new degree of specificity, albeit one temporally and spatially displaced. Rory describes at length his service as a member of the famed Forty-Second Highland Regiment in Spain during the Napoleonic wars. Blind's note, to Louis Lafond's 1885 *Une crise sociale en Écosse: les Highlands et la question des crofters*, underscores the contribution of Highland men to the national project: 'La population des Crofters, des Highlands et des Iles . . . est une pépinière de bon travailleurs et de bons citoyens pour tout l'empire' (p. 99).[22] Lafond's observation of the suitability of the Gaels for supplying the army and navy seems hardly original enough to offset the potentially alienating effect of citing a foreign expert in a foreign tongue, but the lengthy passage Blind quotes makes explicit her naturalistic perspective, discussing people in terms of habitat and arguing for the outlying regions of Scotland as an ideal nursery ('pépinière') for the workers required to staff the British empire.

---

[22] *A Social Crisis in Scotland: The Highlands and the Crofters Question*: 'The population of crofters, of the Highlands and Islands . . . is a nursery for good workers and good citizens for the entire empire.'

The interplay between the particular and the universal in Blind's text as a whole thus starts to come into focus: nineteenth-century naturalistic inquiry looked to the specifics of organisms and their life cycles to reveal larger patterns, clues to universal processes or mechanisms. It moved human reproduction and its consequences – and hence mothering – to the centre of history. The fate of the empire, for Blind, is linked not analogously but metonymically, through a chain of natural causes, to the bodies of women, whose environments and whose labour are crucial to the successful maintenance of culture.

The patterns evident in this human nursery are thus by no means purely natural ones, for the poem represents through the fate of one kinship structure the decisive human destruction of an entire human habitat, a single crofting community, which represents the entire crofting community of Scotland. Part of what is at work here is a realist metonymy emerging from Blind's belief in its political efficacy. In her 1883 monograph *George Eliot*, which defends the extent to which Eliot drew on science and attests to Blind's ease with naturalist, positivist, and other intellectual currents that were so formative for the great prose poet of the 'evolution of society', Blind argued that the novelist had demonstrated the extent to which 'a truthful adherence to nature' placed the artist 'in the very vanguard of social and political reforms; as in familiarising the imagination with the real condition of the people, he [sic] did much towards creating that sympathy with their wants, their trials, and their sufferings, which would eventually effect external changes in harmony with this better understanding' (pp. 88, 107). The poet cum scientist can describe a selective sample of organisms that provide insight into general processes, at the same time that the poet cum realist can strive for reform through poetry's established mode of affect by offering individualised objects of sympathy or identification.

Relating the individual to the general is here at least as political as it is natural, which Rory's case underscores as the poem dwells on the irony of the soldier's relation to the state. Personally, Michael's father has suffered a cruel fate:

> His father had come home one winter time
> From some fierce battle waged on fields of Spain,
> Where he and fellows like him helped to gain
> The day for England's king – alas! for him
> That gain was loss indeed: – crippled in life and limb.
>
> (I.xxx, p. 20)

But far from being personal and arbitrary, this is part of a much larger pattern of loss and gain wherein the Highlands gave up thousands of men to fight England's wars and consolidate empire, only to be later repaid by being legally ousted from their homes. Rory boasts: 'Ye'll all have heard / Tell on the Forty-Second? Show us the glen / In Highland or in Island sent not its bonny men!' (II.xvii, p. 37) Just as the opening of the poem indicated that the singular boulder was produced and then (dis-)placed in the landscape by vast geological processes, so too allusion to Britain's wars reveals the population in an apparently isolated and idyllic corner of the world as subject to global politics. This point is intertwined with the climax of the poem's pathos. In the narrative's most startling disjunction, the description of Mary's parturition in the midst of a gale, barely sheltered by the ruined keep, is abruptly checked by Rory, who stumbles in too disoriented to recognise his own son or realise what is taking place. He embarks on a monologue which tries to reconcile his sense of national identity with what is happening to him:

> So they're burning in the glen,
> But I, ye ken, I'm of the Forty-Secon'!
> I've served my country well as it has me, I'se reckon.'
>
> And therewith burst into a husky song
> Of doughty Highland deeds, and, crazed with wrong,
> Dozed off, nor knew how busy death was there,
> Nor that as his new grandchild felt the air
> And edge of the inhospitable night,
> It shuddered back from life's brink in affright,
> Dragging its mother after.   (IV.xvii–xviii, pp. 82–3)

The jarring interruption of the narrative sequence by Rory's ramblings challenges the reader to reflect on the political ironies at work in the Clearance. Unable in the face of such ideological contradiction to sustain a sense of identity forged in patriotic service, he goes mad.

As the poem mounts towards this twinned physical and ideological crisis, the gulf between poetic centre and surrounding apparatus narrows. The factor echoes his master's self-justifying Malthusian theories[23] when he condemns the crofters as

---

[23] Mary Jacobus' analysis of Malthus' feminisation of the population problem suggests a related thread of ideological debate in Blind's poem. *First Things: The Maternal Imaginary in Literature, Art, and Psychoanalysis* (New York, 1995), pp. 83–96.

Cumbering the ill-used soil they hack and scratch,
And call it tillage! Silly hens that'd hatch
Their addled eggs, whether they will or no.   (III.xxv, p. 54)

The poem soon also provides economic analysis: 'But in these latter
days men's lives are cheap, / And hard-worked Highlanders pay worse
than lowland sheep' (III.xxvii, p. 55). The muted dialogue between
notes and poetic text thus picks up, both in the poetic language and as
the notes become more dense.

Blind's preface addresses the issue of the relationship between the
text and historical record briefly but directly:

I seem to hear many a reader ask whether such atrocities as are
described in 'The Heather on Fire' have indeed been committed
within the memory of this generation. Let him be assured that this is
no fancy picture; that, on the contrary, the author's aim has been to
soften some of the worst features of the heart-rending scenes which
were of such frequent occurrence during the Highland Clearances.
Many of them are too revolting for the purposes of art; for the ferocity
shown by some of the factors and ground-officers employed by the
landlords in evicting their inoffensive tenantry, can only be matched
by the brutal excesses of victorious troops on a foreign soil.   (p. 1)

She alludes only cursorily to contemporary debates, leaving the notes
to answer any doubts about historical accuracy. Excerpted entirely from
publications about the Clearances, these cite some of the most
prominent voices in the fierce debate of the 1880s, ranging from the
Napier Commission's 1884 report,[24] to Edinburgh classics professor
John Stuart Blackie's The Scottish Highlanders and the Land Laws: An
Historico-Economical Enquiry,[25] to the eye-witness accounts of Donald
Macleod.[26] Blind's support for the details of her narrative includes
Macleod's recollection of one expulsion:

[24] Report of the Commissioners of Inquiry into the Condition of the Crofters and
Cottars in the Highlands and Islands of Scotland. PP 1884 XXXIII–XXXVI.
[25] John Stuart Blackie, The Scottish Highlanders and the Land Laws: An
Historico-Economical Enquiry (London, 1885).
[26] Macleod's book first appeared as letters to the Edinburgh Weekly Chronicle
(see Alexander Mackenzie, The History of the Highland Clearances [Inverness,
1883]), then in pamphlet form as History of the Destitution in Sutherlandshire
(Edinburgh, 1841), then in an expanded edition as Gloomy Memories in the
Highlands of Scotland: Versus Mrs. Harriet Beecher Stowe's Sunny Memories, or, A
faithful picture of the extirpation of the Celtic race from the Highlands of Scotland in
Toronto in 1857.

Some old men took to the woods and the rocks, wandering about in a state approaching to or of absolute insanity; and several of them in this situation lived only a few days. Pregnant women were taken in premature labour, and several children did not long survive. . . . I was present at the pulling down and burning of the house of William Chisholme, Badinloskin, in which was lying his wife's mother, an old bedridden woman of nearly one hundred years of age, none of the family being present. . . . Fire was set to the house, and the blankets in which she was carried out were in flames before she could be got out. She was placed in a little shed, and it was with great difficulty they were prevented from firing it also. Within five days she was a corpse. (p. 110)

As the material from Lafond indicates, however, the eighteen pages of notes balance historical testimony with commentary. One of the lengthiest excerpts is from *Land Nationalisation* by Alfred Russel Wallace, best known now as the man who hurried Darwin into publication of the theory of evolution.[27] A vocal exponent of evolution, Wallace also published influentially on many other issues. He in fact stumbled on the theory of natural selection while reassessing Malthus' work on population, and unlike Darwin he eagerly applied his conclusions as a naturalist to social and religious questions.[28]

As I have already suggested, the insistent imagery of reproduction in *The Heather on Fire* emerges from an evolutionary framework which places the Clearances in the context of imperceptibly slow but irresistible natural processes within which each organism contributes to change. This framework raises questions not only about the relationship between the natural and the social, but also about causality and the possibilities for human agency in political situations such as those the poem laments. Blind's reference to Wallace reveals her poetic strategy as intimately connected to debate over Scottish land reform.

Harriet Beecher Stowe's 1854 defence of the Sutherland landlords who hosted her Highland visit represents their 'Improvements' as 'an almost sublime instance of the benevolent employment of superior wealth and power in shortening the struggles of advancing civilisation'.[29] In the 1880s the Duke of Argyll similarly claimed that

[27] Alfred Russel Wallace, *Land Nationalisation: Its Necessity and Its Aims* (London, 1882).
[28] Charles H. Smith, ed. and intro., *Alfred Russel Wallace: An Anthology of His Shorter Writings* (Oxford, 1991).
[29] Harriet Beecher Stowe, *Sunny Memories of Foreign Lands*, 2 vols (Boston, 1854), 1: 313.

the 'old Celtic customs' of land tenure and use must give way in favour
of the settled laws of 'advancing civilisation' but his position as an
authority on evolution gave the pronouncement additional force.[30]
The debate over land reform in Scotland in fact emerged as one among
committed Darwinists. Social Darwinists such as Argyll argued that
private property had a natural basis;[31] with Herbert Spencer he opposed
government interference to protect weaker, that is, less well adapted,
members or groups of society against the operations of a natural social
order which could progress solely through the survival of the 'fittest'
individuals or races.[32] Wallace, however, considered evolution insuffi-
cient to explain people's moral capacities and 'flatly denied that we
should allow it to operate in social issues now that man was able . . . to
modify his environment, both organic and inorganic, and thus control
the forces of nature'.[33] Influenced by Henry George, he revised the
theory of value in political economy to place land and labour ahead of
capital, becoming a socialist.[34]

Blind's own view emerges from her lecture, published a few months
after *The Heather on Fire*, on 'Shelley's View of Nature Contrasted
With Darwin's'. She criticises the lack of 'historic realism' in *Pro-
metheus Bound*, lamenting that Shelley was 'debarred from casting into
a poetic mould the modern scientific conception of evolution and the
struggle for existence' (p. 18). Such realism, she argued, would depict
humanity

emerging from a semi-brutal, barbarous condition, and continually
progressing to higher stages of moral and mental development. For
the true conflict consists in man's struggle with the irresponsible

[30] George Douglas Campbell, 8th Duke of Argyll, 'A Corrected Picture of the
Highlands', *Nineteenth Century* 1055 (November 1884), p. 690. The article
challenges the Napier report. See also 'Isolation, or Survival of the Unfittest',
which asks 'who *were* the Hebrideans?' [emphasis mine], answers that they were
due to their geographic isolation a throwback culture, and asserts, 'The laws of
nature cannot be suspended in favour of any men simply because they speak
Gaelic.' *Nineteenth Century* 1641 (November 1889), pp. 13, 33.
[31] George Douglas Campbell, 8th Duke of Argyll, 'The Prophet of San
Francisco,' *Nineteenth Century* 979 (April 1884), p. 542.
[32] Wallace criticised Spencer's views on land reform in 1891. See Smith,
p. 511.
[33] Harry Clements, *Alfred Russel Wallace: Biologist and Social Reformer* (London,
1983), p. 78.
[34] Clements, pp. 165–74, 229. Wallace also supported broadening women's
educational and work opportunities.

forces of Nature, and the victory in his conquest over them, both as regards the subjection of his own lower animal instincts and in his continually growing power through knowledge of turning these elemental forces, that filled his savage progenitors with fear and terror, into the nimblest of servants. (pp. 18–19)

Thus, although Blind writes as an atheist and Wallace as a spiritualist, they share the conviction that human evolution is as much social as natural, and involves a triumph over rather than adherence to the basic instincts that justify competition and violence in a Social Darwinist model. Three years after *The Heather on Fire*, Blind published another ambitious poem, *The Ascent of Man*, a series of lyrics representing the entire span of human history, from the first inklings of creation when, 'Struck out of dim fluctuant forces and shock of electrical vapour, / Repelled and attracted the atoms flashed mingling in union primeval', to contemporary society with its war, rape and pillage, noisy factories, starving infants, and 'woman's nameless martyrdom'.[35] Wallace contributed a laudatory preface to the second, posthumous, edition a decade later.[36]

In *The Heather on Fire*, although the female body is charged with literal human reproduction – 'brooding care' (I.xiv, p. 12) – the imagery of reproduction and nurturing activities applies equally to men. Early on the 'old familiar sights of their own native glen' are as dear to the returning fishermen as 'is her first-born's earliest lisp / To a young mother' (I.v, p. 7). Michael kisses his old mother's face and hair 'As it might be a babe's, with tender care' (I.xxviii, p. 19), and the crofters are later compared to mothers who love best the offspring who give them the most trouble: 'So do these men, matched with wild wind and weather, / Cling to their tumbling burns, bleak moors, and mountain heather' (III.iii, p. 43). On the morning of the eviction, in an extended pastoral passage, both female and male children of the household engage in domestic activities or nurturing. After their expulsion, in their pitiful refuge in the ruined castle, Michael feeds them 'with a mother's tenderness' (IV.viii, p. 78).

Michael is one of the poem's 'patient and laborious men' (I.xix, p. 14), Highlanders who are valorised rather than feminised by repeated association with women's labour, with reproduction, and with nurturing. One of the key differences between Blind's pastoral

[35] Mathilde Blind, *The Ascent of Man* (London, 1889), pp. 7, 104.
[36] Mathilde Blind, *The Ascent of Man*, 2nd edn (London, 1899).

and an Edenic one lies in her conception of labour. In a Christian context, labour is an undesirable effect of the fall, and women's postlapsarian labour and men's is sharply differentiated. Although her Highlanders by and large engage in a gendered division of labour, in keeping with historical record, Blind seems at pains to dispel the sense that such division is biologically ordained. Women are active partners in the economic activities of the isles, and Michael enjoys a loving equality with Mary, 'faithful partner of his arduous life: / Both toiling late and soon' (III.ii, p. 43). It is as much the waste of salutary labour as the unwarranted human suffering that defines the crime of the Clearances here. When Michael returns from sea to find 'Sore labour's fruits all wasted in a night' (III.lxii, p. 73), both the labour of their hands and the reproductive labour of their bodies have been destroyed.

The tragedy of *The Heather on Fire* is the extinction of a community which, although it contains hardship and conflict, and is vulnerable (and possibly culpable) in its patriotism, is a better foundation for the amelioration of society than the individualist, economically rapacious, and at times sadistic order of society represented by the landlord and his agents. *The Ascent of Man* lays out what is required for human redemption, when humanist Love,[37] the animating force embedded in evolutionary processes, begs:

> Oh, redeem me from my tiger rages,
>   Reptile greed, and foul hyæna lust;
> With the hero's deeds, the thoughts of sages,
>   Sow and fructify this passive dust;
> Drop in dew and healing love of woman
>   On the bloodstained hands of hungry strife,
> Till there break from passion of the Human
>   Morning-glory of transfigured life.   (p. 109)

The sharing of labour, melding of gender roles, and evidence in the Highland men of a nurturing sensibility conventionally associated with women combine within Blind's conceptual framework to suggest that, far from being a primitive or degenerate race, the crofters are an

---

[37] This differs from Helen Groth's reading of Christian ideology as central to the poem in 'Victorian Women Poets and Scientific Narratives', in Isobel Armstrong and Virginia Blain (eds), *Women's Poetry, Late Romantic to Late Victorian: Gender and Genre, 1830–1900* (Basingstoke, 1999), p. 336.

advanced people capable of progressing beyond the slavery to base desires defined by society as masculine.

Poetry for Blind is a major means of transcending the human tendency towards competition and selfishness. *The Ascent of Man* characterises it as the highest of the representational arts, one whose creative powers exceed life itself:

> The poet, in whose shaping brain
> Life is created o'er again
> With loftier raptures, loftier pain;
>   Whose mighty potencies of verse
>   Move through the plastic Universe,
>   And fashion to their strenuous will
>   The world that is creating still.   (p. 54)

It gives tongue to 'silent generations' (p. 54) and allows nations to communicate across time, although the use of the world 'still' here suggests the fragility of the envisioned possibilities intimated elsewhere in Blind's work.

Clearly the displaced, destroyed, and otherwise silenced generations of the Skye crofters motivate *The Heather on Fire*. But this poem is also haunted by gendered anxieties about agency and voice. At the centre of the poem is the failed attempt by a woman to intervene in history. After Mary's initial attempt to inspire the sympathy of the factor fails, and he orders her cottage burnt, she is momentarily frozen and 'dumb' (III.xxxviii, p. 61), struck mute. However, she regains presence and voice, resembling a 'warrior queen': 'Cowards!' she cried once more, 'thirst ye for children's blood?' (III.xxxix, p. 61). Her words barely pause the course of events:

> Her regal presence and her flashing eyes,
> Raised as in supplication to the skies,
> Awed even these surly men, who still delayed
> To shove her back, and make a sudden raid
> Upon her cottage; – brutal as they were,
> The motherhood that yearned through her despair
> Awed them a moment – but a moment more
> They'd hustled her aside and tramped towards the door.
>   (III.xl, p. 62)

This fleeting moment of agency nevertheless leaves the building in flames, and if the grandmother is almost consumed by them, another

creature actually perishes inside the cottage. This is a half-fledged lark
rescued and nurtured by the now ailing child, after harvesters' scythes
caused the mother to abandon her nest. The bird's fiery death not only
suggests the futility of the child's intervention but also metonymically
links the trampling of larks' nests by farmer's feet – in which activity
the Highlanders are complicit – to the cruel events of the poem,
suggesting that human activity may always occur at the cost of 'lower'
organisms, of the disruption of mothering, and of the silencing of song.
In 'On a Forsaken Lark's Nest', a poem published with *The Ascent of
Man*, Blind returned to the same scenario, contemplating the 'heartful
of song that now will never awaken':

> Poor, pathetic brown eggs! Oh, pulses that never will quicken!
> Music mute in the shell that hath been turned to a tomb!
> Many a sweet human singer, chilled and adversity-stricken,
> Withers benumbed in a world his joy might have helped to illume.
> (p. 139)

The Ascent of Man itself contains a parallel image: man's soul 'finding
rest nor refuge anywhere, / Seems doomed to be her unborn offspring's
grave' (p. 50).

The only imaginative writer among Blind's extensive footnotes is
Walter Scott, cited at the moment when the despairing Michael,
realising he has no choice but to embark with his remaining children
on the ill-fated ship, decides to do so like a man. Stripped of their
population, Scott says, 'the Highlands may become the fairy-ground
for romance and poetry, or the subject of experiment for the
professors of speculation, political and economical' (p. 91). Either
eventuality, he implies, is a mockery of pseudo-engagement in the
wake of atrocity. Blind's poetic strategy in *The Heather on Fire*
initially invokes the first possibility – the tradition of nostalgic
lament for a doomed but noble and poetic[38] race – only to dispel
it in a nuanced representation of the forces that have depopulated the
Highlands. She employs an elevated poetic discourse often under-
stood to convey the universality of the human life cycle and
emotions, but interweaves with it other discourses which, with the
paratexts invoking the debates over crofting, land reform, and
national identity, serve to anchor the poem in a particular history

---

[38] Compare W. R. Lawson, 'The Poetry and Prose of the Crofter Question',
National Review 4 (1885), pp. 592–606.

and political analysis. These discourses include the political, the economic, the historical, and the scientific, but operate in the service of an innovative poetics, which, as Isobel Armstrong has argued, is still strongly invested in affect.[39]

Blind's poeticisation of the political seeks to arrive at the ineffable possibilities of the future through a careful account of the past that produced it, charging poetry with a delineation of the delicate historical processes that shape human culture through a dialogue of natural processes and social agency. It thus anticipates Patricia Yaeger's insistence that 'while history-making has its dangers, silence is more dangerous still'. Yaeger draws on Mary O'Brien's *The Politics of Reproduction* to argue that, notwithstanding problems with meta-narratives, feminism requires 'new reproductive narratives so that motherhood, birth, and the unspoken dramas of gestation and parturition will enter the real, will enter history, will be seen as important or "true"'.[40] Blind presents one such strategic narrative by invoking and interrogating the relationship between what Joan W. Scott singles out as two of the major sites of fantasy used to consolidate Western feminist identity: embodied political speech and motherhood.[41] The images of natural reproduction that Blind employs to perform this poetic work imbue apparently insignificant details of human life with the grandeur of cosmic creation, gesturing towards a new kind of historical epic. In using such images to authorise her political poetry, she builds on other writers before her. However, Blind's poetics in *The Heather on Fire* must be understood in relation to the terms in which the late Victorian struggle over land tenure in the Scottish Highlands was debated. What might appear an essentialist poetics founded on a transhistorical biological determinism can be understood as also, and at the same time, an astute literary response to the divergent applications in her time of the theory of evolution to human affairs. Far from anchoring traditional gender roles, Blind's poem attempts to articulate her 'still and mute-born vision' in an innovative poetic mode that challenges the terms in which the Victorians conceived the political: it places women's child-bearing bodies at the centre of history, but hinges the future on a common commitment to nurturing and a more equitable sharing of

[39] Armstrong, *Victorian Poetry*, p. 377.
[40] Patricia Yaeger, 'The Poetics of Birth', in Donna C. Stanton (ed.), *Discourses of Sexuality: From Aristotle to AIDS* (Ann Arbor, 1992), pp. 295, 296.
[41] Joan W. Scott, 'Fantasy Echo', *Critical Inquiry* 27: 2 (2001), pp. 284–304 (p. 293).

various forms of labour. Imbued with a sense of the latent power of women's political poetry but equally of its vulnerability in attempting to bring muted possibilities for the future into dialogue with the hostile conditions of the present, *The Heather on Fire* embodies a revisionary evolutionary poetics.

Towards a New History:
Fin-de-Siècle Women Poets
and the Sonnet

NATALIE M. HOUSTON

IN RECENT YEARS, the study and teaching of nineteenth-century women poets have been greatly facilitated: new anthologies have made texts available for general readers and for classroom use, and a wide range of historical and critical studies have begun to explore the richness of these poets' lives and works. The gradual and necessary process of recovering these works to our contemporary critical attention has resulted in expanded possibilities for teaching and writing the literary history of the Victorian period. This recovery work has been especially important for the *fin-de-siècle* period: several recent studies have demonstrated how the gendered language traditionally used to discuss *fin-de-siècle* literary practice tended to obscure the existence of female aesthetes and the ideological and historical conditions for women writers at the end of the nineteenth century.[1] Both the standard twentieth-century accounts of the male *fin-de-siècle* decadent or aesthetic poets and the focus on New Women novelists in more recent feminist criticism ignored many important women poets. To re-examine these writers not only recovers an important aspect of late-Victorian literary culture, but also reshapes the categories we use to write the literary history of the *fin-de-siècle* period.

As a feminist scholar and teacher, I have participated in the process of historical recovery of the work of women poets, and believe it to be fundamental to enhancing our historical understanding of the nineteenth century. Yet as a textual historian concerned with the material structures of literature – the production, reception, and distribution of texts during the Victorian period – I must confess to being wary of the very category with which I began this essay. To describe an alternative tradition of Victorian women poets, as useful as that can be, risks

[1] See, for example, Talia Schaffer and Kathy Alexis Psomiades (eds), *Women and British Aestheticism* (Charlottesville, 1999); Talia Schaffer, *The Forgotten Female Aesthetes: Literary Culture in Late-Victorian England* (Charlottesville, 2000); and Linda Hughes's introduction to her *New Woman Poets: An Anthology* (London, 2001).

145

obscuring the complicated material history of literature's place within Victorian culture at large. John Guillory suggests that both the defenders of a traditional male-centred canon and the proponents of a newly expanded canon for study and teaching rely on an 'ideology of tradition', which 'collapses the history of canon formation into an autonomous history of literature, which is always a history of writers and not of *writing*'.[2] The focus on individual writers or groups of writers is central to how we organise our syllabi and our scholarship; to try to imagine what a different kind of literary history might look like goes against many of our basic assumptions. Guillory suggests that a history of writing should first explore 'what genres of writing count as "literature" in a given historical context, a question that logically precedes the question of what criteria of value may affirm or deny the canonicity of particular writers'.[3] Yet our methodological tools for considering the questions of literary history and canons of taste tend invariably to rely upon lists of writers.

In this essay, I want to explore an alternative approach to writing literary history that maintains a double focus: on what kinds of writing 'count as literature' and why; and on the relation of that cultural value to the politics of gender. To do this, I examine selected poems by Mathilde Blind (1841–1896), Michael Field (Katherine Bradley [1846–1914] and Edith Cooper [1862–1913]), and Rosamund Marriott Watson (1860–1911) through the lens of genre, reframing these texts by considering the cultural meanings of the sonnet form in the later nineteenth century. The complexities of these poets' lives and works challenge bio-historical critical categories like feminist poet, aesthete, or New Woman.

Mathilde Blind, born into a politically radical German family, was a respected scholar of Shelley and Byron, and a close friend of Ford Madox Brown. Her social and literary connections with the Pre-Raphaelites as well as with Mona Caird and other Victorian feminists are reflected in her extremely varied volumes of poetry. The intense lesbian relationship and poetic collaboration of Katherine Bradley and Edith Cooper, who published under the single name of Michael Field, was marked by their interest in classical and pagan mythology, aestheticist synesthesia, and new ways of representing sexuality. Eccentric and somewhat reclusive in their later years, they knew Oscar

---

[2] John Guillory, *Cultural Capital: The Problem of Literary Canon Formation* (Chicago, 1993), p. 63.
[3] Guillory, p. 64.

Wilde, Vernon Lee, and other poets, and were especially close to Charles Shannon and Charles Ricketts, the publishers of *The Dial*. Rosamund Marriott Watson lived a very unconventional life by Victorian standards, divorcing two husbands, and taking the name of her last partner without marrying him. She published essays and poetry under three names: R. Armytage, Graham R. Tomson, and Rosamund Marriott Watson. Andrew Lang promoted her poetry and she was published in the *Yellow Book*, one of the central documents of 1890s aestheticism.

The lives and works of these poets, like many other Victorian women writers, offer divergent paths for critical interpretation. Both their aestheticism and their politics require further explication, and all too often have been seen as contradictory. Examining these writers' use of the sonnet form adds to the rich picture now developing of Victorian women's poetic practice. By beginning with the question of form, of 'what counts as literature', we can then begin to ask what the sonnet form offered women poets in particular, and investigate how genre might usefully complicate gender-based criticism.

The Victorian Sonnet

Recent accounts of the nineteenth-century sonnet have focused on its revival in the late eighteenth century and its importance in understanding Romantic period poetic theory and practice.[4] The sonnet was adopted by popular women poets like Charlotte Smith, Anna Seward, and Felicia Hemans before being taken up by Coleridge and Wordsworth as a vehicle for descriptive poetry. Although Wordsworth omitted Smith from his account of how he began to write sonnets, claiming direct inspiration from Milton, gift books and anthologies of sonnets published before 1840 demonstrate the popularity of sonnets by both female and male poets of the Romantic period.[5] Restoring women

[4] See, for example, James Chandler, 'The Pope Controversy: Romantic Poetics and the English Canon', in Robert von Hallberg (ed.), *Canons* (Chicago, 1984), pp. 197–226; Stuart Curran, *Poetic Form and British Romanticism* (Oxford, 1986); Jennifer Wagner, *A Moment's Monument: Revisionary Poetics and the Nineteenth-Century English Sonnet* (Cranbury, 1996); and Susan Wolfson, *Formal Charges: The Shaping of Poetry in British Romanticism* (Stanford, 1997).
[5] See, for example, [George Henderson (ed.)] *Petrarca: a Selection of Sonnets from Various Authors with an Introductory Dissertation on the Origin and Structure*

poets like Smith and Hemans to our historical account of the Romantic period has fruitfully complicated older paradigms of Romanticism and has ensured the sonnet's place in studies of nineteenth-century literature. Yet the position of the sonnet within Victorian poetics has remained largely unexplored. Traditionally, the sonnet has not been thought of as an important Victorian poetic form, in part because many twentieth-century accounts of Victorian poetry focused on the dramatic monologue as the most artistically and politically significant Victorian form.[6]

But the material history of Victorian literature reveals that the sonnet was widely used throughout the Victorian period: at least 17 anthologies devoted exclusively to the sonnet were published in Britain, and many more devoted special sections to publishing favourite sonnets; newspapers and general periodicals frequently published sonnets on current events; and hundreds of poets included sonnets among their published works. Although sonnet sequences like Elizabeth Barrett Browning's *Sonnets from the Portuguese* (1850), George Meredith's *Modern Love* (1862) and Dante Gabriel Rossetti's *The House of Life* (1870/1881) are perhaps the best-known Victorian sonnets today, these amatory sequences were not representative of most Victorian sonnet writing. Most Victorian sonnets were not published in sequences, and, rather than expressing romantic attachments, they tended to focus on descriptions of landscape and especially scenes of travel; portraits of famous people, friends, and family; moral or political reflections on specific events or issues; and moments from everyday life.[7]

To discover what made the sonnet 'count as literature' for its Victorian readers, or to assess its cultural meaning and value, we can turn to the extensive field of sonnet criticism published between 1840 and 1900. In addition to the critical introductions included in many of the sonnet anthologies, a large number of reviews and critical essays in

of the Sonnet (London, 1803) and Capel Lofft (ed.), *Laura: or an Anthology of Sonnets, (On the Petrarchan Model,) and Elegiac Quatuorzains: English, Italian, Spanish, Portuguese, French, and German*, 5 vols (London, 1814).

[6] The classic text is Robert Langbaum, *The Poetry of Experience: The Dramatic Monologue in Modern Literary Tradition* (New York, 1957); for a more recent account see Isobel Armstrong, *Victorian Poetry: Poetry, Poetics, and Politics* (New York, 1993).

[7] George Sanderlin, 'The Influence of Milton and Wordsworth on the Early Victorian Sonnet', *ELH* 5 (1938), pp. 225–51; William T. Going, *Scanty Plot of Ground: Studies in the Victorian Sonnet* (The Hague, 1976).

general periodicals like the *Athenaeum*, *Contemporary Review*, *Eclectic Review* and *Quarterly Review* debated rules for the sonnet's form and promulgated basic facts of its long history. Critics and defenders of the sonnet argued about its fitness for the English language, its place in a national literary tradition, and the challenges its restricted form posed for poets and readers alike.[8] For many Victorian poets and critics, the sonnet was an historically self-conscious form of poetry, because the sonnet form itself explicitly registers its long history, creating opportunities for poetic revision and critical debate.

Because the sonnet's two dominant rhyme structures (the Petrarchan, or Italian form *abba-abba-cde-cde* and the Shakespearean, or English form *abab-cdcd-efef-gg*) mark its history as one of national transmission and translation, Victorian critics were concerned about defending its place in a British literary tradition: 'it would be as reasonable to complain that English watches were not genuine, because the first watch was invented by a German, as that the sonnet does not form a genuine portion of English verse, because the first sonnets were written by Italians'.[9] Early in the nineteenth century, most critics attacked the sound and structure of the Shakespearean form as overly harsh, but as the position of Shakespeare as England's national bard became solidified in Victorian criticism, new evaluations of his sonnets led to a greater openness about sonnet form.[10] Although later critics still tended to prefer the Petrarchan form of the sonnet, many poets wrote sonnets in hybrid forms that combined elements of each, such as a Petrarchan octave pattern joined to a Shakespearean sestet. Victorian critics endlessly debated the proper application of the sonnet's rules and their artistic consequences: 'Where the rules which govern the structure of the Sonnet are strictly observed, the subject will be set forth in the first quatrain, illustrated in the second: confirmed by the first tercet, and concluded in the second.'[11] Such critical accounts meant that most Victorian readers of poetry had at least a working

[8] Natalie M. Houston, 'Valuable by Design: Material Features and Cultural Value in Nineteenth-Century Sonnet Anthologies', *Victorian Poetry* 37: 2 (1999), pp. 243–50.
[9] [John Dennis], 'The English Sonnet', *The Cornhill Magazine* 25 (May 1872), pp. 581–2.
[10] See Margreta de Grazia, *Shakespeare Verbatim: the Reproduction of Authenticity and the 1790 Apparatus* (Oxford, 1991) and Peter Stallybrass, 'Editing as Cultural Formation: The Sexing of Shakespeare's Sonnets', in Marshall Brown (ed.), *The Uses of Literary History* (Durham, 1995), pp. 129–41.
[11] Review of *A Collection of English Sonnets*, by R. F. Housman, *Eclectic Review* ser. 4, vol. 1 (1837), p. 594.

knowledge of the form's history and structure. Adherence to the
sonnet's rules was seen by some critics as overly fussy and by others
as fundamental: 'the fitness and unfitness of certain forms and measures
to certain themes and moods have been universally recognised . . . The
rational explanation of the pleasure derived from obedience, and the
repulsion aroused by disobedience to any Art-canon, is probably not far
to seek.'[12] Such claims that the sonnet form was more rational, more
healthy, or more musical than other forms of poetry were common in
the critical discourse of the period, which constructed the sonnet's
value in explicit cultural terms.

The small size of the sonnet was seen to increase its value: 'It is a
special advantage of this form of composition, that it necessitates the
precision of language and the concentration of thought, which are of
priceless value in poetry. In the sonnet every word should have a
meaning – every line add to the beauty of the whole; and the exquisite
delicacy of the workmanship should not lessen, but should rather assist
in increasing the stability of the structure.'[13] Sonnets were frequently
described with metaphors of gems or gold, suggesting the concentrated
worth of each word in the poem. The sonnet's small size made it a
compact, portable source of cultural capital, concentrating the value of
literature into an easily memorised poem:

> We do not intend to select even one sonnet for quotation out of the
> hundred and fifty-four which Shakespeare has left us. The choicest
> of them are, or ought to be, familiar; but if any young reader is still
> unacquainted with this golden treasury of thought and imagination,
> we counsel him to obtain a pocket edition of the poems, and carry it
> about with him until he gain a familiarity with its contents.[14]

For some critics, the sonnet was the repository of valuable thought;
others recognised the value of its economical size for busy modern
readers:

> The stirring of the poetic impulse is very markedly at work among us
> at present, and there is no more remarkable sign of the times than
> the steadily growing public appreciation of the sonnet as a poetic
> vehicle. For one thing, its conciseness is an immense boon in these

---

[12] Henry G. Hewlett, 'English Sonneteers: Mr. Charles Turner', *Contemporary Review* 22 (September 1873), p. 633.

[13] Dennis, p. 582.

[14] Dennis, p. 588.

days when books multiply like gossamer-flies in a sultry June; it is
realised that if good a sonnet can speedily be read and enjoyed, that
if exceptionally fine it can with ease be committed to memory, and
that if bad it can be recognised as such at a glance, and can be
relegated to oblivion by the turning of a single page.[15]

The work of interpreting the sonnet's condensed expression was seen as
a valuable means of disciplining readers' taste and habits: 'The
sympathetic reading of a good sonnet is an exercise of poetic faculty
hardly different in order, although inferior in degree, from that
involved in its production.'[16] Critics prescribed slow, reflective, reading
and re-reading as the best approach to understanding the sonnet, and
suggested that it could improve the reader's intellect.

Although the difficult work required to write a good sonnet was
generally hailed as a mark of the form's literary and cultural value, the
existence of rules for the form suggested that anyone could learn to
write sonnets. Although some critics, like Arthur Hugh Clough and
Leigh Hunt, celebrated the sonnet as a kind of democratic vehicle for
poetic expression, other critics were more anxious about this: 'Its
extreme artificiality is at once a test and a temptation, – a test, since
it is only a true poet who can make artificiality serve the purposes of
art; and a temptation, since the artificial construction – the mere form
– can be easily built up and filled out with words by the simplest
handicraftsman in verse.'[17] Some of the critical claims about the
sonnet's value thus operate as a kind of defence against the idea that
the sonnet was an artificial or apprentice form.

Victorian critics generally emphasised the reflective or descriptive
uses for the sonnet form: 'our English sonnet has been generally the
growth of quiet thought and of an imagination fostered under the eye of
nature'.[18] These critics took pains to distinguish the nineteenth-cen-
tury uses for the sonnet from the Renaissance sonnet sequences written
by Shakespeare, Sidney, and others, disavowing the adulterous passions
expressed in those works as inappropriate for poetry. The history of the
sonnet's disappearance in the eighteenth century and revival in the
nineteenth was often framed in moral and cultural terms, whereby

[15] William Sharp (ed.), *Sonnets of This Century* (London, 1886), p. xxvi.
[16] [C. W. Russell], 'Critical History of the Sonnet', Part One, *Dublin Review* n.s.
27 (1876), p. 403.
[17] [C. E. Norton], 'The Book of the Sonnet', *North American Review* 104 (April
1867), p. 628.
[18] Dennis, p. 590.

descriptive or philosophical sonnets were seen as the result of a more refined cultural landscape. The formal grounds for championing the Petrarchan form of the sonnet, for example, were separated from the cultural context of Petrarch's love poems. Following the publication of Elizabeth Barrett Browning's *Sonnets from the Portuguese* in 1850, some poets experimented with reworking the amatory form of the sonnet to represent modern sentiments, but in general amatory topics were relatively rare in Victorian sonnet work.

Throughout the nineteenth century, women poets who wrote sonnets were included in the sonnet anthologies and discussed in the criticism. The sonnets of Elizabeth Barrett Browning were especially praised, and Charlotte Smith, Anna Seward, Felicia Hemans, Christina Rossetti, Eliza Cook, Adelaide Procter, Dora Greenwell, Augusta Webster, Alice Thompson, Emily Pfeiffer and many others were frequently mentioned in accounts of important sonnet writers.[19] Because the discourse around the sonnet was largely concerned with formal and aesthetic issues, and because Victorian critics emphasised the descriptive uses for the form, Victorian sonnet criticism rarely takes up gender explicitly or even metaphorically. Throughout the century, it was acknowledged that women poets wrote sonnets, but the form itself did not have especially gendered connotations.

Aestheticism and the Sonnet Form

A large part of the appeal of the sonnet form in the Victorian period was the understanding that it could offer for consideration defined, individual moments of sensory or psychological perception for later reflection. In 1873, William Davies concisely summed up the prevailing critical views:

> A word may be said as to the uses and advantages of the sonnet. It is capital for embalming the moods of a moment – those sentiments and feelings which contain a sort of completeness in themselves. It forms an admirable setting for a beautiful prospect, a noble act, a splendid character, whereby they may be contemplated

---

[19] See, for example, Alexander Japp, 'The English Sonnet and its History', *Gentleman's Magazine* 275 (1893), p. 276; James Ashcroft Noble, 'The Sonnet in England', in *The Sonnet in England & Other Essays* (London, 1893), pp. 55–7; and [C. W. Russell], 'Critical History of the Sonnet', Part Two, *Dublin Review* n.s. 28 (1877), p. 150.

again in miniature, as it were, when their outward form is no longer with us.[20]

The sonnet was seen as a kind of documentary form able to record perceptions or emotions for later review. The importance of each word in a sonnet gave weight to each detail, and the poem's small size focused the reader's attention on things that might be overlooked in a longer descriptive poem.

Because the sonnet was established in Victorian criticism as a useful poetic vehicle for capturing descriptive details about scenes, events, or sensory perceptions, it was well suited to the aestheticist project elaborated by Walter Pater and by two generations of poets marked by his influence. In the conclusion to *The Renaissance*, Pater articulated what was a widespread Victorian recognition, that human consciousness creates coherence from infinitesimal individuated sense-perceptions:

> That clear, perpetual outline of face and limb is but an image of ours . . . a design in a web, the actual threads of which pass out beyond it. This at least of flamelike our life has, that it is but the concurrence, renewed from moment to moment, of forces parting sooner or later on their ways . . . a drift of momentary acts of sight and passion and thought.[21]

The representational qualities assigned to the sonnet form itself made it an obvious choice for many poets interested in exploring detailed impressions of colour or sound, or recording moments of experience. In Pater's account, our experience is made up of an infinite series of subjective, transitory perceptions:

> those impressions of the individual mind to which, for each one of us, experience dwindles down, are in perpetual flight . . . each of them is limited by time, and . . . as time is infinitely divisible, each of them is infinitely divisible also; all that is actual in it being a single moment, gone while we try to apprehend it . . . to a

---

[20] [William Davies], 'The Sonnet', *Quarterly Review* 134 (January 1873), p. 204.
[21] Walter Pater, *The Renaissance: Studies in Art and Poetry* (London, 1935), p. 218. The concluding essay was written in 1868 but not published until the 1873 *Studies in the History of the Renaissance*, which was later retitled. Concerned that 'it might possibly mislead some . . . young men', Pater removed the Conclusion from the second edition (1877) but restored it to the third (1888) with slight changes.

single sharp impression, with a sense in it, a relic more or less
fleeting, of such moments gone by, what is real in our life fines
itself down.[22]

For Pater, the goal is to heighten one's ability to perceive those
multiple, individual moments at the finest level of perception possible:
'A counted number of pulses only is given to us of a variegated,
dramatic life. How may we see in them all that is to be seen in them by
the finest senses?'[23] Dante Gabriel Rossetti's famous prefatory sonnet to
The House of Life proclaimed that 'A sonnet is a moment's monument',
and many other poets, including Ernest Dowson, Alfred Douglas, and
Arthur Symons, were also drawn to the sonnet form as a means for
exploring such moments of perception.

The desire to fix or describe precise moments of experience reflected
much larger cultural models of chaos and flux in the later Victorian
period. As Gillian Beer notes, Victorian science began to account for
various invisible forces at work in the physical world: 'Wave theory,
acoustics, radiation, all seemed to indicate that our senses are con-
tracted and that we are battered by continuous events beyond their
registration.'[24] Such new scientific ideas percolated throughout the
culture more generally, in part because the metaphorical language of
flux and waves was already familiar. Late-Victorian aesthetic theory
shared this language with writings in many other fields. Theodore
Watts-Dunton, who was associated with the pre-Raphaelite circle,
proposed a new model of the sonnet form in his poem 'The Sonnet's
Voice: A Metrical Lesson by the Sea-Shore', which was first published
in the *Athenaeum* in 1881, and explicated in several articles.[25] Watts-
Dunton suggested that the rhyme scheme *abba abba cddc cd*, a
Petrarchan variant which was popular with Victorian poets, was
modelled on the ebb and flow of a wave, because the sestet's *cddc*
rhyme in lines 9–12 echo the structure of the octave. Watts-Dunton
and other critics who took up his theory claimed that the sonnet 'wave'
was a more natural form, and that it constituted a distinctive British
contribution to sonnet literature. This Victorian form was thought to

---

[22] Pater, pp. 219–20.
[23] Pater, p. 220.
[24] Gillian Beer, *Open Fields: Science in Cultural Encounter* (Oxford, 1996),
p. 296.
[25] Several of these articles were reprinted in Theodore Watts-Dunton, *Poetry
and the Renascence of Wonder* (London, 1916).

soften the traditional division of syntax and subject between the sonnet's octave and sestet:

> The Italian form demands two parts to the sonnet-thought, but they are as the two parts of an acorn; the later English form requires also two sides to the sonnet-thought, but they are as the two movements of the wave. In the one, the parts are separate and contrasted, yet united; in the other, they are blended, the same in substance, distinct only in movement.[26]

Thus the same interest in flux and force that animates Pater's examination of sense perception runs throughout late nineteenth-century sonnet theory and practice. Although a full account of the aesthetic sonnet in the later nineteenth century is not possible here, three uses of the sonnet form were particularly important for late Victorian aestheticism: the capture of a moment, or 'embalming' that Davies mentions; the ability to record fine details within the sonnet's closely limited structure; and its openness to a symbolic or allegorical register.

Women Writers and the Sonnet

Fin-de-siècle poets frequently used the sonnet as a vehicle for exploring the kind of analysis of sense perceptions that Pater suggests. Rosamund Marriott Watson's 'An Autumn Morning' (1889), for example, opens with a series of impressions:

> A sunny autumn morning, calm and stilled,
>   Smiles on the bare, burnt meadows; down the lane
>   The hedge-fruits ripen, fresh with last night's rain,
> Among broad leaves the sun begins to gild;
> The crisp low-breathing air no frost has chilled,
>   Sweet with pine-fragrance, stings the sense again,
>   With joy so keen it meets the lips of pain
> With dim desires and fancies unfulfilled.
>
> Ah, swift and sudden as a swallow's flight
>   These flitting golden glimpses come and go;
>   The Unseen clasps us through the veil, and, lo!

---

[26] Hall Caine, *Sonnets of Three Centuries: a Selection Including Many Examples Hitherto Unpublished* (London, 1882), p. xxiii.

Our blood stirs strangely with a deep delight –
Old dreams, vague visions, glimmer on our sight,
   All we have known, and all we may not know.[27]

The sonnet draws a connection between sensory experience and
human desire, suggesting that pleasure and insight are merely fragment-
ary glimpses of the full range of experience. It is sensory perception
itself, as much as the dreams and visions of the sonnet's final lines, that
is incomplete, even when recorded in as much detail as the octave
presents. The muted analysis in the sestet created by Watson's use of
Watts-Dunton's 'wave' rhyme scheme turns on the sonnet itself,
potentially describing the act of revisiting such impressions through
poetry, as well as the initial experience.

   Mathilde Blind's 'Haunted Streets' (1893) also uses the 'wave' form
to record a common sensory experience, the illusion of seeing a familiar
face among a crowd:

Lo, haply walking in some clattering street –
Where throngs of men and women dumbly pass,
Like shifting pictures seen within a glass
Which leave no trace behind – one seems to meet,
In roads once trodden by our mutual feet,
A face projected from that shadowy mass
Of faces, quite familiar as it was,
Which beaming on us stands out clear and sweet.

The face of faces we again behold
That lit our life when life was very fair,
And leaps our heart towards eyes and mouth and hair:
Oblivious of the undying love grown cold,
Or body sheeted in the churchyard mould,
We stretch out yearning hands and grasp – the air.[28]

A momentary sense perception, however illusory, like those created by
the kaleidoscope in lines 3–4, creates emotions and brings up fragments
of memory. The feelings described here are resolutely non-narrative,
limited not only by the sonnet's structure, but by the experience itself.

[27] Texts for Watson's poems come from her volume published under the pen
name Graham R. Tomson, *The Bird-Bride: A Volume of Ballads and Sonnets*
(London, 1889). All verse quotations reproduce the conventions of indenta-
tion and line spacing of the original source.
[28] Texts for Blind's poems come from Mathilde Blind, *Songs and Sonnets*
(London, 1893).

The sonnet offered late-Victorian poets a strategy for representing and analysing such fragments of experience. The 'undying love grown cold' in line 12 encapsulates the problematic of temporal change and the sonnet recognises that our emotions (here figuratively located in the heart) long for continuity or stasis. In Blind's exploration of the links between feeling and perception, human emotions, too, become perceptions to be recorded: the projection of a seemingly-familiar face, the leap of the heart, the desiring hands. Despite the disappointment of the fade to air at the sonnet's close, the poem refuses to judge, instead only recording a moment of perception. The sonnet form allows Blind the flexibility to eschew gendered pronouns altogether and to present this experience as a general human one.

Michael Field's 'Ebbtide at Sundown' (1908) suggests that there is beauty to be found within the moment of loss:

> How larger is remembrance than desire!
> How deeper than all longing is regret!
> The tide is gone, the sands are rippled yet;
> The sun is gone; the hills are lifted higher,
> Crested with rose. Ah, why should we require
> Sight of the sea, the sun? The sands are wet,
> And in their glassy flaws huge record set
> Of the ebbed stream, the little ball of fire.
> Gone, they are gone! But, oh, so freshly gone,
> So rich in vanishing we ask not where –
> So close upon us is the bliss that shone,
> And, oh, so thickly it impregns the air!
> Closer in beating heart we could not be
> To the sunk sun, the far, surrendered sea.[29]

Loss and change are fundamental aspects of the natural world, and this sonnet claims a kind of wisdom and beauty in representing or recording a particular moment of transition, as do the individual grains of sand in line seven. The poem's final lines suggest that the emotions brought up by observing the tide are integral to that experience, rather than the distinct responses of a particular observing mind.

Understanding the significance of the sonnet for Victorian readers as a means for recording sense perceptions and experience helps contextualise these poems. In content and style, each of the three descriptive sonnets I've discussed here resemble those written by male

[29] Text from Michael Field, *Wild Honey from Various Thyme* (London, 1908).

poets of the same period, and their deliberate distance from any kind of personal statement or opinion seems at first to resist political analysis. But it is, I think, precisely because the sonnet form was relatively free of gendered associations, that women poets took it up for these kinds of investigations of temporality and sense perception. Recognising the form of these poems as having distinct meaning beyond the work of any particular poet helps us to see the ways in which female aesthetes participated in larger literary conventions and discourses.

Because the sonnet form was praised for its ability to present visual details, Victorian poets often used sonnets to comment on works of art, and the poems and paintings of Dante Gabriel Rossetti were of course influential in this regard. Michael Field's 1892 volume of poems, *Sight and Song*, consists entirely of poems about paintings in various museums that Bradley and Cooper visited. Two are in sonnet form, including this description of a painting of the martyred Saint Katharine of Alexandria by Bartolommeo Veneto:

> A little wreath of bay about her head,
> The Virgin-Martyr stands, touching her wheel
> With finger-tips that from the spikes of steel
> Shrink, though a thousand years she has been dead.
> She bleeds each day as on the day she bled;
> Her pure, gold cheeks are blanched, a cloudy seal
> Is on her eyes; the mouth will never feel
> Pity again; the yellow hairs are spread
> Downward as damp with sweat; they touch the rim
> Of the green bodice that to blackness throws
> The thicket of bay-branches sharp and trim
> Above her shoulder: open landscape glows
> Soft and apart behind her to the right,
> Where a swift shallop crosses the moonlight.[30]

The sonnet's hybrid form, strong enjambment, and the non-indented design of the sonnet on the printed page eschew the rhythm of question and answer, or situation and analysis, that was common in the Italian sonnet form and its contemporary variant described by Watts-Dunton. Instead of offering interpretation, this sonnet presents itself as an enclosed work of art like the painting. In choosing the present tense to catalogue the visual elements of the artwork, the sonnet echoes the

---

[30] Text from Michael Field, *Sight and Song* (London, 1892).

painting's freezing of a key narrative moment: the Virgin-Martyr perpetually stands, her fingers shrink, and the shallop crosses. Lines four and five highlight the static temporality of both painting and sonnet, by disrupting the present tense with a reminder of the historical referent behind these works of art. The sonnet, like the painting, is a work created of blocks of deliberate colour, as the liminal edge of green in line ten reveals. The power of this sonnet's close focus on descriptive detail concentrates in lines eight and nine, in 'the yellow hairs are spread / Downward . . . they touch the rim' – that surprising plural individuates the strands of hair, sharpening the focus of the poem. No longer simply a moment from an historical and religious narrative, nor even the sympathetic account of her eyes and mouth prevented from feeling further, this poem presents the shock of the particular detail within the compelling narrative. The condensation of the sonnet form so important to Victorian critics allows for the presentation of such details without much interpretation: the reader is required to work to figure out the meanings of the sonnet, just as a viewer of the painting must interpret the significance of the colour scheme, the setting, and the symbology of the shallop.

Rosamund Marriott Watson's 'Boucher' (1889) offers another exploration of the timelessness of both visual and poetic portraiture:

'Lead me this evening to my painter's chair'
  (Dying, he said); 'lay here upon my knee
  The palette – now the pencils give to me,
And set my Venus on the easel there,
So that the sunlight gleams upon her hair
  And her white body, risen from the sea:
  Leave us – alone awhile we twain would be;
I who must die, and she for ever fair.'

Above the flocking Loves, the sea's blue rim,
  A shadow followed as the sun-rays fled;
  Grey, up the ivory breast, the golden head,
It stole; but, steadfast through the twilight dim,
  Still on his idol gazed the sightless dead,
And still the rose-crowned goddess smiled on him.

This sonnet subtly interrogates various male fantasies: the stylised women painted by Boucher; the symbolic representation of Venus as a naked woman arising from the sea; and the perfect communion between artist and his created work. The sonnet's sestet questions these idealisations (carefully set apart from the text of the poem with quotation marks) by offering the vivid picture of death as shadow in line 11. The moment captured in this sonnet, emphasised by 'still' in lines 13 and 14, is simultaneously comforting in its eternity, and ironic, as the human actions of gazing and smiling are not real. Watson's choice of the sonnet form to present this scene enhances the poem's critical impetus, since the sonnet was often discussed as a kind of verbal portrait or miniature.

In 'Beauty' (1893), Mathilde Blind also takes up the trope of deathless art, adopting the metaphor of paint to describe an emotional effect:

> Even as on some black background full of night
>   And hollow storm in cloudy disarray,
>   The forceful brush of some great master may
> More brilliantly evoke a higher light;
> So beautiful, so delicately white,
>   So like a very metaphor of May,
>   Your loveliness on my life's sombre grey
> In its perfection stands out doubly bright.
>
> And yet your beauty breeds a strange despair,
>   And pang of yearning in the helpless heart;
> To shield you from time's fraying wear and tear,
>   That from yourself yourself would wrench apart,
> How save you, fairest, but to set you where
>   Mortality kills death in deathless art?

The sonnet's Italian form presents a problem and solution in the relation between octave and sestet. Beauty becomes not only a thing to be admired, but a problem to be solved, in that it creates the desire to stave off change. The solution proposed here, of course, is 'deathless art', which creates a space preserved from time's decay. Blind uses the sonnet form to easily reference in shorthand the trope of deathless love and the immortality conveyed by framing one's emotions in verse, which was well established in the sonnet tradition by Shakespeare. In this sonnet, Blind thus asserts her right as a woman poet to frame beauty in deathless art, just as the amatory sonneteers of past centuries did. Significantly, however, this is a single sonnet, not part of a traditional amatory sequence, and the poem's speaker and object are unspecified, even as to their gender. The reference to metaphor in line six reveals the poem as a self-conscious collection of conventions about beauty, art, and the sonnet form itself, which place any possible interpretation in question.

In the prefatory essay to his sonnet anthology, William Sharp compared the sonnet to a technology of vision: 'those who have studied it love it as the naturalist loves his microscope – and veritably, like the microscope, it discloses many beautiful things which, if embedded in some greater mass, might have been faintly visible and incoherent' (p. xxviii). Michael Field's irregular sonnet 'White Madness' (1908) operates with this kind of precision, seeking out the beautiful, interesting anomaly in nature:

> White flowers as robes for Solomon fine spun
> There are; and others that grow white themselves,
> Distraught, made very bashful by the sun,
> Turned to particular as gnomes and elves.
> Thus a gold daffodil grows white and dumb,
> Trembling a little; even for this cause
> 'Mid lusty forest hyacinths a' hum,
> One silver cluster into light withdraws;
> Untangled from their massy group one sees
> Thus from dark bell-heads clear fritillaries:
> And there beside are violets, so shy
> They would not bear the name we love them by,
> That in white madness, witless and undone,
> Creep through unhaunted hedgerows to the sun.[31]

This poem uncovers analysis within the language of description as the sonnet catalogues different whitened flowers. The emphasis on the emptying of colour, the flowers made white, silver, light, and clear, makes the list an arrangement of similarities within the different species. The sonnet finds beauty in nature's contrasts, in a sequence that seems arranged by colour rather than by anything scientific or geographical. Like other aesthetic sonnets, 'White Madness' submerges opinion or interpretation in its focus on the interplay of colour and colourlessness. The draining of each flower's colour is equated with a bashfulness congruent with the traditional meaning of white violets, which were usually linked with modesty or innocence. The poem's focus on these particular examples offers a picture of traditionally feminine virtues (shyness, modesty) as alienation, difference, and eventual madness beneath the powerful sun. Each of these sonnets

---

[31] From Field, *Wild Honey from Various Thyme*.

that focus on particular visual details satisfies aesthetic conventions and presents a highly finished surface that intentionally conceals its ideological import.

Following the publication of Dante Gabriel Rossetti's *House of Life* (1870/1881), many poets wrote sonnets with figurative personifications or allegorical terms for philosophical or emotional concepts, moving the sonnet away from recording realistic perceptions and towards purely imaginative or conceptual landscapes. The sonnet's small size and association with the visual arts encouraged such symbolic representations. Rosamund Marriott Watson's 'An Unbidden Guest' is in many respects typical of this strand in aesthetic uses for the sonnet form:

> I said, my dwelling-place is passing fair,
>   My dusk, dim chamber where the daylight dies:
>   No sun doth blind, no tears may vex mine eyes;
> Cast out alike are Glory and Despair.
> My soul is banishèd – I wot not where.
>   I thrust him forth, unheedful of his cries,
>   Long years ago: full vain is thine emprise,
> O shrouded Stranger from the outer air!
>
> He smiles, a bitter merriment is his!
>   His footsteps falter not, but still draw nigh;
>   He holds a crystal cresset-flame on high.
> 'So, friend, at last we meet again – is *this*
>   The home forbidden me in years gone by?
> Behold, how desolate and bare it is!'

Watson explores the tension between contentment and passion using familiar aesthetic tropes of the soul's habitation that draw on Tennyson as well as Rossetti. The sonnet stages emotional emptiness as a false retreat, as the personification of the soul returns to menace the speaker. The language and images are very derivative, and the poem is not one of Watson's most interesting texts – and yet its very status as a kind of pastiche of Pre-Raphaelite language suggests that the sonnet form offered women poets access to a variety of poetic discourses.

If the sonnet encouraged some poets to adopt symbolic personification, its small framework also provided for the deconstruction of poetic symbols, as in Blind's 'A Symbol' (1893):

Hurrying for ever in their restless flight
  The generations of earth's teeming womb
  Rise into being and lapse into the tomb
Like transient bubbles sparkling in the light;
They sink in quick succession out of sight
  Into the thick insuperable gloom
  Our futile lives in flashing by illume –
Lightning which mocks the darkness of the night.

Nay – but consider, though we change and die,
  If men must pass shall Man not still remain?
  As the unnumbered drops of summer rain
Whose changing particles unchanged on high,
  Fixed, in perpetual motion, yet maintain
The mystic bow emblazoned on the sky.

Blind uses the Italian sonnet form to present a philosophical question and pose a solution that draws on Victorian science to provide a secular answer to the mystery of human existence. Although the rainbow can be analysed into its constitutive particles to show that perpetual motion creates the appearance or illusion of stasis, the 'mystic' or symbolic meaning of the rainbow persists, and the sonnet suggests some equivalent larger meaning behind the sum of individual human lives.

It is the submerged quality of the gender issues in most of the sonnets I've instanced here that brings me back to my original theoretical questions. Understanding Victorian critical beliefs about the sonnet form helps to contextualise these poems as cohering with other literary and critical practices – or, in Guillory's words, these were definitely poems that 'counted as literature'. The sonnet form offered women poets, as it did male poets, a vehicle for shaping selected observations, whether philosophical or descriptive. The sonnet suited dominant aesthetic interests in the later part of the century, in offering close focus on particular sensory details and a literal framing of art images. The artful construction of the sonnet's form meant that its structure, too, cohered with the aesthetic principles held by many poets.

So, if understanding the values Victorian poets and readers associated with the sonnet form helps explain the interest these poets might have had in it, what might this begin to tell us about women poets specifically? A precise answer would require further investigation into the production and reception histories of sonnets by women poets. The formal and aesthetic qualities outlined above mean that the texts themselves have little obvious political content or even any gendered pronouns. They resist political interpretation and demand that we expand our methodologies for thinking about Victorian women poets and their relationship to aestheticism, and to literary form more generally. Recognising how these and other women poets were drawing on the literary resources of their culture to shape their art in ways that frequently side-stepped many Victorian assumptions about gender and literary production might help us to imagine how we might begin to revise some of our own critical assumptions. By the end of the nineteenth century, the sonnet form was widely used by male and female aesthetic poets to describe similar themes and enact similar aesthetic principles. Victorian sonnet theory, unlike that of the novel, made very few distinctions based on gender. That apparent absence of distinction might well prove an important starting point for new historical explorations of the intersections of genre and gender.

Reassessing Margaret Veley's Poetry: The Value of Harper's Transatlantic Spirit

JOSEPH BRISTOW

I

IN THE OPENING PAGES of the major 1990s anthologies that drew attention to many long-forgotten nineteenth-century women poets, readers encountered various editorial justifications for the reprinting of a divergent body of materials that previously remained subject to scholarly neglect. 'Over the last two decades', Isobel Armstrong and I observed in 1996, 'researchers have gradually begun to rediscover the work of women poets of the nineteenth and earlier centuries.'[1] 'This process of rediscovery', we commented, 'has been one of the most intellectually exciting developments within the field of literary history' (p. xxiii). Even though it would be hard to contest either of these statements, the aesthetic or cultural value of these rediscovered works has not always stood at the centre of critical debate. To be sure, in *Victorian Women Poets: An Anthology* (1995) Angela Leighton declared that 'it is the sheer variety of this poetry, in verse form as well as subject matter, which makes it worthy of recovery and reassessment'.[2] As a consequence, Leighton believed that such recovery and reassessment would occasion an equally broad extent of critical reactions because the very 'range and energy of Victorian women's poetry make it still, today, worth being read, wept over, laughed at and enjoyed' (p. xl).[3] But while the diversity of what Leighton characterised as a 'forgotten tradition of verse' has doubtless prompted a broad repertoire of readers' responses, modern critics still prove somewhat reluctant to elaborate the terms on which they might

---

[1] Isobel Armstrong and Joseph Bristow, 'Introduction', in Armstrong and Bristow with Cath Sharrock (eds), *Nineteenth-Century Women Poets: An Oxford Anthology* (Oxford, 1996), p. xxiii.
[2] Angela Leighton, 'Introduction II', in Leighton and Margaret Reynolds (eds), *Victorian Women Poets: An Anthology* (Oxford, 1995), p. xl.
[3] I am not sure whether in her use of 'laughed at' Leighton really means there might be some worth in readers responding in tones of derisive mockery towards the work of women poets who have been recently recovered and reassessed.

evaluate poetry that is, given its indisputable range, a necessarily uneven canon of writing.

Instead, an enthusiastic acquisitiveness that has amassed numerous ballads, lyrics, and narrative poems continues to drive much of the eager rediscovery of nineteenth-century women writers of poetry. Such recovery and reassessment certainly results in a welcome re-mapping of Victorian literary history. To begin with, the work of reclamation undertaken by anthologists makes it abundantly clear that from 1800 to 1900 women made an immense contribution to the publication of poems in a wide variety of print media, including album books, literary journals, newspapers and political pamphlets. Yet the editorial principles that guide the selection of some poems and not others in this type of research has inevitably provoked a number of vexed questions and generated several methodological dilemmas. Should anthologies that aim to rediscover neglected women poets gather together works that are identifiably distinguished? If that is the case, then which critical assumptions might inform any claims on the distinction of a work? Or should inclusions have representative status, in so far as they are supposed to embody a particular kind of poetry that is prominent in the period? Moreover, should the type of poetry represent a specific author's use of it or a larger generic formation? The answers to these queries unavoidably rely on editorial predilections.

In her thoughtful assessment of the 1990s anthologies, Linda M. Shires contends that the selection that Leighton made with Margaret Reynolds helpfully complicates the 'received history of the Poetess' by concentrating attention on an expansive tradition that can be traced from Felicia Hemans to Christina Rossetti and beyond.[4] At the same time, however, Shires observes that the editors' emphasis on the history of the poetess excludes working-class and colonial writers throughout *Victorian Women Poets* – 'an omission that gives a flavour of elitism to the selection' (p. 603). Meanwhile, Shires acknowledges that the samples of poetry that Armstrong and I took from some one hundred and one nineteenth-century women authors was carried out in a spirit that would permit 'readers to form their own judgements' about the value of the material (p. 604). In many respects, we withheld from discussing the cultural worth of what were by and large writings that belonged to mostly uncharted territory whose most significant features were still not entirely in critical view. It would of course be

---

[4] Linda M. Shires, 'Victorian Woman's Poetry', *Victorian Literature and Culture*, 27 (1999), pp. 601–9 (p. 602).

unfair to suggest that editorial deliberations over the making of anthologies remain limited to which of these differing models of selection could or should be preferable. But the point is that the modern restitution of innumerable women poets whose reputations faded quickly from cultural memory after their deaths accentuates the urgency of justifying why we might lend value to their writings beyond the plain fact that they happen, in all their diversity, to exist.

The present discussion confronts the lasting problem of how we might estimate the worth of rediscovered nineteenth-century women poets by concentrating not so much on the diversity of the forms in which they worked as the divergent outlets in which they placed their writings. Tracing these patterns of publication involves coming to terms with the rather erratic manner in which these writers would rise and fall before the public's gaze. Increasingly, scholars have witnessed how some of the seemingly most marginal poetry that at times appeared in slim volumes produced in modest runs from avant-garde publishers such as John Lane and T. Fisher Unwin also went through editorial procedures that believed it held value for a much larger audience. By far the greatest readership lay in the periodical press, especially the monthlies that originated in the United States. In this regard, *Harper's New Monthly Magazine* counted among the most widely circulated literary magazines of the late-Victorian era that gave prominence to the work of a select group of English women writers whose poetry would receive renewed attention during the mid-1990s. Established in 1850 by Harper and Brothers, this impressively illustrated periodical had some thirty-five years later achieved remarkable sales of 200,000 copies at home and some 35,000 copies in Britain.[5] By that time, as American journalist Poultney Bigelow recalled, '*Harper's* had more circulation, even in England, than any English magazine.'[6] Bigelow observed that 'many English people spoke to me of *Harper's* as their own' because the long-standing editor, Henry Mills Alden, understood 'the spirit of a transatlantic public' (1: 309).

In this essay I consider some of the inferences that we can make about the value that *Harper's* endowed upon an English woman writer who achieved a solid reputation in both the British and American periodical press before her untimely death in 1887.

---

[5] Eugene Exman, *The House of Harper: One Hundred and Fifty Years of Publishing* (New York, 1967), p. 79.
[6] Poultney Bigelow, *Seventy Summers*, 2 vols (London, 1925), 1: 309, quoted in Frank Luther Mott, *A History of American Magazines*, 5 vols, *Volume IV, 1850–1865* (Cambridge, MA, 1938), p. 399.

During the early 1880s, the journal featured Margaret Veley, a
London-based author who achieved noticeable success in reaching
the numerous buyers of a range of well-regarded magazines origin-
ating on both sides of the Atlantic, including *Blackwood's Edinburgh
Magazine*, *Macmillan's Magazine*, and the *Spectator* in Britain, and the
Century Illustrated Magazine in the United States. The circulation of
the American monthlies far exceeded that of any of the British
periodicals in which Veley published her fiction and poetry, and only
the *Century* – as *Scribner's Monthly* became known in 1881 – outsold
Harper's, with sales reaching 222,000 copies in the United States in
the late 1880s.[7]

Recent scholarship has revealed that the rediscovered Veley
belonged to a thriving literary culture in London that provided the
necessary contacts for her to publish in the aforementioned celebrated
magazines. Ana Parejo Vadillo has disclosed the centrality of a number
of English women poets of the 1880s – including A. Mary F. Robinson,
Graham R. Tomson and Augusta Webster – to the parties and salons
of London in which they could not only 'meet to discuss their work
and ideas' but also experience 'a source of intellectual encouragement,
cultural intercourse and literary prestige'.[8] In this context, the letters
of Vernon Lee throw considerable light on the high position that
women writers held in the metropolitan literary world. Lee recorded
she dined at the home of Leslie Stephen, editor of the *Cornhill*, where
she met the art critic 'Sidney Colvin & some aesthetic rich brewers
called Cyril Flowers . . . and Miss Velly [*sic*], a shy little woman who
has written two very good novels in the *Cornhill*, called *For Percival*
[1878] and *Damocles* [1882]'.[9] *Harper's* maintained a strong interest in
well-published women writers who benefited from the acquaintances
that could be made at such literary at-homes in London. In his second
paper on 'London as a Literary Centre', for example, R. R. Bowker
contended that the 'catalogue of successful women novelists is even
greater in England than that of men, and mere mention is but poor

[7] This figure is cited in Arthur John, *The Best Years of the* Century: *Richard
Watson Gilder*, Scribner's Monthly, *and the* Century Magazine, *1870–1909*
(Urbana, IL, 1981), p. 233.
[8] Ana Parejo Vadillo, 'New Woman Poets and the Culture of the *Salon* at the
Fin de Siècle', *Women: A Cultural Review*, 10: 1 (1999), pp. 22–34 (p. 23).
[9] Vernon Lee, 'To Matilda Adams Paget', 16 July 1884, in *Vernon Lee's
Letters*, ed. Irene Cooper Willis (London, 1937), p. 156. Lee's misspelling of
Veley relates to the pronunciation of what was originally a French family
name.

apology to the reader of them in lack of more adequate attention'. Bowker, like Lee, comments on Veley's position as 'a favourite novelist' with readers of the *Cornhill*.[10] But it is not just Veley's first work of fiction, *For Percival*, which caught Bowker's eye in Stephen's commercially successful periodical. He also observes how Veley's poems – particularly 'The Level Land', which *Harper's* featured in November 1880 – showed 'a deep poetic gift' (p. 26). Consequently, Veley's recent passing, at the age of forty-four, amounted to a 'sad loss to literature' (p. 26).

Bowker's words certainly carried great authority because of the venue in which they appeared, and before moving to an exploration of Veley's contributions to *Harper's* it is vital to understand the broader direction that the magazine had been taking since 1850. 'By the 1870s', Matthew Schneirov remarks, 'it would not have been uncommon to find a copy of *Harper's Monthly* on a typical middle-class centre table along with a Bible, a book or two of poetry, a stereoscope, a well-illustrated travel book, and perhaps a scrapbook'.[11] Part of the journal's appeal to what might be characterised as genteel taste lay in its serialisation of novels that had already won favour in England. Alden, who edited *Harper's* from 1869 to 1919, states that its handsome sales initially depended on reprinting 'great fiction' by English writers such as Edward Bulwer Lytton, Charles Dickens and George Eliot at a time when these authors' writings were not 'readily accessible' to American readers in book form.[12] Moreover, when *Harper's* 'began its career', Alden contends, 'there were no really great writers of fiction' in the United States. Even though, as Frank Luther Mott points out, Alden's claim is rather misleading (not least because 'Emerson, Hawthorne, Melville, Longfellow, and Lowell were in their prime'), it was none the less true that America 'had no great popular novelists' who were 'proved and sure and profitable'.[13]

Thus Alden is probably correct to state that the 'vast majority' of American readers remained dependent upon a magazine which should 'undertake to meet its need by the publication serially, but in their entirety, the best current novels of the day' (p. 50). Notably, in

[10] R. R. Bowker, 'London as a Literary Center: Second Paper', *Harper's New Monthly Magazine* 77 (1888), p. 26.

[11] Matthew Schneirov, *The Dream of a New Social Order: Popular Magazines in America, 1893–1914* (New York, 1994), p. 48.

[12] Henry Mills Alden, *Magazine Writing and the New Literature* (New York, 1908), p. 51.

[13] Mott, p. 387.

December 1864, when Harper and Brothers' finances suffered greatly
because of the Civil War, the appearance of Wilkie Collins's *Armadale*
and Charles Dickens's *Our Mutual Friend* supposedly restored the
monthly journal's sales to their antebellum heights. The absence of
international copyright still meant that Harper and Brothers cut
advantageous deals with English authors based on gentlemanly agree-
ments where it made fixed payments for reprints without royalties. In
1880, for example, Thomas Hardy started receiving £100 an episode for
A Laodicean, an arrangement that earned him a total of £1,300.[14] It
would take until that year before *Harper's* rose to the challenge of
serialising works of American fiction. Twelve years previously, as
Nancy Glazener observes, the literary nationalism evident in the
pages of the revived but short-lived *Putnam's Monthly* showed that
'loyalty to American authors' could be 'an asset for magazines'.[15] While
it was the case that *Harper's* had long published short stories by United
States authors (it had, however, ignored Southern writers), its serial-
isation of American novels began with Henry James's *Washington
Square* – a work that shared the same volume as *A Laodicean*.

Although *Harper's* maintained a strong interest in English writing
throughout the 1880s, it gradually shifted in emphasis away from
reprinting fiction by British writers to promoting a greater number of
novels by authors raised in the United States. The December 1880
issue, in which *Washington Square* runs to its close, features almost
exclusively American writers such as James T. Fields and Sarah Orne
Jewett. Then again, some of the United States contributors wrote on
English topics. Fields's and Jewett's fiction appears alongside an article
on 'The English Lakes and Their Genii' by another compatriot, the
radical Unitarian Moncure D. Conway, who maintained close contact
with the journal during his residence England from 1864, when he was
commissioned to write on the Shakespeare tercentenary, until the early
1880s. The only English author present in this number is the
seventeenth-century poet Robert Herrick, whose lyrics are finely
illustrated by one of *Harper's* leading in-house artists, Edwin Austin
Abbey. Undoubtedly, some issues went against this general trend. The
April 1884 number contains works by no less than four English male
writers: chapters from serials by William Black (*Judith Shakespeare*) and

[14] The information about Hardy's earnings in *Harper's* appears in Simon
Gatrell, *Hardy the Creator: A Textual Biography* (Oxford, 1998), p. 230.
[15] Nancy Glazener, *Reading for Realism: The History of a U.S. Literary Institu-
tion, 1850–1910* (Durham, NC, 1997), p. 262.

Charles Reade (*The Picture*); a poem by the elderly Richard Hengist
Horne; and a commemorative essay on Edward Bulwer Lytton by
biographer C. Kegan Paul. These English authors' works sit next to
such articles as 'The Second War of Independence' by American
abolitionist, historian and social reformer Thomas Wentworth Higgin-
son. But it is noticeable that seven months later the only English
writers visible in *Harper's* are ones, like Herrick, who made their mark
in the past: William Wordsworth (his 1833 'Long Meg' poem) and
Oliver Goldsmith (accompanied by one of Abbey's illustrations of *She
Stoops to Conquer*). Conspicuously, the contemporary poetry contained
in this issue includes American Walt Whitman's 'Of That Blithe
Throat of Thine', a work eventually collected in the 1889 edition of
Leaves of Grass – his long-evolving poem inspired by democracy in the
United States.

Even more significant perhaps is the fact that in 1885 *Harper's*
signed the American novelist William Dean Howells for a salary of
$10,000 a year to produce a novel annually and contribute an editor's
column monthly. In his 'Editor's Study', which appeared in each
number until March 1892, Howells famously lambasted what he saw
as the decisive failure of the English novel. In March 1889 he
castigated English culture for its 'mania for romanticism' when in his
view realism justified the function of the novel because of its 'truthful
treatment of material'.[16] Despairing of the apparent English preference
for 'romance', Howells championed home-grown fiction of local colour
by regional writers such as Grace King whose work focused on life in
New Orleans.

But that is not to say that Howells's desire to uphold the independ-
ence of American realists from the outmoded romancers of the Old
Country meant that this journal became in any respect insular from the
London literary world on which it had drawn so liberally in previous
years. At the same time as it strengthened its commitment to
American novels, *Harper's* wished to broaden its market by establishing
a separate European edition of the magazine, whose contents for a
while differed from the numbers issued in New York City. A further
initiative came with the opening of a busy London office in 1883. Two
years later, the Scottish writer Andrew Lang informed an American
correspondent that he felt 'horribly hustled' as London editor of

---

[16] [W. D. Howells], 'The Editor's Study', *Harper's New Monthly Magazine*, 79
(1889), p. 966.

Harper's.[17] By the spring of 1886, the experienced American publisher
James R. Osgood travelled from Boston to London as the representative
of *Harper's* publisher.[18] Later, when the 1891 International Copyright
Bill was passed, Osgood established the firm of Osgood, McIlvaine &
Co, which took responsibility for publishing the European edition of
Harper's Magazine as well as the popular *Harper's Weekly* (which began
in 1857). In 1893 Harper's began serialising George Du Maurier's
Trilby, the tale of atelier life in the bohemian world of 1850s Paris that
would become in the single-volume form the first so-called bestseller.
By any account, during the *fin de siècle Harper's* unquestionably looked
as if it had risen to the pinnacle of transatlantic prosperity and literary
prestige. Within a matter of years, however, the flotation of Harper and
Brothers led to unforeseen losses and unbearable loan payments. The
limited company went into receivership in the first week of December
1899. Renamed in 1900 as *Harper's Monthly Magazine*,[19] the journal
would later suffer from the fierce competition of mass-market maga-
zines such as *McClure's*, which began in 1893, and *Cosmopolitan*, which
enjoyed a circulation of 300,000 in 1897.[20] Soon afterwards, *Harper's*
discontinued in the genteel form that had come to enshrine what
Bigelow claimed was the 'spirit of a transatlantic public'.

How, then, was poetry valued in *Harper's*, and what was it worth
when the journal stood at its transatlantic zenith? While it has not
been possible to identify the amounts that this famous monthly paid for
each poem, the records of the non-illustrated *Atlantic* – whose sales
declined to 12,000 in 1881 – show that in 1857 such works attained a
fee of $50. (Prose was rated at $6 a page, increased to $10 if the author
was established.)[21] These were significant sums. Poetry, however, was

---

[17] Andrew Lang, 'To Brander Matthews', 20 April 1885[?], in Marysa Demoor
(ed.), *Friends over the Ocean: Andrew Lang's American Correspondents, 1881–
1912*, Werken Uitgegeven door de Faculteit van de Letteren en Wijsbegeerte,
No. 176 Aflevering (Gent, 1989), p. 66.
[18] For information about the growth of *Harper's* I have relied on the following
sources: Exman, *The House of Harper*; J. Henry Harper, *The House of Harper: A
Century of Publishing in Franklin Square* (New York, 1912); and Mott, pp. 383–
405.
[19] The European edition of the journal was titled *Harper's Monthly Magazine*
before 1900.
[20] Schneirov observes that in 1906, the year after William Randolph Hearst
bought *Cosmopolitan*, it informed its readership that its circulation had reached
400,000; the magazine focused not only on literature and art but also current
affairs (p. 87).
[21] Information about the sales figures and fees paid by the *Atlantic* appears in
James Playsted Wood, *Magazines in the United States*, second edition (New York,

hardly as prominent as prose in the American monthlies. According to Arthur John, poetry accounted for a mere one per cent of the contents of *Harper's* in 1871, a figure that increased to a modest two per cent nine years later.[22] During the same period, fiction occupied roughly a third of each 950-page volume. Such a meagre quantity may well give the impression that poetry was a minor affair in *Harper's*. In any case, the 1880s were still a period in which some of the poems published in United States monthlies might not be worthy of serious attention. The label 'magazine poetry' remained a pejorative term in certain quarters. In his history of the *Century*, John states that in the November 1872 issue of *Scribner's Monthly* 'every line of verse was written by a woman'; this 'army of female bards', John complains, 'filled every spare half page with pious songs and tributes to nature' (p. 67).

John, however, also observes that 'a higher level of craftsmanship' was evident in the work of male American poets, such as Edmund Clarence Stedman, R. H. Stoddard and Bayard Taylor (p. 68). Moreover, the poets Brander Matthews and Henry Cuyler Bunner, both of whom proved highly responsive to the 'British revival of French metrical forms, introduced the rondeau, the ballade, and the triolet to the United States through the pages of *Scribner's* (June 1878)' (p. 68). John's comment points to a significant aspect of what might be termed the literary cosmopolitanism of monthlies like the *Century* and *Harper's*. These affluent magazines provided the opportunity for American writers to engage in a new type of interaction between different cultures. Granted, we might view Matthews and Bunner imitating the considerable revival of interest in the fixed forms of Provençale poetry that was in many respects inspired by Lang's *Ballads and Lyrics of Old France* (1872). Yet, in the broadening context of these transatlantic periodicals, the appearance of such poems in *Scribner's Monthly*, the *Century* and *Harper's* showed that these magazines were finely produced vehicles that enabled a highly mobile two-way literary traffic between New York City and London that kept apace of recent developments in literature.

In relation to these transatlantic literary dialogues, the thoughtful

1956), p. 66, quoted in Jean M. Parker, '*Atlantic Monthly*', in Alan Nourie and Barbara Nourie (eds), *American Mass-Market Magazines* (Westport, CT, 1990), p. 33, and Mott, p. 506. The *Atlantic's* sales had been much higher in previous years. In 1870, they topped 50,000 before the appearance of Harriet Beecher Stowe's controversial essay on George Gordon Byron lost a large proportion of the readership.
[22] Arthur John, *The Best Years of the* Century, pp. 43, 44.

work of anthologist, critic and poet Edmund Clarence Stedman
remains particularly noteworthy. In 1873–75 Stedman contributed a
series of informative articles on 'Victorian Poets' to the *Century*.
Published in a single volume in 1875 and updated in a revised edition
of 1887, Stedman's *Victorian Poets* holds many distinctions, not least
the open-mindedness with which it approaches an eclectic range of
writers who represent diverse areas of nineteenth-century English
culture. Just as significant, Stedman's book was the first to make the
epithet Victorian familiar to his contemporary audience. His compa-
triot R. H. Stoddard remarked that this comprehensive study was so
great that it amounted to 'the most important contribution ever made
by an American writer to the critical literature of the English poets'.[23]
Stedman adopted an independent-minded approach to extending his
readers' awareness of writers whose reputations were still in the process
of formation. His willingness to pay attention to the emerging talents
of literary London would lead to a number of further critical projects.
The first was his lengthy essay, 'Some London Poets', which *Harper's*
commissioned in the early 1880s. In his correspondence, Stedman
modestly claimed that this substantial discussion was 'sketchy' and
'gossipy' (2: 34, 35). Somewhat deferentially, he assured Algernon
Charles Swinburne – whose poetry caused offence to Josiah Holland,
editor at the *Century* – that he was 'somewhat watchful' of Swinburne's
'position in America', since he wished to ensure that this English
contemporary 'should here be comprehended justly' (2: 34). In 'Some
London Poets', the flattering portrait of Swinburne, whose sexually
controversial *Poems and Ballads* (1866) had scandalised the British
press, reveals how the nine wood-block exquisite engravings aimed to
distinguish a discussion that shows considerable sensitivity to the
making and breaking of modern poetic reputations.

Stedman's essay opens with a fine medallion portrait of Horne, the
now ageing poet who enjoyed passing fame with his allegorical poem
Orion (1843). While Stedman delays mentioning Horne until the end
of his essay it is surely significant that his discussion culminates in the
terrible critical neglect that has befallen an elderly genius. 'I wonder',
he comments, 'how many London authors realise how brave a genius of
the old-fashioned stamp is passing his last days among them, and how
very tender and helpful they might be to him.' In the preceding pages,

[23] R. H. Stoddard, *Recollections*, quoted in Laura Stedman and George M. Gold
(eds), *Life and Letters of Edmund Clarence Stedman*, 2 vols (New York, 1910), 2:
10.

Stedman provides fair-minded assessments of the work of mostly budding writers. Notably, practically every poet whom Stedman mentions has never since held an enduring place in the literary canon. He begins by expressing admiration for the collaborative critical work of a band of young men, all members of London's Savile Club, who contributed one-third of the essays to a recent attempt to assess England's poetic heritage: Thomas Humphry Ward's four-volume *The English Poets* (1880), which would run to many editions. 'The Savile Club', Stedman observes, is 'a comparatively modern but cozy and characteristic institution', which enables a rising generation of literary men – including Lang and Dobson – to lunch together.[24] Among this grouping is Edmund Gosse, whom Stedman says is a Civil Servant in the Board of Trade. (Soon afterwards Gosse became the English editor of the *Century*.) There follow some briefer comments on Philip Bourke Marston and Arthur O'Shaughnessy, whose careers had been cut short through ill health. More sustained, however, is Stedman's attention to the 'British sisterhood of song' (p. 884). If Stedman displays a democratic attitude toward up-and-coming writers, then he makes it most visible in the seriousness with which he takes emergent women poets.

Even though Stedman claims that 'no female poet of modern times has equalled Mrs. Browning' who died in 1861 (p. 884), he quickly turns to the work of a number of women writers whose names would eventually become familiar again through the anthologies of the 1990s. Among critics of the late-Victorian period Stedman almost single-handedly acknowledged the politically charged work of Augusta Webster, born in 1837. Her monologues, he contends, are 'ambitious . . . and marked by a strength and breadth not thought to be the special traits of woman's work' (p. 884). Having expressed such feminist sympathies, he considers the women poets of a younger generation who have been catching attention. 'Fresh names, like that of Miss Veley', he comments, 'are occasionally inscribed upon drifting sprays of verse' (p. 886). But the writer he deems worthy of closest attention is twenty-four-year-old A. Mary F. Robinson, whose first two collections – *A Handful of Honeysuckle* and *The Crowned Hippolytus* – appeared in 1878 and 1882 respectively. He regards Robinson 'as the surest among new aspirants to fulfil the predictions made for her' (p. 886).

[24] Edmund Clarence Stedman, 'Some London Poets', *Harper's New Monthly Magazine*, 64 (1882), p. 875.

While Stedman, like most reviewers of Robinson's early work, immediately detected its debt to 'Pre-Raphaelitish atmosphere' (p. 886), he senses that 'Dawn Angels', dating from 1878, is so 'very beautiful' that he reprints it on the page that follows her portrait (see figure 3). In 1895, Stedman would gather 'Dawn Angels' in his *Victorian Anthology, 1837–1895*, a selection that ranks alongside Alfred H. Miles ten-volume *The Poets and Poetry of the Century* (1892–97) in its comprehensiveness, since it contains works by no less than three hundred and forty-three authors. By this later point, Robinson's reputation was secure. She had published no less than six collections, as well as several volumes of prose in English and French, along with articles that included her appraisals of the poetry of Anna Laetitia Barbauld, Joanna Baillie and Felicia Hemans in Ward's *English Poets*. But in the mid-1880s Robinson's standing would take a turn that Stedman did not expect, and it is instructive to consider briefly why this undoubtedly gifted woman poet would not fare particularly well in the United States magazines of the 1880s. In 1884, Robinson published *The New Arcadia*, a volume that takes a deeply sceptical approach to lyric poetry. 'I have lost my singing voice', Robinson states in her concluding poem 'Song'. 'My hey-day', she remarks, 'is over.'[25] Throughout, Robinson not only sings songs that look critically at lyric form. She also elaborates ballads that scrutinise social hardship in a rural world where nature is far from consoling. In 'Man and Wife', for example, we read about an elderly married couple whose rural impoverishment means that they must end their days in isolation from each other in the poorhouse.

On the basis of *A Handful of Honeysuckle*, readers were not prepared for this ironic depiction of modern Arcadia. Robinson's first collection, after all, employed refrains that suggested that she respected a poetic heritage whose aestheticism descended from such works as 'Sister Helen' and 'Troy Town' by Dante Gabriel Rossetti: the recently deceased artist and poet on whom she wrote with authority in *Harper's* in October 1882. The American *Atlantic*, for instance, found *The New Arcadia* most disagreeable: 'The main of her volume consists of stories of country life; but they are very far from being idyllic.' From this reviewer's perspective, Robinson undermined the belief that 'there is a great deal of beauty in nature, which has a refreshing and ennobling influence upon most minds, and accordingly aids the true function of

---

[25] A. Mary F. Robinson, *The New Arcadia and Other Poems* (London, 1884), p. 175.

Figure 3 Engraving of a photograph of A. Mary F. Robinson, *Harper's New Monthly Magazine*, 64 (1882), p. 225.

the poetic art, which is to lift up, refine and inspire us'.[26] Later, the
London-based *Athenaeum* would recall the 'coarse wretchedness' of *The
New Arcadia* while sensing that her new collection, *An Italian Garden:
A Book of Songs* (1886), evinced a return to lyric that none the less
displayed her imagination 'spending itself too long in vagueness and
dreaming and sweetly told conceits'.[27]

The negative reception of *The New Arcadia* cannot explain why
Robinson failed to place her poetry in *Harper's* until 1901.[28] None the
less, it points to the kinds of difficulty that an ambitious woman poet
could encounter when attempting to produce poetry that went against
the grain of reviewers' expectations in the United States. Certainly, in
the 1880s Robinson would publish poetry in other magazines such as
Oscar Wilde's mostly feminist *The Woman's World* in London. But at
the time of Stedman's notice Robinson failed to enjoy the prominence
that Veley secured in *Harper's* – the journal that chose not to present
portraits of Veley but commission high-calibre illustrations for her
work. As I explain below, there were possible reasons why Veley
succeeded in *Harper's* where Robinson failed. But Veley's success was
brief. In years to come her 'drifting sprays of verse', as Stedman styled
them, disappeared so quickly that the process of recovering her
intelligent poetry would literally involve resuscitating her 'transatlan-
tic spirit' out of thin air.

II

In March 1880 Margaret Veley published the first two of the five poems
that she would place in *Harper's*: a longer work titled 'The Level Land',
which filled a page, and a short twelve-line lyric titled 'October'.

---

[26] [Anonymous], 'Recent Poetry', *Atlantic Monthly*, 54 (1884), p. 121.
[27] [Anonymous], Review of A. Mary F. Robinson, *An Italian Garden: A Book of
Songs*, *Athenaeum* (17 April 1886), p. 517.
[28] 'Solitude', a quatrain by Mary Robinson, appears in *Harper's Monthly
Magazine*, 102 (1901), p. 282. In the preface to her 1902 *Collected Poems*,
A. Mary F. Robinson – whose married names were first Mme James Darmest-
eter and then Mme Emile Duclaux – remarks that she has decided to publish
under the name that she bore when she first wrote poetry. During her two
marriages she published an extensive amount of critical prose in French. 'As
regards the English public, Madame Duclaux has given no proof of her
existence; she has, she hopes, before her a modest future of French prose, and
and leaves her English verses to Mary Robinson': see Mary Robinson, *The
Collected Poems: Lyrical and Narrative* (London, 1902), p. vii.

Harper and Brothers had good reason to draw attention to Veley's name. In August that year they issued her prose narrative titled Mrs. Austin in the Harper's Half-Hour Series, in which Hardy's 'Fellow Townsmen' also appeared. Harper and Brothers acted as the United States publisher of her next two novels, Rachel's Inheritance; or, Damocles and Mitchelhurst Place (1884). By any account, Veley belonged to Harper and Brothers' stable of contemporary English writers whose work strengthened their responsiveness to 'the spirit of a transatlantic public'. On the one hand, Veley's fiction represented what the publisher deemed were the best English novels for an American audience. On the other hand, the poems she had accepted in New York City travelled back to London in a respected periodical that sought to bring increasing attention to United States literature.

What, then, might have attracted this transatlantic journal to 'The Level Land'? The answer, in part, derives from the conspicuously liberal outlook of Veley's poetry. On first hearing, however, the poem scarcely sounds progressive in style. In lines of mostly iambic pentameter, Veley's speaker yearns not for 'a world above' that is 'Star-like, unknown' but a 'level land': 'A land of sunny turf and laughing rills, / A land of endless summer, sweet with dew'.[29] But once the poetic voice depicts the landscape of the 'level land' it becomes clear that the poem is in fact attempting to create a new aesthetic. Veley's admiring perspective on the 'new beauty' that she witnesses in this location controverts one of Edmund Burke's memorable assertions, dating from 1757, about types of vastness that fail to reach the breath-taking proportions of the Sublime: 'A level plain of a vast extent on land', Burke observes, 'is certainly no mean idea; the prospect of such a plain may be as extensive as the prospect of an ocean; but can it ever fill the mind with any thing so great as a prospect of the ocean itself?'[30] In refuting Burke's viewpoint, Veley's fluent syntax shifts between couplets and interlaced rhymes in order to contend that the 'new beauty' of such a plain is also different from the feminine 'delicacy' and 'fragility' that Burke associates with the altogether smaller scale of the Beautiful (1: 275). 'The beauty of women', he remarks, 'is considerably owing to their weakness, or delicacy.' Similarly, the Beautiful for Burke

[29] Margaret Veley, 'The Level Land', Harper's New Monthly Magazine, 61 (1880), p. 856.
[30] Edmund Burke, 'A Philosophical Enquiry into the Origin of Our Ideas of the Sublime and the Beautiful', in T. O. McLoughlin, James T. Boulton and William B. Todd (eds), The Writings and Speeches of Edmund Burke, 4 vols to date (Oxford, 1997), 1: 230.

remains visible in the 'vegetable beauties' of 'flowery species' such as 'the delicate myrtle . . . the almond . . . the jessamine' and 'the vine' (1: 275). To be sure, the 'land's delight' of Veley's poem emanates from blossoms that figure as 'women queenly souled'. Yet Veley's womanly flowers, as her phrasing suggests, are far from fragile or weak in Burke's sense of these terms. In her view, they belong to a communitarian vision of a social world in which 'wayfarers are gay', all participating in a harmonious environment in which 'words said or sung, / Sweet wordless looks, and music finely strung / Belong to all'. Together, the members of this harmonised community respect 'beauty that has been' while 'feast[ing] afresh' on 'new beauty'. Small wonder that this flat landscape features neither 'laughter . . . of lofty scorn' nor 'satire born / Of hidden pain and weariness of heart'. In every sense, this busily peopled world – one markedly distinct from Robinson's dystopic new Arcadia – embraces an ideal of social equality.

Veley's poetic voice therefore adopts an innovative perspective that longs for the potential democracy of a world that might otherwise appear featureless. But, given Veley's evident unwillingness to produce a purely expressive poetry, her poem takes a critical turn. Within a matter of lines, the speaker explains why it proves difficult for her to sustain such a liberating vision. Once she reflects on the ways in which everyday life might develop on the level land, the communitarian ideal quickly breaks down because the thought of disagreement among 'contending creeds' reminds her that discordant notes may well 'mar the music of river reeds'. The allusion to piping music is significant because it shows us that the speaker understands that in rejecting the ascendant trajectory of the Sublime she recognises that she might reduce the land into a state of fanciful lyricism. How, then, might the poetic voice find a more balanced – if not level – perspective on the expansive plain that she has outlined?

Veley's speaker sets out to answer this question in the concluding lines. She recognises that experiencing 'perfect slumber' amid 'the soft sighing of the water's brink' on this level plain would make her oblivious to 'the strife of Right and Wrong'. In tones that echo Tennyson's 'The Lotos-Eaters' (1832, revised 1842), the first-person voice dismisses such 'torpid creeping of the blood' as the 'Dream of a fool'. Momentarily, she admits that 'There rises from the sod . . . / Dimly, an infinite ascent to God' – one that gestures towards the Sublime. But no sooner has she gone back on her word in order to 'strain upward toward an atmosphere / Of sovereign calm' than she contends that the 'spell' of the level land cannot disappear. 'It lurks', she says, 'in written page and carven stone, / And blossom from our laboured gardens tell / Of fair lands golden-crowned with asphodel'. In other words, the exquisite environment that combines the fertility of nature with the fruits of human labour may be a 'vision sweet and vain'. But its 'new beauty' cannot be ignored, since the very real world that she inhabits keeps pointing towards human longing for social concord – a type of harmony, we might infer, that puts 'The Level Land' in implicit dialogue with the avowedly democratic ideals of Whitman's *Leaves of Grass*.

'The Level Land', then, embodies a style of progressive liberal idealism with which many of *Harper's* contributors – such as Conway, Higginson and Whitman – were associated. 'October' also turns its gaze to a regenerative future. In three quatrains Veley's optimistic lyric voice addresses natural cycles of growth and decay, suggesting that we should not feel 'Anxious' as we witness the falling 'autumn leaves' announce the departure of 'summer-time'. Instead, we must remember that nature does not preserve any 'little leaf or flower that she has seen'. As a matter of course, 'new blossom and a tender green' will bud. Such sentiments emerge more forcefully in 'Almond Blossom', which appeared in *Harper's* in August 1881. Here, once again, Veley's poetry stands alongside two of Herrick's lyrics, both of which are illustrated by Edwin Austin Abbey. But on this occasion, in an issue that serialises *A Laodicean* and Constance Fenimore Woolson's *Anne*, Veley's poem is the subject of a frontispiece that features one of Abbey's distinctive designs (figure 4). The fact that Charles Parsons, art editor at the New York office, asked Abbey to undertake this work says much about the value that *Harper's* wished to confer upon the ten triplets that comprise this thoughtful lyric.

Unlike 'The Level Land' or 'October', in 'Almond Blossom' Veley adopts the voice of a man addressing his female beloved. Here he attempts to persuade her that she should not 'regret' the fact that the pink flowers that she clutches will eventually wither. 'They are not dead', he assures her, since they belong to a 'world unworn' – one that can never diminish because it ensures that nature continues to 'sleep' and 'waken' in accordance with the cycle of the seasons.[31] Thus the blossoms 'laugh our dreams of ancient days to scorn'. In fact, he goes further in rejecting any yearning his beloved may have for the past by claiming that even the 'great works' of human endeavour that were

---

[31] Margaret Veley, 'Almond Blossom', *Harper's New Monthly Magazine*, 63 (1881), p. 345.

Figure 4 Edwin Austin Abbey, 'Frontispiece – Almond Blossom', in *Harper's New Monthly Magazine*, 63 (1881), p. 322.

'designed to last' cannot endure, since the blossoms will fall in a 'lightly woven chain' around the ruins of monuments whose glory has long vanished. Implicitly, the male lover remains critical of the nostalgia expressed in John Milton's 'Lycidas' (1637), where the poetic voice apostrophises 'the laurels . . . myrtle brown, with ivy sere': 'I come to pluck your berries harsh and crude'.[32] Milton's pastoral proceeds to summon the 'Sicilian muse' (line 133) to inspire the 'vales' (line 134) to 'purple all the ground with vernal flowers' (line 141) and 'strew the laureate hearse where Lycid lies' (line 151). In 'Lycidas', Veley's speaker suggests, Milton sought to monumentalise a 'world' depicted by Virgil and Ovid that 'was doomed to pass'.

Yet in 'Almond Blossom', even if the seventeenth-century world that produced Milton's neo-classicism has long vanished, it remains the case that the natural environment continues to generate the same flowers that Milton 'plucked for Lycidas'. Accordingly, Veley's speaker asserts that it is necessary to acknowledge that we will one day 'leave the flowers behind' because it is humanity, rather than nature, which must inevitably 'pass' along 'an unknown way'. At the same time, he seeks to assure his beloved that he does not wish to dismiss the romantic splendour of the present moment. Undoubtedly, the 'rosy petals' will continue to 'strew, as now, the turf beneath the trees' into the 'twilight centuries'. But that is not to say that either he or she should forget that today the 'Pink sprays of almond', even only 'for a little space', lend a 'supreme and solitary grace' to her 'musing smile' and 'blossom-perfect face'. It is a charming ending to an unassuming lyric that, like 'The Level Land', quietly examines received wisdom about the orthodox cultural values accorded to greatness. Here Veley gently criticises Milton's pastoral elegy by praising nature's capacity to disclose the grandiose pretensions of the belief that 'great works', including perhaps 'Lycidas', can and should endure forever.

By now the tone of Veley's poetry should be plain: its democratic spirit, which dispenses with any craving for the days of yore, strives to imagine a non-hierarchical perspective on the modern social body. Edwin Austin Abbey's illustration, however, does not emphasise the progressive sentiments of Veley's 'Almond Blossom', since his chosen design shows that the poem served as an occasion for him to elaborate his developing interest in making accurate representations of historical costume and informed depictions of the English countryside. By 1881

---

[32] John Milton, 'Lycidas', in Milton, *Complete Shorter Poems*, 2nd edn, ed. John Carey (Harlow, 1997), ll. 1–3.

Abbey's reputation as an illustrator was almost second to none. Michael Quick contends that at an early age Abbey, who trained in Philadelphia, 'was the first of American artists to see in illustration the promise of a worthwhile, life-long career'.[33] While still in his twenties, Abbey emerged not only as *Harper's* best draughtsman. As Quick points out, Abbey's contributions to William Cullen Bryant's *History of the United States* (1876–81) together with his fine illustrations of Herrick's poetry also stand as 'milestones in the history of the illustrated book in America' (p. 20). Both Bryant's volumes and Herrick's poems encouraged Abbey to research the history of dress, and his later drawings for an edition of Goldsmith's *She Stoops to Conquer*, which appeared in 1884, extend his interest in providing his contemporary audience with the exact features of male and female attire in their original context. Abbey's ability to capture past literary moments with such precision attracted Henry James's praise in an essay that considered the growing eminence of *Harper's* illustrators: 'the peculiar sign of his talent is surely this observation in the remote . . . Remote in time (in differing degrees), remote in place, remote in feeling, in habit, and in their ambient air, are the images that spring from his pencil, and yet all so vividly, so minutely, so consistently seen.'[34]

Since he wanted to ensure that Abbey's historical representations of English culture obtained even greater authenticity, Charles Parsons encouraged the artist to spend a period of time across the Atlantic in order to research both the settings for the Herrick edition and the environs of Stratford-upon-Avon for an illustrated volume of Shakespeare's plays. After leaving New York City in 1878, Abbey would reside in England for much of his remaining life, producing a large number of illustrations for *Harper's* before turning to oils and making his mark at the Royal Academy. His correspondence with Parsons reveals that by early 1880 he was tackling a large quantity of work: 'I think I had better give up the rest of De Mille's story [*The Castle in Spain*], if you must have it by the first of July . . . I am anxious to get at and finish a number of the Herrick things before the end of the year. I have half a dozen or so on the stocks, and these with Miss Veley's things and the other work I have – the Holland, the Effigies, the

---

[33] Michael Quick, 'Abbey as Illustrator', in *Edwin Austin Abbey (1852–1911)* (New Haven, CT, 1974), p. 20.
[34] Henry James, 'Our Artists in Europe', *Harper's New Monthly Magazine*, 79 (1889), p. 56.

Thames, Surrey, and a number of other things – will keep me busy for some time.'[35] Abbey's comments clearly show that his illustrations of Veley's poetry counted among his priorities. The resulting frontispiece strikes a balance between representing the romantic theme of 'Almond Blossom' and displaying his interest in placing figures from the era of Goldsmith in particular in genuine English settings. Moreover, Abbey's drawing – which bears some resemblance to his illustrations of *She Stoops to Conquer* – is the result of a decidedly transatlantic spirit: it draws on an American artist's wish to depict English landscape and historical costumes more precisely for a largely United States audience. Simultaneously, it underscores the work of an up-and-coming poet based in London whose political sympathies concur with the American liberalism evident throughout *Harper's* in the 1880s.

Two years after 'Almond Blossom' appeared in *Harper's* Abbey produced another frontispiece, this time based on Veley's 'A Town Garden': a five-stanza poem in iambic tetrameter that expresses sadness at the 'Dim flowers' and 'scanty, smoke-incrusted leaves' that struggle to survive beneath a 'murky sunset' (see figure 5).[36] Here, too, the subject-matter, which is expressly modern, focuses on rethinking pastoral – this time in a type of urban setting that would absorb the attention of Veley's contemporaries such as Tomson.[37] Abbey's accompanying design, however, is noticeably different from his drawing for 'Almond Blossom'. Here he represents an identifiably 1880s urban backyard where the wretched shrubs, as Veley puts it, look 'sapless' in 'leaf and stem'. The bare bricks of a row of tall terraced houses, ones that look familiar to a London suburb of the time, provide the bleak background to the shadowy garden wall. A female figure, with downcast eyes, none the less concentrates on nourishing the feeble plants with her watering-can. In this impressive drawing readers of *Harper's* witnessed a distinctive change in Abbey's style. His realistic attention

[35] Edwin Austin Abbey, 'To Charles Parsons', 17 February 1880, quoted in E. V. Lucas, *Edwin Austin Abbey, Royal Academician: The Record of His Life and Work*, 2 vols (London, 1921), 1: 98.
[36] Margaret Veley, 'A Town Garden', *Harper's New Monthly Magazine*, 67 (1883), p. 405.
[37] It is worth comparing Veley's 'A Town Garden' to Tomson's 'In a London Garden' where the poetic voice discerns 'Loose-dripping discs of limpid yellow lustre' from a gas-lit street lamp that 'shines through' the 'hanging linden leaves': see *A Summer Night and Other Poems* (London, 1891), p. 3. Tomson, who would after 1895 publish under the name Rosamund Marriott Watson, had unrivalled success among English poets of the 1880s and 1890s in placing her poems in the United States monthlies.

Figure 5 Edwin Austin Abbey, 'Frontispiece – A Town Garden', in *Harper's New Monthly Magazine*, 67 (1883), p. 326.

to landscape, particularly the fine execution of grass and foliage, owed much to the influence of his collaborator Alfred Parsons. The finely detailed frontispiece accords with the overall sentiment of Veley's carefully argued poem. Certainly, the woman who replenishes the soil is Abbey's invention. But this is a thoughtful addition that comple- ments the poetic voice which at first expresses despair about the 'rose against a wall' dying 'by inches in the gloom'.

As she ponders the fading rose, however, Veley's speaker resists the temptation to 'transplant' the 'poorest blossom' and 'set' it beneath 'the arching sky' in the manner of pastoral. Better, she thinks, for the feeble plant to 'Bestow' its 'life instead of flowers'. In the process, she argues, the 'dole / Of lingering leaves shall not be vain' because they will be 'Worthy to wreathe the hemlock bowl / Or twine about the cross of pain'. In other words, 'A Town Garden' concludes by stating that it would be mistaken to think that the 'garden caught in a brick-built trap' had no value, since the stunted growths may well create a vivid impression of noble sacrifice. By alluding to the bowl of hemlock and the cross of pain, Veley creates a striking comparison between the different forms of persecution that led Socrates, on the one hand, and Jesus Christ, on the other hand, to forfeit their lives for the benefit of future generations.

But if Abbey comprehended Veley's attempt to discern some special worth in the 'Prisoned and perishing' flowers of her town garden, barely any future readers could see much merit in preserving her poetry. Her attempts to transvalue traditional aesthetic ideals, whether in connec- tion with the Sublime or with pastoral, failed to persuade even one of her greatest sponsors, Leslie Stephen, that she ranked as highly as *Harper's* – which published another of her lyrics in 1884 – seems to have thought.[38] Writing to Charles Eliot Norton in January 1888, Stephen reported Veley's recent passing 'about a month ago':

> Her poor old mother who is paralytic & desolate wishes to publish some of her poems & I am going to arrange this for her. It is a sad ending to a life which, I suspect, was not a very bright one. The poems, I think, showed real talent but – well, not quite of the first order.[39]

---

[38] The fifth and final poem that *Harper's* accepted is 'Of the Past': *Harper's New Monthly Magazine*, 68 (1884), p. 366.

[39] Leslie Stephen, 'To Charles Eliot Norton', 11 January 1888, in John W. Bicknell (ed.), *Selected Letters of Leslie Stephen*, 2 vols (Basingstoke, 1996), 1: 354.

Later that year, Stephen furnished a lengthy preface to A *Marriage of Shadows and Other Poems*, and his somewhat uninspiring remarks provide the basis for the sparse number of subsequent commentaries on her life and work. While it was Stephen's task to honour the poet, he chose for the most part to temper the fact that Veley 'was a decided liberal in both political and religious matters'.[40] Nowhere does he permit any taint of controversy to affect the writer's reputation as a woman whose 'extreme gentleness of manner' and 'extreme diffidence' (p. ix) ensured that she endured a 'quiet and uneventful life' (p. vii). Moreover, even though Stephen notes in passing that Veley became closely acquainted with Luke Ionides – friend to many distinguished literary figures, including Dante Gabriel Rossetti – he occasionally distracts the reader by focusing on such a 'minor virtue' as the 'character and delicacy' of her 'pre-eminent . . . handwriting' rather than her considerable literary output (p. xiii). But in the few letters by Veley from which he offers extracts, Stephen discloses that the poet was not perhaps as 'delicate' as he might like to suggest. Reflecting on her use of 'asphodel' in 'The Level Land', Veley was shocked to learn that this much-poeticised plant possessed 'a nutritive and medicinal root, shaped like a small turnip' (p. xxiii). In the end, she concluded that she knew 'no more of amaranths and asphodel' than she 'did before, since the poet's flowers – Mr. Tennyson's for instance – are evidently not related to their earthly namesakes' (p. xxiv). Here Veley's wry wit not only strikes a note of self-mockery but also deflates the supposed pretentiousness of a revered poetic tradition.

The London periodicals were quick to appreciate such excerpts. But critics reached differing conclusions about the poetic value of A *Marriage of Shadows*. The *Saturday Review*, for instance, felt that her 'biography' was 'more interesting than the essays in verse', and added that 'she acted wisely when she gave most of her time and work to prose', since in poetry Veley spoke 'in a tongue of which she was not really mistress'.[41] The influential *Athenaeum* thought that she was 'exceptionally successful in light verse' rather than the ambitious title poem, which seeks to show that 'the land of shadows of veritable men and women' possesses 'some strange existence truer than that of

[40] Leslie Stephen, 'Preface', in Margaret Veley, A *Marriage of Shadows and Other Poems* (London, 1888), p. ix.
[41] [Anonymous], Review of Veley, A *Marriage of Shadows*, *Saturday Review*, 11 August 1888, pp. 185–6.

their flesh and blood prototypes'.[42] In other words, 'A Marriage of Shadows' – an eerily abstract and sensuous work – seemed marred by its otherworldliness. Altogether more encouraging was the *Spectator*, the journal that accepted her earliest poems. It found much to commend, especially her 'execution in its most perfect form', together with the 'intensity of feeling' that ensured that her poetry rose 'to a level far above that of even excellent amateur verse'.[43] Yet, even then, the reviewer sensed that her work had not reached its full potential. 'Miss Veley, if she had lived', the *Spectator* concluded, 'might have surpassed greatly as a poet the considerable reputation she had made as a novelist' (p. 1033). Thereafter, until the mid-1990s recovery of her once highly visible reputation, her poetry would be consigned to lasting obscurity – except for the one extraordinary occasion when the prominence of her name in *Harper's* allowed her transatlantic spirit, at greater length than ever before, to arise from beyond the grave.

Paradoxically, it was the fact that Veley's poetry had almost disappeared entirely from view that meant it accrued special value for psychical researchers some forty years after her death. In 1927, Miss Margaret Head and Mr V (the pseudonyms of two automatists) channelled the poet's spirit during a series of sittings that involved detailed interviews with the long-deceased author and the production of a substantial quantity of automatic writing, including a number of octosyllabic verses rapidly transcribed at three lines per minute that were presumed to originate from Veley's posthumous imagination. In the *Proceedings of the Society for Psychical Research*, W. H. Salter detailed all of the available printed sources – including Stephen's 'Preface', together with entries in the *DNB* and Allibone's *Dictionary of English Literature* – that elucidated Veley's career. Furthermore, Salter checked the biographical information channelled by Mr V against the directories of Essex, the county in which Veley resided from birth until moving to London in 1880. Even though it is clear to anyone who has read Stephen's 'Preface' that most of the details uttered at these sittings were readily accessible, the transcripts of the communications none the less retain special interest in both the history of psychical research and the critical reclamation of nineteenth-century women poets.

To begin with, Mr V's mediation of Veley's spirit provided a significant test of his powers as a medium. In 1923 Mr V aroused

---

[42] [Anonymous], Review of Margaret Veley, *A Marriage of Shadows, and Other Poems*, *Athenaeum*, 22 September 1888, p. 377.

[43] [Anonymous], 'Miss Veley's Poems', *Spectator*, 28 July 1888, pp. 1032–3.

considerable attention after channelling the spirit of Oscar Wilde with
the assistance of one of the most admired, indeed highly literary,
mediums of the day. Hester Travers Smith, who aided Mr V at several
sittings, rose to fame by communicating the thoughts of such departed
luminaries as Francis Bacon and William Shakespeare. As Helen
Sword observes, Travers Smith – the daughter of eminent literature
professor Edward Dowden – grew up 'watching the literary elite of
Dublin pass through her house'.[44] Wilde of course came from a family
that belonged to Dublin's cultural elite. Strikingly, in Travers Smith's
company Mr V replicated Wilde's Greek hand and distinctive signa-
ture. Meanwhile, at her ouija board Travers Smith produced the
author's posthumous commentary on the works of various writers and
thinkers whose reputations rose after Wilde's death in 1900. Moreover,
these sittings also featured communications that adopted a distinctly
Wildean turn of phrase: 'Being dead', Wilde's spirit languidly confessed
through Mr V, 'is the most boring experience in life.'[45] Such revela-
tions stirred up publicity in the *Sunday Express*. As Salter knew, Mr V's
revelations about Wilde's life could have been gleaned from the
increasing quantity of biographical sources, including Arthur Ran-
some's critical study of 1912 that managed to shift what had been a
rather anecdotal discussion of Wilde's scandalous career on to a more
serious level of inquiry. For example, the spirit's gibes at Galsworthy's
Justice (1910) – a polemical drama about prison reform – clearly related
both to Wilde's famous abhorrence of realism and his infamous prison
sentence at Reading Gaol: 'I have carefully digested what our friend
[Galsworthy] has said about a subject he knows nothing of.'[46] Not
surprisingly, in order to defend her authority as a medium Travers
Smith felt obliged to declare that she 'had forgotten most of his [i.e.
Wilde's] life'; at the same time, she stated that Mr V knew just as little
as she did of the none the less notorious Anglo-Irish writer's career.[47]

[44] Helen Sword, *Ghostwriting Modernism* (Ithaca, NY, 2002), p. 13.
[45] Hester Travers Smith, 'The Return of Oscar Wilde', *Occult Review*, 38
(1923), p. 81. During this sitting, Mr V communicated Wilde's spirit while
Travers Smith touched Mr V's hand.
[46] Hester Travers Smith, 'The Return of Oscar Wilde: Part II', *Occult Review*,
38 (1923), p. 150.
[47] Hester Travers Smith, *Psychic Messages from Oscar Wilde* (London, 1924),
p. 100. Travers Smith added: 'Even now I refrain from reading Ransome's Life
in case I should have further sittings.' Travers Smith's book both reprints from
the *Occult Review* the records of the sittings that channelled Wilde's spirit and
adds information about the communications that Wilde's spirit made through
her ouija board.

In communicating the comparatively obscure Veley's spirit Mr V may have thought that he stood on altogether less questionable ground because he was recovering the life and work of an author about whom 'few people nowadays have even heard, although she was a person of some note in her own generation'.[48] Disingenuously, Mr V professed not to have any knowledge about Veley – in all but one regard: he recalled reading 'Almond Blossom' in the 1881 volume of *Harper's*, which remained in his family, some time before. Mr V's eagerness to justify his standing as a communications channel, however, hardly lies in his insincere claim that his only contact with Veley's writing came through a back issue of *Harper's*. At the end of Salter's lengthy commentary, Mr V provides a forty-page analysis that compares the style of the poems collected in A *Marriage of Shadows* with the automatic scripts. The result is the most comprehensive discussion of Veley's poetry to appear before Staci L. Stone's largely factual essay of 1999.[49] Of 'The Level Land', for example, Mr V comments: 'She was content to use the language of the precursors of the Romantic Revival. The "peaceful plains", "the everlasting hills" . . . "the laughing rills" – all the well-worn pieces of the pre-romantic currency are to be found in her verse, and sometimes the old coins ring a little thin' (p. 338). But if 'the diction is undistinguished', then 'there must be some compensation in the way of rhythmic life or metrical subtlety' (p. 339). As a consequence, Mr V attends to Veley's virtuosity in metre, focusing on 'the free almost conversational rhythm of "A Japanese Fan" – a poem that appeared in the *Cornhill* in 1876. Mr V observes that the 'poetic form', which alternates octosyllabics with lines of trochaic dimeter catalectic, 'serves to sustain and accentuate the undertones of gentle but grim irony that run beneath the forced vivacity' (p. 340).

Mr V could have added that 'A Japanese Fan' – which the *Athenaeum* reviewer admitted was 'one of the best such *vers de société* poems ever produced' (p. 377) – shrewdly questions the value of the elegant object that she mentions in the title. The speaker, whose sex is

---

[48] W. H. Salter, 'Some Automatic Scripts Purporting to Be Inspired by Margaret Veley, Poet and Novelist (1843–1887)', *Proceedings of the Society for Psychical Research*, 38 (1929), p. 282. This document is divided into two parts: the first is Salter's account of the sittings further page, while the second focuses on Mr V's analysis of Veley's poetry and the 'spirit verses' that he channelled. Further page references appear in parentheses.
[49] Staci L. Stone, 'Margaret Veley', in William B. Thesing (ed.), *Victorian Women Poets, Dictionary of Literary Biography, Volume 199* (Detroit, MI, 1999), pp. 289–97.

not specified, asks a companion: 'Do you wonder why I prize it? / Care
to know?' (*Marriage of Shadows*, p. 70). The poetic 'I' proceeds to mock
the inability of the listener (whose sex also remains ambiguous) to
acknowledge the 'beauty' in a foreign artefact whose tremulous 'beat'
has 'Set' her 'passion to a music / Strangely sweet' (p. 74). To clarify the
meaning of the fan, the persona translates the 'little square of writing'
(p. 76) beside the 'lady, small of feature, / Narrow-eyed, / With her hair
of ebon straightness / Queerly tied' (p. 71). It turns out that the
Japanese characters which the speaker claims to understand tell the
tale of a beautiful woman who 'played the traitor' to a male lover
(p. 75). The story thus interpreted implies a somewhat cautionary
lesson to the speaker's auditor who fails to appreciate the 'value' of the
'picture' that he or she is 'scorning / With a glance' (p. 71). Likewise, as
Virginia Blain discerns, the fact that 'A Japanese Fan' withholds the
gender of both speaker and auditor creates a 'teasing posture' of sexual
indeterminacy that enables a range of erotic identifications, including
same-sex ones, to run through the supple rhythms of Veley's prosody.[50]
Undoubtedly, Veley's carefully alternated long and short lines – which,
like several of her other poems, produce an unconventional assessment
of the cultural worth of what she describes – bear an uncanny relation
to any attempt to evaluate her writing.

The intellectual and rhythmic superiority of 'A Japanese Fan', along
with a number of lyrics, comes keenly into focus when Mr V begins to
compare the 'script verses', signed 'M. Veley', which he channelled in
the presence of Miss Hunt. One such work, titled 'Sunset Street',
emerged at the first sitting on 22 May 1927. By his own admission, this
'spirit poetry' is 'invariably melodious and well finished and charming
in sentiment even though it does not reach a high imaginative level'
(p. 346). While it might appear that Mr V presents 'spirit poems' like
'Sunset Street' as possible evidence of Veley's minor status as a writer,
his transcriptions imply that no matter how hard he studied the poet's
work he could not emulate the standard she achieved. Ultimately, to
the sceptical mind Mr V's exploitation of Veley's poetry casts suspicion
on his response to his earlier encounter with 'Almond Blossom' in
Harper's: 'I cannot remember that it had ever excited in me any special
curiosity as to its author' (p. 331). Such a comment resembles a
disavowal, since it may well have been the case that Mr V wished to

[50] Virginia Blain, 'Sexual Politics of the (Victorian) Closet; *or*, No Sex Please
– We're Poets', in Isobel Armstrong and Virginia Blain (eds), *Women's Poetry:
Late Romantic to Late Victorian, Gender and Genre, 1830–1890* (Basingstoke,
1999), p. 146.

understand more about a writer who, unlike most English poets of the time, placed her writing in a widely read transatlantic journal of great prestige. One can only speculate about what might have motivated his fascination with Veley's poetry, especially those works that contemplate the afterlife from an unorthodox position. In her thought-provoking sequence 'A Marriage of Shadows', for example, Veley imagines a parallel world in which shadows possess a ghostlike independence from their human origins, enabling forms of intimate touching and mingling that would be socially proscribed in everyday life. This phantasmal poem dramatises the 'marriage' of insubstantial presences that bear more than a passing resemblance to the spirits who strove to revive their lives and work through the distinctly literary mediumship of Mr V.

At least one psychical researcher remained convinced that Mr V's communication of Veley's spirit proved that the poet's voice had re-entered the modern world. In 1929 Rene Sudre with Mr V's permission disclosed that the medium was 'none other than Mr S G Soal, lecturer [in mathematics] at the University of London and one of the most distinguished of all English metapsychists'.[51] Dismissing the 'hypothesis of conscious fraud', Sudre discounts the DNB and Harper's as 'feeble sources' that 'would not be adequate to permit [Soal] to play her role from the double viewpoint of biographical information and literary composition' (p. 384). In other words, Sudre believed that Soal's sittings showed that the living maintain a 'relation constant but unknown with an impersonal or depersonalised world of spirit' (p. 385). Unfortunately, Soal's subsequent career as a psychic would raise an increasing number of questions about the legitimacy of his methods, especially his influential response to J. B. Rhine's monograph on extra-sensory perception that appeared in the United States in 1934. In the mid-1930s, Soal progressed to a series of parapsychological tests that elaborated Rhine's card-guessing experiments which aimed at proving telepathic communication. Soal, according to Ray Hyman, introduced more safeguards against error than any previous researcher in the field: his 'randomised targets', together with 'sophisticated checks for randomness' and 'the most appropriate statistical procedures', sought to be foolproof.[52] For many years, Soal impressed

---

[51] Rene Sudre, 'The Margaret Veley Case, and Survival', Psychic Research, 23: 7 (1929), p. 380.
[52] Ray Hyman, 'A Critical Overview of Parapsychology', in Paul Kurtz (ed.), A Skeptic's Handbook of Parapsychology (Buffalo, NY, 1985), p. 50.

Notes on Contributors

Joseph Bristow is Professor of English at the University of California, Los Angeles. His books include an edited collection, *Wilde Writings: Contextual Conditions* (2002). He has recently edited Wilde's *The Picture of Dorian Gray* for Oxford University Press. At present, he is writing a study of Victorian poetry, sexual identity, and sexual desire.

Susan Brown teaches English at the University of Guelph. Her ongoing research in Victorian women's writing, literary history, and humanities computing will soon emerge in the collaborative Orlando Project (www.ualberta.ca/ORLANDO/).

Glennis Byron is a Reader in English Studies at the University of Stirling. She is the author of *Letitia Landon: The Woman Behind L.E.L.* (1995), *Dramatic Monologue* (forthcoming 2003), various articles on nineteenth-century poetry and the Gothic, the editor of *Dracula. New Casebook* (1999) and, with David Punter, *Spectral Readings: Towards a Gothic Geography* (1999).

Alison Chapman is Lecturer in English Literature at the University of Glasgow. She is the author of *The Afterlife of Christina Rossetti* (2000) and the co-editor, with Richard Cronin and Antony H. Harrison, of *A Companion to Victorian Poetry* (2002). Together with Jane Stabler, she has co-edited *Unfolding the South: Nineteenth-Century British Women Writers and Artists in Italy* (2003).

Natalie M. Houston is an Assistant Professor of English at the University of Houston. She has published articles on Victorian women writers, nineteenth-century poetry anthologies, and the poetry of the Crimean War. Her edition of M. E. Braddon's *Lady Audley's Secret* is forthcoming from Broadview Press, and she is currently completing a book on the cultural history of the Victorian sonnet.

Michele Martinez is a Visiting Assistant Professor of English at Trinity College in Hartford, Connecticut, and currently at work on a book entitled *Sister Arts and Artists in Nineteenth-Century England.*

Patricia Pulham is Lecturer at Queen Mary, University of London where she teaches nineteenth-century literature and contemporary poetry. She has published articles on the work of the late-Victorian writer Vernon Lee, and is currently co-editing a collection of Lee's supernatural tales to be published by Broadview Press in 2004.

Marjorie Stone is Professor of English and Women's Studies at Dalhousie University. She is the author of *Elizabeth Barrett Browning* (1995) and the forthcoming collection, co-edited with Judith Thompson, *Literary Couplings and the Construction of Authorship: Writing Couples and Collaborators in Historical Context.* She is currently working on a project entitled *The Black Dove's Mark: Nineteenth-Century Literary History and the Elizabeth Barrett Browning Archives.*

Index

Veley, Margaret (cont.):
'Marriage of Shadows, A' 188–9, 193
Marriage of Shadows, A 188–9, 191
Mitchelhurst Place 179
'October' 178, 181
'Of the Past' 187 n.38
'Town Garden, A' 185–7
Vellutello, Alessandro 105–6, 110
Veneto, Bartolommeo 158–9
Venus 159–60
Vickers, Nancy J. 26
Victoria Regia 31
Virgil 105, 181
vision 125–6, 158–61, 161–2
see also: perception
voice 37, 58, 63–7, 71–7, 79, 81–4, 90–4, 96, 97, 125–6, 141–2, 179, 180, 181–3

Wagner, Jennifer, 147 n.4
Wallace, Alfred Russel 137–9
Waller, John F. 6, 100
Waller, R. D. 104 n.14
Walton, Izaak 103 n.13, 106 n.20
Ward, Thomas Humphry 176
Wars, Thomas Humphry 175
Watson, Rosamund Marriott (Graham R. Tomson) 7, 146–7, 168
'Autumn Morning, An' 155–6
'Boucher' 159–60
'In a London Garden' 185 n.37
'Unbidden Guest, An' 162
Watts-Dunton, Theodore 154–5, 156, 158
'Sonnet's Voice, The' 154–5
Webb, Richard D. 41
Webster, Augusta 1, 2, 5, 31, 79–80, 85, 86–7, 96, 152, 168, 175

'Castaway, A' 79–80, 91
'Circe' 86, 91–2
'Happiest Girl in the World, The' 88
'Medea in Athens' 86
'Painting, A' 86–7
'Poets and Personal Pronouns' 90
'Sister Annunciata' 88
Wendorf, Richard 103, 112
Westenra, J. C.
'Love's Inquest' 20–1
Westmacott Jr., Richard 18
Weston, Anne Warren 46
Whipple, Charles K. 34
Whitla, William 99 n.3, 105
Whitman, Walt 171, 181
Wiffen, Benjamin J. 35
Wilde, Jane Francesca (Speranza) 131 n.17
Wilde, Oscar 146–7, 178, 190
Williams, Isaac 102 n.11
Wolfson, Susan 147 n.4
Woman's World, The 178
women's poetic tradition 60, 145–6, 163–4, 165–6
see also: literary history
Wood, James Playsted 172 n.21
Woodhouselee, Alexander Tytler Lord 106, 110–11, 113
Woolson, Constance Fenimore 181
Wordsworth, William 11–12, 147, 171
working class women's poetry 2, 166
Wortley, Lady Emmeline Stuart 3–4
'The Lady Ashley' 22–5, 26, 28

Yaeger, Patricia 143
Yee, Shirley 44, 53 n.42
Yellin, Jean Fagan 48
Yellow Book 147
Yorkshire Literary Annual, The 12

Lightning Source UK Ltd.
Milton Keynes UK
UKHW020002230820
368628UK00003B/231